Bargainin' For Salvation

Bargainin' For Salvation

Bob Dylan, A Zen Master?

Steven Heine

continuum

NEW YORK • LONDON

2009

The Continuum International Publishing Group Inc
80 Maiden Lane, New York, NY 10038

The Continuum International Publishing Group Ltd
The Tower Building, 11 York Road, London SE1 7NX

www.continuumbooks.com

Library of Congress Cataloging-in-Publication Data

Heine, Steven, 1950-
Bargainin' for salvation : Bob Dylan, a Zen master? / Steven Heine.
  p. cm.
Includes bibliographical references.

ISBN-13: 978-0-8264-2950-6 (pbk. : alk. paper)
ISBN-10: 0-8264-2950-5 (pbk. : alk. paper)

1. Dylan, Bob, 1941- Songs. Texts. 2. Dylan, Bob, 1941—Criticism and interpretation.
3. Rock musicians–United States–Biography. 4. Creation (Literary, artistic, etc.)–
Religious aspects–Zen Buddhism. I. Title. II. Title: Bob Dylan, a Zen master?

ML420.D98H45 2009
782.42164092--dc22   2009009919

Typeset by Newgen Imaging Systems Pvt Ltd, Chennai, India
Printed in the United States of America

Contents

Acknowledgments

I am grateful to Colleen Sheehy, Director of Education at the Weisman Art Museum, for organizing a symposium on Dylan, "Highway 61 Revisited: Dylan's Road from Minnesota to the World," held in conjunction with an exhibit at the University of Minnesota in Minneapolis from March 24–27, 2007. Having the opportunity to present a paper there on the topic of Dylan and Zen stimulated my thinking about writing this book and also gave me the opportunity to meet so many wonderful people toiling in the field of Dylanology.

During the weekend of the conference, I made the first of what was to be several trips to see Dylan's hometown of Hibbing, MN, and had a chance to meet many more fascinating and very helpful individuals who are promoting various ways of examining and highlighting Dylan's life work. Among these are Joe and Mary Keyes, proprietors of Howard Street Booksellers, and Bob and Linda Hocking, who own and run Zimmy's restaurant, both in downtown Hibbing near the High School where Dylan first performed and across from the Androy Hotel where his family celebrated his bar mitzvah party. The Keyes and the Hockings are among the main organizers of the Dylan Days Festival that convenes every year in May in conjunction with Dylan's birthday and they are largely responsible for keeping hope alive, so to speak, in Hibbing, where many old timers at once respect Dylan's privacy and are indifferent to his celebrity.

I had so many enjoyable and moving experiences that, with their approval, I began to call Zimmy's the "Vatican of the Church of Dylanology" because that is where the main rites and rituals generally take place, and Howard Booksellers the "Lourdes," since it is the site for visions and healings. During my visits to Hibbing, I had the privilege of talking to several figures who were important in the formative high school years, including Dylan's teachers B. J. Rolfzen and Charley Miller as well as his band mate and fellow motorcyclist Leroy Hoikkala.

My son Aaron, who told his high school buddies that *Masked and Anonymous* was his favorite film and "Mr. Tambourine Man" his favorite song, went with me on several of these pilgrimages to Hibbing. I have also appreciated ongoing conversations with my old friends Dan Leighton, Paul Swanson, and Dale Wright regarding Dylan's music in relation to Buddhism and Japanese culture more generally. Other friends and colleagues who were very supportive of this project include Chuck Prebish, Sorching Low, John Tucker, and Victor Forte.

I am particularly grateful for the help of several assistants and friends who read or worked with me on thinking through the manuscript. These include Joanna Garcia, who brainstormed the discography, typology, and pyramid, and was a heck of an editor; Anna Scharnagl, who also helped in editing after a job interview/audition that included a rendition of "If Not For You"; Emily Hutchinson, aka mapmaker extraordinaire; Daniella Piñeros, who helped collect more books and notes than you could shake a stick at; and Therese Sollien, who got involved late in the game but offered comments that hit the nail right on the head.

Finally, I thank Jeff Rosen and his office staff for permission to reprint Dylan lyrics and liner notes relevant to the discussion of his music-making.

List of Illustrations

FIGURES

TABLES

Preface

Satori in Amsterdam— I'll Let You Be in My Dreams If I Can Be in Yours

PERSONAL AND IMPERSONAL PERSPECTIVES

Any book on Bob Dylan's music is bound to feature two interlocking perspectives: the impersonal, or an objective examination and assessment of his works; and the personal, or an expression of the author's subjective awareness of and interest in the significance of Dylan. Both perspectives reflect a high level of sensitivity to the important influences of Dylan's music felt both individually and communally. This book primarily highlights the impersonal side in discussing affinities between the radical relativism and disillusionment manifested in some stages of Dylan's career and the irreverent, topsy-turvy rhetoric of Zen Buddhist thought that defies all truth claims. I am using the preface as a vehicle for commenting on personal perspectives that led me to engage in this effort.

Like many fans who came of age in the 1960s, Dylan's music was the soundtrack of my adolescence and college years. I frequently tell my students that there are two events from that era that everyone recalls vividly—where they were in November 1963 when President Kennedy was assassinated; and when it was in the summer of 1965 that they first heard "Like a Rolling Stone," the opening snare drum roll of which Bruce Springsteen has said once kicked open the doors of his mind. For me, hearing that song for the first time was one of several epiphanies—or instantaneous flashes of insight that Zen Buddhists refer to as Satori experiences—in understanding and appreciating the full impact of Dylan's music.

A couple of other instances of Dylan-based Satori moments come to mind. First, I remember sitting around a campfire at summer camp in 1963 when one of the older campers pulled out a guitar and sang "Blowin' in the Wind" with a wonderful emulation of Dylan's voice and spirit. Having learned of the song initially through the Peter, Paul, and Mary version, hearing it sung the "right" way was a breakthrough moment. About a year later, I reached a Satori when I heard a medley of Dylan songs sung the "wrong" way by a pop singer (it may have been John Davidson) on a TV variety show. What struck me despite the tame, abbreviated versions of the music was that there could be a single author/composer who was responsible for so many different kinds of songs that had such a penetrating effect on American political consciousness and popular culture.

Needless to say, Dylan's influence along with my enthusiasm for it continued to grow. Then the most profound Satori of all took place while I was in college and made a trip to Europe during winter break with one of my roommates. Dylan's style of singing has always made it difficult to understand all the words of the songs unless you can read the lyrics. In a period that was several decades before the internet made lyrics accessible at the click of a mouse, it was not easy to get a chance to read through and study the words to Dylan songs. As I recall, about the only way to obtain the lyrics was to purchase a guitar book for each of the albums which included the words along with the chords. But these books were hard to come by, and buying them all would have been an inconvenient and overly expensive proposition for a poor student who did not play guitar.

How was a devoted follower supposed to make sense out of the eleven-minute, ten-verse "Desolation Row" without being able to pore over the lyrics printed on a page? In late December 1968, about a year after the release of *John Wesley Harding* with its impenetrable songs and a few months before *Nashville Skyline* was produced with its deceptively simple cliché-based lyrics, my roommate and I flew from Paris to Amsterdam on the way to London. We got lodging at a bed and breakfast along one of the canals. The rooms were tiny and the heating minimal during a very cold spell that winter.

One day while wandering around town in search of the perfect slice of herring or basket of fries with mayonnaise, I stopped in a bookshop. While browsing the shelves, lo and behold, I found a bootleg edition of all of Dylan's lyrics. I bought a copy immediately and then sat around the lobby of the hotel showing other Americans my proud new possession. A friend teased me by asking if I intended to chant the contents of the book from cover to cover, forwards and backwards. I told them I would consider the suggestion.

Shortly after this, one time very late at night a local resident came by and invited several of us to join him in the back of his van parked on the street just outside the hotel in order to partake of an imported intoxicant of the kind generally imbibed with a pipe as a possible starting point for negotiating an acquisition. I joined the group and suddenly found myself rather inebriated, but instead of enjoying this I realized I felt rather cold and claustrophobic and decided to head back inside to go to bed. My roommate followed and when we got upstairs, I realized all over again that in the miniscule room the heat was insufficient. On top of this I was fed up with my friend who was overly attached to my schedule and agenda, and was not showing enough initiative of his own.

With my mind racing around these unpleasant thoughts, I could not get to sleep and I also knew that it was too cold to go for a walk and it would be uncomfortable sitting in the lobby. As a Japanese poet's saying indicates, "I do not like where I am but have no place to turn. How can I seclude myself?" Instead of leaving the room, I lay down next to the radiator underneath a pile of blankets topped off with my wool coat, but I was still shivering and feeling as uptight as I have ever felt. My only consolation was the volume of Dylan lyrics. I opened my book, which was organized by song title listed in alphabetical order, and started reading feverishly through each line of every song.

Then I got to "Desolation Row," the most obtuse and mysterious of songs and my eyes fell on the eighth verse, which I realized has a resonance with the view in Eastern thought, especially Buddhism, that the world is illusory:

> Now at midnight all the agents
> And the superhuman crew
> Come out and round up everyone
> That knows more than they do
> Then they bring them to the factory
> Where the heart-attack machine
> Is strapped across their shoulders
> And then the kerosene
> Is brought down from the castles
> By insurance men who go
> Check to see that nobody is escaping
> To Desolation Row.

The comment about insurance men links the metaphysical realm to the everyday world in an insidious way that is reinforced by the image of the castle, which I had to believe was influenced by Franz Kafka's famous novel.

This song adds the contemporary element of showing how the system—for Dylan, it is a bizarre and twisted mockery of the American Dream—tries to enforce its grip on the illusory world so that the only sane option is to recognize the insanity or to become, as Gunter Grass once put it, "crazy for sanity." Authority for Dylan and Buddhism is seen to be nothing more than a projection of human desire. Meanwhile, both forms of thought praise the integrity of those rare individuals who resist the corruption and hypocrisy that false leaders do not want to allow to be questioned. Somewhat like a Zen Buddhist master, Dylan suggests at the end of the song that a genuine hero must act spontaneously on the imperative to seize the day and smash down the proverbial "Gateless Gate" by challenging false authority held by officials representing an oppressive social system. The state of solitude and detachment from the absurdity of social contests and conflicts is an ideal shared by Dylan and Zen masters.

As I was gazing at the printed page, my mind conjured an image of labyrinths constructed by Dylan in every verse of the song that reflected the problematic side of life's condition. In highlighting the inaccessibility of the center of the labyrinth that appeared in my mind in psychedelic technicolor of immense proportions, the insight provided by the final lines of each verse served to explode the labyrinthine construction before my very eyes. "Nobody is escaping" in the penultimate line of the verse on a deeper level actually meant the opposite, which is that I really and truly could escape precisely by seeing that the impossibility of rescue is all too concise and too clear. But let us not talk falsely now . . . In other words, by understanding how Dylan's lyrics functioned as the catalyst for a Satori, I had a Satori of my own making about the degree of insight encompassed by his lyrics.

Over the course of a few decades, I remained an avid Dylan fan despite the intricate twists and turns of the styles of his musical productions and public personae. Although I admit to becoming a bit of a doubting Thomas around the time of his gospel conversion, I still found that Dylan's songwriting was a major intellectual and cultural influence on my worldview.

Turn the calendar ahead nearly forty years from the time of my Satori in Amsterdam. On August 29, 2006, the anniversary of Katrina, while awaiting a hurricane to hit Miami (which proved to be a false alarm) I listened intently to *Modern Times* which was released that day. What a revelation! Not only had Dylan fulfilled the promise of a trilogy previewed by the two preceding albums, *Time Out of Mind* in 1997 and *"Love and Theft"* in 2001, but he had, I felt, surpassed his greatest lifetime achievements in capturing a worldview based on resigning oneself to relative, multiple truths while seeking passionately yet vainly for the absolute source of truth.

What was the key to the success of *Modern Times*, and of the whole resurgence of Dylan's career that began around 1989 with the production of *Oh Mercy* and that was also confirmed by the release of *Tell Tale Signs* in October 2008, just at the time I was completing the manuscript? I fully agree with the assessment of the recent album by Mikal Gilmore:

> The alternate studio takes, undisclosed songs, movie tracks and live performances that make up the three discs of *Tell Tale Signs* (also available as a two-disc package) depict Dylan's development from 1989 to 2006—which is to say they're closer to Dylan's here and now than any earlier volumes. Also, *Tell Tale Signs* is less an anthology than an album in its own right . . . this collection bears witness to Dylan's reclamation of voice and perspective. He had been a singular visionary who upended rock & roll by recasting it as a force that could question society's values and politics, but he relinquished that calling as the society grew more dangerous. By the end of the Eighties, he had undergone so many transformations, made so many half-here and half-there albums, that he seemed to be casting about for a purpose. What did he want to say about the times around him? Did he have a vision anymore or just a career?[1]

These became my burning questions, or my koan (a pedagogical puzzle or riddle that triggers the insight and illumination of a Satori) to use Zen Buddhist terminology. I wanted at once to follow and to make sense of Dylan's new spiritual path as explained in "Ain't Talkin'": "All my loyal and much loved companions/ They approve of me and share my code/ I practice a faith that's been long abandoned/ Ain't no altars on this long and lonesome road."

Probing this query brought me back to the idea of connecting Dylan & Zen, as I saw numerous elements of affinity that could be systematically explored. First, both Dylan and Zen masters start their discourse of seeking spiritual liberation by evoking the angst and anguish, suffering and torment of human existence or what is known in American popular music as the deep blues. To better understand the roots of Dylan's musical approach to this theme, I made a journey down Highway 61 starting in Memphis and exploring the Mojo Triangle. This links the towns of Clarksdale, the epicenter of the Mississippi Delta and site of the proverbial Cross Roads, with Greenwood, where on a hot July day in 1963 Dylan sang "Only a Pawn in Their Game" before an audience of mostly black civil rights activists, and Greenville, which suffered greatly during the Mississippi flood of 1927. I also visited smaller enclaves such as Moorhead, where the Southern crosses the Yellow Dog; Tutwiler, which was the home of W. C. Handy; and Ruleville near Maggie's, er, I mean Parchman Farm.

From this trip, I came to realize that the Blues, which arose among the most impoverished and submissive classes in modern America who had nothing to lose by telling the truth as they saw it, with its formulaic expressions regarding concrete objects and activities that reflect angst conveys a universe of insight into the nature of transcendence. Despite obviously vast differences of history and culture, this tradition, it seemed to me, has much in common with the inventiveness of Zen Buddhist literature, which was developed by the elite classes in medieval China who chose to forsake the conventional route to fame and fortune in order to undertake the lifestyle of an itinerant outsider.

Other links between Dylan and Zen are that both challenge the (il)legitimacy of social authority and do not hesitate to question the questioner at every turn. In pursuing authenticity and autonomy, they prefer to communicate the sense of paradoxical reality through obtuse, indirect language that draws attention to an experiential rather than abstract level of truth. For both Dylan and Zen, the self is a floating, constructed image that realizes a genuine level of awareness by remaining attuned to the transient joys of the flux and relativism of the illusory world.

Based on these thoughts, I became convinced that the merits of *Modern Times* as a kind of culminating album in Dylan's illustrious career (hopefully there are more to come) and of the hard-foughtfought challenge of pursuing the lonesome faith with no altars has much to do with Dylan's ability to achieve, finally, a middle-way standpoint. The middle path represents a constructive compromise that overcomes his previous tendency to lurch back and forth between extremes of the certainty of finding a single answer and the uncertainty that there was not any answer at all.

In fall 2006, in response to a call for papers I started planning a presentation dealing with linkages between Dylan and Zen for an international symposium on Dylan's musical influences that was held at the University of Minnesota in March 2007. At the conference, I learned a great deal by participating on a panel with other speakers who explored Jewish and Christian themes in Dylan's works, as well as from several speakers including my good friend Paul Swanson, who is from Minnesota and lives in Japan, on the impact of Dylan on Japanese popular culture.

In April, just a few weeks after the conference I returned for the first time in decades to Amsterdam. On the last day of this visit—during which I had presented several lectures on Zen Buddhism, in particular dealing with my specialty focus on the philosophy of Dogen who was founder of the Soto Zen sect in medieval Japan—I accompanied my Dutch friend/host on a walk around the canal district. She suggested that we make a purchase in a local shop to celebrate the occasion and while a bit under the influence I stumbled on the bed and breakfast where the initial Satori in Amsterdam had taken place.

The circle was unbroken, I felt, and I told my friend that when I die I hope to be buried with the collected writings of one of history's great spiritual/poetic masters whose name is five letters beginning with "D"—and it's not Dogen.

Chapter 1

Dylan's Zen Rock Garden

Leaving His Heart in That Kyoto Temple

DYLAN'S SPIRITUAL INFLUENCES, EASTERN AND WESTERN

It has been said, "Religion looms large in Dylan's worldview."[1] During every phase of his career, Bob Dylan has portrayed himself as an outcast or misfit, a drifter or wanderer, or a stranger in a strange land toiling in perpetual exile yet struggling to gain redemption by breaking through the ever-challenging gates to heaven. From the mournful pleas of the "Man of Constant Sorrow" on his first album *Bob Dylan* (1962) to awaiting mixed blessings "When the Deal Goes Down" on the recent *Modern Times* (2006), Dylan's ongoing quest for elusive paradise has continued unabated.

As a critic of Dylan points out, "Folklore, ethnomusicology, linguistics, anthropology, literary criticism, and philology: none of these can be left aside in a thorough attempt to gain insight into the rich dynamics and designs of Bob Dylan's performance artistry."[2] The same must also be said for the field of religious studies, and while the main focus has been on various aspects of Western traditions, this book makes the case for injecting Eastern mysticism into the multidisciplinary, multicultural mix because of Dylan's wide-ranging affinities with Zen Buddhism, which are in small part historical/biographical and in large part spiritual/intellectual.

Dylan's songwriting was greatly influenced by American folk/blues music as well as Beat poetry and a variety of other literary sources. In considering the role of religious imagery, the most prominent source of inspiration seems to be an extensive use of biblical references. Whether their significance is interpreted from either a Judaic/Old Testament or a Christian/New Testament perspective, citations from the Bible appear in just about every album. This includes, but is by no means limited to, his gospel stage that began in the late 1970s and endured until the early 1980s.[3] But is the Bible the sole factor needed to assess the spiritual dimensions of Dylan's life work?

It is clear that Japanese culture, Zen Buddhism in particular, was making an important imprint on Dylan's approach to music-making during the mid-1970s. This phase, marked by several direct references as well as indirect allusions in Dylan's writings, lasted for several years through the time of his first Far East tour in 1978. It culminated with an explicit mention of Zen gardens that he visited in Kyoto in the album liner notes to *Live at Budokan*, which was released in America in early 1979, just months after his conversion to Christianity in fall 1978 and before the release of the gospel album *Slow Train Coming* in the summer of 1979. The gradual rise yet abrupt fall of an interest in Zen in relation to the awakening of a Christian consciousness is a very important biographical juxtaposition that is generally overlooked in the field of Dylanology. This is primarily because most critics are not sensitive to the issue of Eastern affinities and possible influences. Dylan's relation to Zen may seem a remote and exotic cultural context, but it is critical for understanding his sense of religious experience.

Dylan's initial exposure to Zen undoubtedly came through the auspices of poet and avowed meditator Allen Ginsberg, along with other Beat movement writers who were involved extensively with pursuing the Buddhist dharma either in their narrative writings, such as Jack Kerouac, or in their religious practice and poetry, such as Gary Snyder. Dylan befriended Ginsberg and read the works of other Beats when he first arrived and become ensconced in the bohemian scene that was flourishing in New York's Greenwich Village in the early 1960s. For the members of the Beat cultural movement, the appropriation of a Zen way of living freely and without constraint in the eternal moment was considered a crucial component of their literary endeavors, which expressed an obsessive search for individual freedom and spiritual insight beyond the conventions of modern, mechanistic society.

As early as the mid-1960s, or over a decade before his travels to Japan, there were lyrics in a number of Dylan songs indicating the inception of a Zen-like outlook. These passages deal with the quest to find a haven of solitude and detachment in a world where the boundary between reality and illusion is continually breaking down with each act of social or personal injustice, hypocrisy, and inauthenticity. This spiritual longing for an answer found through naturalism is conveyed in songs such as "Chimes of Freedom," with its expression of compassion for the misunderstood and downtrodden experience during an exhilarating thunderstorm; "It's Alright, Ma (I'm Only Bleeding)," which expresses a strict adherence to intellectual and cultural integrity and disdain for self-deception; and "Desolation Row," which shows that the aloofness of resignation and withdrawal from conflicts petty and grand seems to be the only answer for profound social ills.

In songs in which the Beat literary influence is particularly strong, Dylan seems to reflect the Buddhist attitude of "seeing things as they really are," by overcoming delusion and remaining free of blinders, distortions, or bad faith. Affinities with Zen also are evident in lyrics that express a view of moral causality which resembles the Buddhist notion of karma. Several songs from *Blonde on Blonde* in 1966, including "Stuck Inside of Mobile with the Memphis Blues Again," "Visions of Johanna," and "4th Time Around" refer to the notion that "'Everybody must give something back/ For something they get.'" Another example of Zen inklings is the cycle of songs on *The Basement Tapes* recorded in 1967 (released in 1975) that explore the implications of an experience of nothingness, or the spiritual void, in "Too Much of Nothing," "Nothing Was Delivered," and "You Ain't Goin' Nowhere."

Dylan's possible interest in a Zen outlook was probably influenced by his first wife Sara who was known for her calmness, self-effacing outlook,

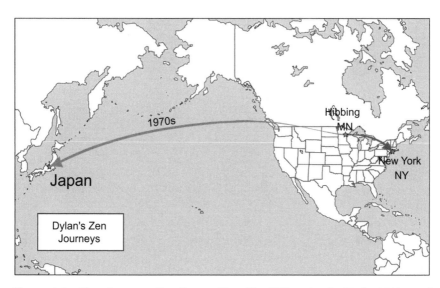

Figure 1.1 Two Journeys Leading to Zen: The Village in the Early 1960s, and Japan in the Late 1970s

and "Zen-like equanimity,"[4] and for teaching Dylan a way of finding quietude within the turbulent lifestyle of concert touring. "An adherent of Eastern mysticism," an observer reports, who did not ask Dylan probing questions,

> she possessed a certain ego-less quality that dovetailed greatly with Dylan's more pronounced sense of ambition ... Possessed of a quiet but unimposing fortitude, Sara furnished him with a much-needed oasis of calm and sincerity away from the high-octane hurly-burly and habitual deceit of the entertainment industry.[5]

An interest in Zen was greatly enhanced by Dylan's travels to Japan ten years later. His music gained popularity and a cult following in Japan beginning in the 1960s, when songs like "Blowin' in the Wind," "Like a Rolling Stone," and "I Want You" were hit singles and he became a role model for Japan's student protest movement during the Vietnam War era. Dylan's arrival for the 1978 tour was eagerly anticipated and documented by scores of journalists. When he was asked at a press conference why he had come to their country, Dylan told Japanese reporters rather playfully that it was because "we are living in a Zen age."[6] Although Dylan sang

Figure 1.2   Dylan 1960s Record Jacket in Japan

unconventional arrangements of his classic songs accompanied for the first time in his career by a backup band with sax, bongo drums, and distaff singers, the reception was very positive. A headline in an entertainment rag back in the states ran, "Dylan Zaps Japs."

Upon leaving Japan at the conclusion of the tour, Dylan spoke fondly of the Zen temples he visited there, including the Kinkakuji Temple (The Temple of the Golden Pavilion) and the most famous Zen rock garden located at Ryoanji Temple in Kyoto. According to the cover of *Live at Budokan*,[7] "The Japanese people can hear my heart still beating in Kyoto at the Zen Rock Garden—Someday I will be back to reclaim it."[8]

SITTING BUDDHA VERSUS PRECIOUS ANGEL

Dylan's "Zen Garden," a stage of his career that included references to Zen or Asian mysticism, was probably first cultivated in 1974 on *Planet Waves*, which includes liner notes that evoke the image of Native American poets seeking to find a glimpse of the Buddha as part of their spiritual journey. In "Dirge," Dylan says cryptically in a way that is similar to "Desolation Row," "I paid the price of solitude, but at least I'm out of debt." This implies that a Zen-like transcendence of ordinary attachments is worth the sacrifice of superficial companionship or seeking the approval of peers.

In an outtake version of "Idiot Wind" recorded for *Blood on the Tracks* a year later, Dylan evokes an ancient Asian religious text, the *I-Ching* or *Book of Changes* (also cited in a 1965 interview): "I threw the *I-Ching* yesterday, it said there might be some thunder at the well./ I haven't tasted peace an' quiet for so long, it seems like livin' hell."[9] Originally composed nearly 3000 years ago and translated many times into English, the *I-Ching* introduces the doctrine of the balance of opposing but complementary forces of Yin (yielding) and Yang (assertive). It is known for its distinctive view of reconciling the conundrum of human choice versus fate determined by external powers through the doctrine of synchronicity, or the confluence of mutually determining factors that defy logical explanation. From the standpoint of synchronic events, there is no such thing as coincidence in the conventional sense of random, arbitrary occurrences, because free will and destiny are interwoven possibilities in each and every action. The reference to "thunder in the well" indicates the occasion of dramatic change or upheaval, and suggests that the consolation of solitude and quietude is not easily attained until the emotions of resentment and doubt are overcome.

In addition, the final verse of an unofficial version of "Simple Twist of Fate" also recorded for *Blood on the Tracks* concludes the anguished love song about missed opportunities amid the misfortunes of fateful circumstances by saying that the complex situation is "leaving me to meditate/ One more time on a simple twist of fate."[10] Here, the notion of fate suggests the inescapability of inevitable circumstances that may cause turmoil or upheaval yet must be accepted with calm resignation.

Furthermore, this album is replete with the notion of seeking moments of insight or artistic epiphany amid the frail beauty and tragedy of a transient world in which "Friends will arrive, friends will disappear," according to "Buckets of Rain," while one is "down the road to ecstasy" in "Idiot Wind." Also, the final verse of "Shelter from the Storm" says, "Well, I'm livin' in a foreign country but I'm bound to cross the line/ Beauty walks a razor's edge, someday I'll make it mine." The phrase "a razor's edge" evokes the title of W. Somerset Maugham's 1930s novel about an American adventurer trying to integrate his experience of Buddhist meditation into the everyday problems of the Depression era. Dylan's approach, which maintains aesthetic distance and detachment yet remains committed to the cause of accepting chaos for self and others without denying the pervasiveness of personal and social turmoil, has an affinity with the Zen goal of attaining the sudden flash of understanding that characterizes an experience of instantaneous awakening or Satori.

In "Up to Me," another song recorded for *Blood on the Tracks* but not included on the official release, Dylan cryptically downplays the typical Christian explanation of moral consequences based on the beatitudes, including the ideals of turning the other cheek and the meek inheriting the earth. According to the lyrics, "We heard the Sermon on the Mount and I knew it was too complex,/ It didn't amount to anything more than what the broken glass reflects." The image of the broken glass nicely conveys the Zen view of accepting multiple, fractured perspectives through the exercise of solving a koan, or a succinct, seemingly unanswerable, double-bind-oriented yet edifying spiritual riddle, such as "The gate to wisdom is not really a gate. How do you pass through a no-gate?"[11] The song indicates that the Asian outlook of taking part in, yet remaining detached from, a fragmented and relativistic universe is more attuned to natural circumstances and therefore of equal weight or perhaps superior to the biblical account of morality.

A few months later in April 1975, Dylan did a radio interview with Mary Travers (of the renowned folk trio Peter, Paul, and Mary, which first made "Blowin' in the Wind" a hit single), in which he chided listeners like Travers who would say they "enjoyed" listening to *Blood on the Tracks*, since it reveals so much inner pain (she conceded that she meant to say "appreciated"). Dylan also discussed with Travers how the Zen notion of time as an eternal present moment helped to inspire the revival of his artistry after a lull in his songwriting during the early 1970s. This period of composing was also greatly influenced by Dylan's elderly painting teacher Norman Raeban.[12] Although Raeban, a descendant of famed Yiddish writer Shalom Aleichem, was not at all involved in and did not introduce him to Zen, he did teach Dylan "a new way of seeing" based on developing a comprehensive scope of perception that has affinities with meditation techniques associated with Eastern mysticism. According to Dylan, this helped to spark his innovative approach to creating narrative structures by integrating past and future vantage points with current perspectives through flashbacks and asides, especially in "Tangled Up in Blue."

In his next album, *Desire* released in 1976, references to Buddhism come to the fore in the hit protest song "Hurricane": "Now all the criminals in their coats and their ties/ Are free to drink martinis and watch the sun rise/ While Rubin sits like Buddha in a ten-foot cell/ An innocent man in a living hell." Dylan ironically evokes the image of a Buddhist meditation hut, which is traditionally "ten-foot square" in honor of the abode of the humble lay saint Vimalakirti, who was said to have bested Buddhist deities in a heavenly debate. This image creates a sense of empathy for the listener with the plight of the unfairly imprisoned black boxer, Rubin "Hurricane" Carter.

Carter was a rising prizefighter who "one time . . . could-a been/ The [middleweight] champion of the world," but who in the racially divided environment of Paterson, New Jersey in the 1960s was framed for a bloody murder he did not commit. Hurricane continued to contest and appeal his case through the legal system while he remained in prison for ten years after Dylan's involvement in the cause, and he was eventually freed from jail in 1985 after serving nearly two decades. Some time later, he was awarded two honorary doctorates of law from universities in Canada and Australia, and his story was featured in a film starring Denzel Washington.

In the song, Dylan's first overtly topical lyric in half a decade (since "George Jackson" recorded in 1970 about another apparently falsely accused black prisoner who in this case died in jail), Hurricane is a kind of modern-day Zen hero. He is said to summon his considerable inner strengths to become spiritually liberated from prolonged physical suffering due to blatant racism and social injustice. By turning incarceration into an opportunity for contemplation and purification in rising above all detractors and obstacles, Carter demonstrates the qualities of patience, fortitude, and equanimity coupled with self-assurance and self-assertiveness. It is very interesting that Dylan chose to cast this issue in terms of Eastern imagery of meditative self-determination rather than the Western ideal of sacrificial martyrdom. He also includes in the liner notes to *Desire* the confession that he has got "a whole lot of karma to burn . . .."

Figure 1.3   1978 Far East/Budokan Tour Program

Figure 1.4   Zen-Style Interior Design

There are several lyrics in *Street-Legal*, Dylan's next album of original material released in 1978, the same year the live album was recorded in Japan, that contain references or allusions to Zen. In particular, a line in "We Better Talk This Over" cites one of the most famous of the enigmatic Zen koans regarding the difficulty of communicating intuitive awareness. "But I don't think it's liable to happen," Dylan says, perhaps mockingly, of the possibility for reconciliation with a romantic partner, and he concludes with the koan, "Like the sound of one hand clappin'."

This album also contains songs influenced by the Mississippi Delta Blues tradition, which has greatly affected Dylan's music-making throughout his career, including "New Pony," a rewrite of a classic 1920s Charley Patton tune "Pony Blues." *Street-Legal* makes a couple of allusions to another great bluesman, Robert Johnson, especially in lines in "Where Are You Tonight? (Journey Through Dark Heat)" about "the juice running down my leg" and about anxiety "killing me by degrees." This highlights that the songs of itinerant yet long-suffering early twentieth-century American Blues singers in pursuit of redemption was a genre crucial to the development of many subsequent forms of modern popular and spiritual music. It bears striking affinities with the attitudes and spiritual poetry created by unconventional Zen pilgrims seeking their path in medieval East Asia.

Another lyric in that song, "There's a white diamond gloom on the dark side of this room and a pathway that leads up to the stars;/ If you don't believe there's a price for this sweet paradise,/ Remind me to show you the scars," evokes the classical mystical experience of enduring the "dark night of the soul" in order to find higher truth.[13] This corresponds to the Zen notion of the edifying quality of suffering that is inextricably linked with the attainment of enlightenment. In addition, this song's classic blues putdown of a foe, "It felt outa place, my foot in his face," sounds a lot like a comparable Zen saying about dismissing a rival, "Why is his nose in my hands?"

In an interview published in *Macleans* in March 1978 just as the Japan concerts were concluding, Dylan responds to a question about whether he sees any conflict between his having an affinity with Existentialism and his upbringing in Judaism. He says that there are many labels that have been pinned on him, including "existentialist Jew" or "Buddhist Jew," but these are all irrelevant for understanding his music. This was months before a major transition in Dylan's religious orientation was about to happen with a new, or possibly revived, interest in Christianity. It turned out by the time of the release of *Street-Legal* in the summer of 1978 that there was yet another twist of faith already taking place, and that Dylan's Zen Garden stage was heading for a collision course with his rather abrupt conversion to fundamental Christianity.

It is interesting that in the mid-1970s as Dylan's interest in Buddhism grew, he was developing a fascination with Jesus as a role model or with identifying himself with the self-sacrificing attitude and martyrdom of Jesus. This is indicated in the self-referential lines, "There's a lone soldier on the cross" in "Idiot Wind" and "In a little hilltop village, they gambled for my clothes" in the penultimate verse in "Shelter from the Storm." It is also evident in scenes in *Renaldo and Clara* in which Dylan and Ginsburg take a break from touring during the Rolling Thunder Revue to reenact the Stations of the Cross at the gravesite of Jack Kerouac in Lowell, Massachusetts. Now Jesus is not symbolic of an internal state of consciousness, for Dylan has converted to the faith which holds to a literal reading of the doctrine "that there'll be no peace, that the war won't cease/ Until He returns."

Following the conversion, the encounter and conflict between the two religious approaches quickly came to a head in 1979 with the album *Slow Train Coming*, in which Dylan repudiates Buddhism as part of embracing a new belief, although some would argue he had long been involved with the gospel but was not consciously aware of or willing to admit his own religious views. After finding a "Precious Angel" (reportedly one of his backup singers) who facilitated his Christian experience, Dylan chides the ecumenical interests of his recently divorced wife who had helped to indoctrinate him to Eastern religiosity. He sings, "You were telling him about Buddha, you were telling him about Mohammed in the same breath./ You never mentioned one time the Man who came and died a criminal's death."

With a Zen light shining on the sitting Buddha seemingly eclipsed and cast aside by the Christian angel's glow, one wonders whether Dylan's affinity with the East would tend to diminish and perhaps disappear altogether. However, the relation between the impact of Christianity, which Dylan seemed to have abandoned by the early 1980s, and other spiritual and cultural worldviews remains complex and contested. One way to answer the question of whether or not Dylan may have lost an interest in Zen and Asian mysticism is that there are important indicators of his continued involvement with Japanese culture that have emerged over the three decades of the post-gospel period.[14]

For example, in the early 1980s, the video of "Tight Connection to My Heart (Has Anybody Seen My Love)" was shot in Tokyo. Originally recorded for *Infidels* but released on *Empire Burlesque*, the song deals with the ambiguous image of an idealized, spiritual "Madame Butterfly." As with so many of Dylan's innovations, this proved to be years ahead of its time. The video's extensive use of imagery from contemporary Japanese society presages other American pop cultural interests in the Orient, such as Gwen

Stefani's chorus known as the "Harajuku Girls" that rose to prominence over twenty years later. Furthermore, during a tour of Japan in the early 1990s, outstanding performances of "A Hard Rain's A-Gonna Fall" and "Ring Them Bells" were delivered in an orchestral setting, unusual for Dylan, as part of the "Great Music Experiment" that was produced in the ancient capital city of Nara.

A few years after this, around the turn of the millennium, a special collection of live Dylan songs was released only in Japan, indicating the continuing high level of interest among fans there. Moreover, it became a sensational story when it was shown that the moderately bestselling book *Confessions of a Yakuza* written by a Japanese doctor infused a dozen passages among the lyrics of "*Love and Theft*," especially in the songs "Floater" and "Lonesome Day Blues," which also includes extensive references to the works of classical poet Ovid.[15] In "Ain't Talkin'" from 2006, Dylan evokes Buddhism as a source of comfort for its insight and compassion when he laments those who would distract and deprive the comforts of contemplation.

In addition to these examples, one of the verses from "Sugar Baby" sounds like a description of the notion of suffering (*dukkha*) that comes straight out of a traditional Buddhist text whether or not Dylan conceived of the song in this way:

> Every moment of existence seems like some dirty trick
> Happiness can come suddenly and leave just as quick
> Any minute of the day the bubble could burst
> Try to make things better for someone, sometimes,
> you just end up making it a thousand times worse.

With its emphasis on self-deception coupled with disappointment and anxiety in relation to feelings of uncertainty and instability generated by the incessant flux of impermanence, the song evokes the Asian mystical worldview. However, it is important to note that the final line of the last verse, "Look up, look up—seek your Maker—'fore Gabriel blows his horn," certainly expresses a typically Western view of judgment day by referring to the inevitability of accounting for a lifetime of sins and transgressions.

DYLAN'S CAREER TRAJECTORY AS SWINGING PENDULUM

The full extent of Dylan's involvement, direct or indirect, with Zen and other branches of Asian mysticism is not clear, but may seem rather limited in scope. How important, then, are affinities with Zen for understanding Dylan's work? Does it play a key role, or is it a veritable blip on the screen compared to other aspects that seem to have had a more dramatic and enduring affect on his religiosity? The factors of Western spirituality include Dylan's Jewish upbringing and conversion to Christianity that lasted for at least a few years, as well as extensive biblical citations through-out his songwriting career. Also included is his fascination with diverse spiritual sources ranging from Blues music and Beat poetry to the classics and the philosophy of Nietzsche as well as the poetry of Rimbaud, along with a wide variety of literary and cultural elements, especially from American folk music and the society it reflects yet seeks to transform.[16]

The juxtaposition and sharp contrast between Dylan's appreciation of the Zen rock garden in Kyoto in 1978 and his reverence for Christ that was awakened less than a year later highlights the fact that there have always been two main worldviews, at times competing and at times com-plementary, in Dylan's mind. Exploring in detail the relation between the worldviews at different stages of his career is one of the central themes of this book.

Various kinds of lyrical or intellectual affinities and indirect connec-tions between Dylan and Zen have taken place throughout different peri-ods of his career, and are by no means limited to the one rather compressed time frame of the mid- to late 1970s (*Blood on the Tracks* through *Street-Legal*). Stepping back from that particular phase to survey his overall pro-duction over nearly half a century, it seems clear that many of the singer–songwriter's lyrics echo the Zen philosophy of seeking enlighten-ment through experiencing life's hardships, continually questioning assumptions and stereotypes, and searching within for a sense of reprieve and transcendence. A Zen perspective appears to play a crucial, if generally indirect role at times of the disillusionment Dylan expressed in stages dur-ing the 1960s and the 1980s in addition to the 1970s. During these phases of his songwriting, Dylan rejected any and all symbols of authority that might obstruct his dedicated pursuit of authenticity and autonomy, which is realized during key moments of Zen-like detachment and compassion.

At the same time, there are many songs in various career stages that reverberate with Judeo-Christian precepts of believing in a higher power, obeying moral codes, and submitting to judgment. Dylan's Judeo-Christian-oriented lyrics evoke a dualistic worldview in the sense that Duality refers to two competing forces, such as good and evil, or heaven and hell. The Duality side is where Dylan is looking for a single higher power to offer solutions to personal and social dilemmas. The higher power provides justice or a sense of retribution for social ills for people that are not following the highest moral standards. In "When the Ships Come In," for example, he writes, "Then the sands will roll/ Out a carpet of gold/ For your weary toes to be a-touchin'/And the ship's wise men/ Will remind you once again/ That the whole wide world is watchin.'" This is a judgmental view dating back to the Old Testament prophets that Dylan has embraced in some periods of his career.

But in other songs, Dylan leans more toward the non-dualistic worldview of Zen Buddhism. The Non-Duality side is where Dylan sees that instead of one single truth that is making a judgment and offering retribution, there are multiple relativistic truths. In the world of the interaction of Yin and Yang forces, all contrasts, including the relation between reality and illusion, break down. A line from the final verse of "Tangled Up in Blue" in 1975, "All the people we used to know/ They're an illusion to me now," is a prime example of Dylan expressing resignation toward the relative, illusory world.

To sum up, the Duality worldview is based on a vertical, top-down sense of the universe in which a monolithic truth creates moral judgment and retribution for transgressions committed both individual and collective. The Non-Duality worldview is based on a horizontal, side-by-side sense in which there is a plurality of truths that coinhabit the universe in Yin/Yang fashion and are best dealt with through stoic acceptance and resignation. Both views make extensive use of paradoxical imagery. For example, a line in "The Times They are A-Changin'" from the early 1960s, "Rapidly fadin',/ And the first one now/ Will later be last" is an example of vertical paradox in which opposites are conjoined but with a clear sense of priority (echoing Mark 10.31, "But many that are first shall be last; and the last first"). On the other hand, a lyric in "Silvio" from the mid-1980s, "I can stroke your body and relieve your pain/ Since every pleasure's got an edge of pain," expresses horizontal paradox in which opposites are forever entwined, and are of equal value and weight.

Dylan's emphasis has swung like a pendulum alternating between the two worldviews especially in his first three decades as a recording artist. During Dylan's folk-protest era of 1963–1964, his lyrics often invoked themes of morality and justice. But during his folk-rock period of 1965–1967, Dylan's work was more quixotic and searching. For example, in "Tombstone Blues" Dylan insists that excessive verbiage reflecting false knowledge must be discarded: "Now I wish I could write you a melody so plain/ That could hold you dear lady from going insane/ That could ease you and cool you and cease the pain/ Of your useless and pointless knowledge."

This is reminiscent of a Zen master, influenced by the Daoist view that it is necessary to unlearn and eventually forget conventional understanding, who comments: "The Dao is not subject to knowing or not knowing.

Knowing is delusion; not knowing is blankness. If you truly reach the genuine Dao, you will find it as vast and boundless as outer space. How can this be discussed at the level of affirmation and negation?" Both Zen masters and Dylan use language in a special, deliberately perplexing way to go beyond ordinary knowing and speaking in order to reach what a medieval mystical text called the "cloud of unknowing." This state-of-mind reflects a kind of intuitive knowledge that surpasses conventional logic and understanding.

Following the dramatic shift that took place in the 1960s, Dylan's lyrics have continued to move back and forth between the Judeo-Christian and the Zen worldviews, with the pendulum swinging between idyllic family life (Duality) and the disappointment of separation (Non-Duality) in the 1970s, and between an affirmation of the gospel (Duality) and frustration with this belief system (Non-Duality) in the 1980s. Dylan's process of exploring different spiritual paths corresponds to the manner in which Zen masters relentlessly seek a constructive compromise between two approaches. One is a dedicated commitment to self-discipline or self-reliance as the key to realization known as the "path of Self Power," and the other is a calm acceptance of fateful circumstances and divine forces operating beyond anyone's control known as the "path of Other Power." Like Zen's approach to multi-perspectivism through "turning the world upside down and topsy-turvy," Dylan is "tough, witty and resourceful and full of reverberating awareness of life's conflicting positions."[17] He demonstrates an ability to hold in his mind disparate realities with a creative tension that brings out the best yet does not interfere with both possibilities.

The zigzag quality lasted, I suggest, until the late 1980s when Dylan began to find a middle path, or a constructive compromise between the extremes. This was first suggested by the song "Man in the Long Black Coat," which juxtaposes two verses, one commenting dualistically that "every man's conscience is vile and depraved" with the following verse remarking non-dualistically that "people don't live or die, people just float." In subsequent albums, he has continued to place side-by-side the respective standpoints and seems comfortable with their compatibility.

Thus, during the most recent phase of his work that has lasted for two decades, Dylan has developed an approach revealing that East versus West, as well as Duality versus Non-Duality, are not always polarized as alternating opposites or engaged in a standoff, but can be linked together as mutually enhancing cross-cultural possibilities of the ongoing, universal spiritual quest. According to a verse in "Nettie Moore," a song about a vengeful yet regretful lover, "The Judge is coming in, everybody rise/ Lift up your eyes/ You can do what you please, you don't need my advice/ Before you call me any dirty names you better think twice." The first two lines evoke dualism, but the final part of the passage suggests the chaos and "mixed-up confusion," to cite the title of Dylan's first official single, regarding multiple, fragmented approaches to truth.

ARE BIRDS FREE?

Dylan's work has demonstrated a remarkable variability that is reflected in his capacity to make the most of a rich variety of genres from blues to rock, country, and gospel that some would say reveal fundamental inconsistencies from the early to the late periods of his career. The genres include personal romantic narratives with profound social significance, such as "Visions of Johanna" or "Tangled Up in Blue"; topical, state-of-the-union message statements, such as "Desolation Row," "Slow Train," or "Political World"; apocalyptic pronouncements, as in "Shooting Star" or asking whether this is "Lincoln County Road or Armageddon?" in "Señor (Tales of Yankee Power)"; barbed-wire fence-straddling howls of desperation, such as "Can You Please Crawl Out My Window" and "Cold Irons Bound"; and confessional, repentant anthems, such as "Ballad of Frankie Lee and Judas Priest," "I Believe in You," and "Not Dark Yet." Underlying these thematic approaches is the ever mysterious presence of Dylan taking on the guise of Alias, the Drifter, Jack of Hearts, Jack Fate, Jokerman, or Man in the Long Black Coat. Accepting chaos while wondering if chaos will ever accept him and remaining busy being born rather than busy dyin', Dylan finds shelter from the storm— most of the time.

While it is important to acknowledge and appreciate diverse Western influences, sacred as well as secular, the main theme of this book is to swing the pendulum, so to speak, by highlighting the spiritual significance of enigmatic Dylan seen in relation to the equally elusive and ambiguous utterances and mannerisms of traditional Zen Buddhism. This is done not to assert the superior impact of Zen, but to help to locate and interpret the fulcrum or leverage point that is crucial for understanding the crisscross paths of dualistic and non-dualistic worldviews in Dylan's career. Dylan's affinity with Zen is not limited to certain periods, but cuts across all phases in reflecting the quest to uphold authenticity and autonomy in a world characterized by the absurdity of disruptive turmoil and petty conflict.

Traditional Zen thought was generally expressed in the "sparse words" of minimalist yet evocative verse, often accompanied by eccentric gestures or body language as well as other forms of creative expression. Zen masters sought to attain liberation from bondage to inhibiting psychological and social structures in pursuit of spiritual freedom, regardless of ideology. Their teachings, preserved in the voluminous records of medieval Chinese and Japanese literary culture, remain alive today in large part by contributing to modern interfaith and cross-cultural exchanges regarding diverse paths to spiritual realization. The inventive philosophical queries and commentaries of Zen discourse had a strong impact on the New York bohemian environment of the 1960s, as evident in the extensive role they played in the life and works of Beat writers, and also bear a striking similarity to Dylan's corpus.

Dylan's work seems Zen-like in puzzling passages about impenetrable paradoxical states of consciousness like, "She knows there's no success like failure, and that failure's no success at all," "I need a dump truck mama to unload my head," and "You know it blows right through me like a ball and chain." In addition, there are quixotic queries influenced by Pete Seeger's "Where Have All the Flowers Gone?," such as "How many times must a man look up/ Before he can see the sky?," "Where have you been, my blue-eyed son?" (following the traditional "Lord Randall"), "What Can I Do for You?," and "[Did] I ever become what you wanted me to be/ Did I miss the mark or/ Over-step the line/ That only you could see?" These recall classic examples of Zen koans such as "Does a dog have Buddha-nature?," "What is the sound of one hand clapping?," and "What is the look on your face before you were born?" In addition, Zen irreverent behavior such as having masters slap or ridicule one another, or cut off fingers or limbs as disciplinary actions, is similar to the smashing of windows in the liner notes to *John Wesley Harding*.

Both Dylan and Zen demonstrate an ability to use language creatively while remaining cognizant of the limitations of verbal discourse in order to convey the heights and horizons, as well as the depths and defeats, of an inner dimension of spirituality characterized by self-reflection and self-correction. Zen frequently depicts a damned-if-you-do and damned-if-you-don't situation with seemingly absurd examples like holding up a container and demanding of a disciple, "Tell me what this is without calling it a water pitcher and without not calling it a water pitcher. Tell me!"

Zen discourse resonates with Dylan's marvelous and haunting inquiry—a true modern-day Zen koan—into the realm and limit of freedom in the concluding (yet inconclusive) verse of "Ballad in Plain D." After bemoaning the loss of someone he genuinely loved through tragic circumstances of betrayal and arrogance, the song's narrator responds to his "friends in the prison," metaphorically speaking, who ask "how good does it feel to be free," by questioning them "so mysteriously": "Are birds free from the chains of the skyway?"

When the capacity of language to express truth is exhausted, Zen masters evoke the importance of maintaining a noble silence, and if asked about its meaning they often maintain a lofty "silence about silence," lest speech corrupts the contemplative moment. Dylan similarly recognizes the value of no-words when he comments in the *Bringing It All Back Home* liner notes that "experience teaches that silence terrifies people the most." Dylan sees that reticence is a useful and sometimes necessary tool to put an end to the blowing of the "Idiot Wind," and to inspire and rouse listeners from their spiritual or ideological slumber.

Yet, Dylan and Zen masters are well aware of the limitations of silence that make it necessary to abandon a reliance on abandoning "words and letters" if it is used in either a passive and aphasic or stubborn and withdrawn way. In those cases, they speak out vigorously from the standpoint of moral outrage or to express social criticism. Dylan has said, "I used to care/ But things have changed," implying a reluctance to get involved and ensnared in the strife and struggles of the world. Underlying or complementing this detachment is a genuine compassionate concern and commitment for the well-being of self and others. According to "Thunder on the Mountain," "Remember this, I'm your servant both night and day." Knowing when to be retiring and when to be proactive in articulating a vision or demanding moral rectitude is an important skill and domain of responsibility taken on by the spiritual master. For Dylan, the Delta Blues musical genre of Charley Patton and Robert Johnson has long been the primary venue that enables forceful yet frequently ambiguous, quixotic expressions of spiritual longing in a way that resembles the elusive, probing quality of Zen Buddhist koans and verse.

There are additional significant similarities between Zen masters and Dylan in their respective dual roles as mystical seekers and recluses, as well as prophets and social critics. Zen became prominent as a medieval Buddhist monastic tradition in which the leading patriarchs attained the heights of spiritual liberation but remained keenly aware of the ambiguities, struggles, and tensions that continue to plague the religious path. Thirteenth-century Japanese Zen master Dogen referred to attaining truth as a matter of "disentangling entangled vines," which can never be fully straightened out. In a parallel way, Bob Dylan is a poetic singer "still searching for another joint" as "revolution is in the air," who glimpses freedom now and again while "knockin' on heaven's door," but keeps wondering "If I could only turn back the clock to when God and her were born." Zen and Dylan take paradox and irony to the level of an art form in seeking to find truth amid the entanglements and distractions of illusory existence.

Here and elsewhere, while primarily influenced by Western religious and literary sources, Dylan's work seems to approach the Zen worldview, which finds liberation through recognizing and resigning to, rather than denying, the transient world characterized by illusion and self-doubt. Dylan emphasizes transforming bad-faith perspectives into wisdom that sees reality as it is and he is still willing and able to accept disillusionment through detachment that does not turn its back on a world of commitment and responsibility. Some prominent examples include the following:

- "I try my best/ To be just like I am,/ But everybody wants you/ To be just like them./ They sing while you slave and I just get bored" ("Maggie's Farm," 1965).
- "Everybody said they'd stand behind me/ When the game got rough/ But the joke was on me/ There was nobody even there to call my bluff/ I'm going back to New York City/ I do believe I've had enough" ("Just Like Tom Thumb's Blues," 1965).
- "In fourteen months I've only smiled once and I didn't do it consciously" ("Up to Me," 1974).
- "Life is sad/ Life is a bust/ All ya can do is do what you must./ You do what you must do and ya do it well" ("Buckets of Rain," 1974).
- "I was lyin' down in the reeds without any oxygen/ I saw you in the wilderness among the men./ Saw you drift into infinity and come back again/ All you got to do is wait and I'll tell you when" ("True Love Tends to Forget," 1978).
- "I gaze into the doorway of temptation's angry flame/ And every time I pass that way I always hear my name./ Then onward in my journey I come to understand/ That every hair is numbered like every grain of sand." ("Every Grain of Sand," 1981).
- "So many roads, so much at stake/ So many dead ends, I'm at the edge of the lake/ Sometimes I wonder what it's gonna take/ To find dignity" ("Dignity," 1989).
- "I've been down on the bottom of a world full of lies/ I ain't looking for nothing in anyone's eyes" ("Not Dark Yet," 1997).

Similarly, Dogen's majestic philosophical/poetic essay titled *Shobogenzo* "Genjokoan," which can be translated as "Realizing Enlightenment in Everyday Life," at once embraces a relativist worldview that is resigned to the delusory status of everyday concerns and invokes the sense of ultimate awareness as dynamic and evolving yet always somehow incomplete and in need of renewal: "When dharma [Buddhist truth] does not fill your whole body and mind, you think it is already sufficient. When dharma does fill your body and mind, you understand that something is missing."[18] This paradoxical irony further resembles Dylan's song, "Trying to Get to Heaven," which includes a line about emotional loss that also plays with the tension in the ultimate casting off of illusion that comes with spiritual insight. Dylan says, "Just when you think you've lost everything, you find out you can always loose a little more," crooning "lo-o-o-o-ose," sung low over a few extra measures for added emphasis.

As an expression of their mystical vision, Dylan and Zen both speak poetically with paradoxical phrasing about the true wisdom embedded in the harmonious world of nature. One of the most important aspects of the worldview of Zen, known for its exquisite rock gardens, calligraphy, tea ceremony, and other forms of art and ritual, is that it seeks to go beyond pessimism by affirming the frail beauty of concrete reality while recognizing and accepting transience and relativism. According to a Dogen verse, "To what shall I liken the world?/ Moonlight, reflected in dewdrops,/ Shaken from a crane's bill." Beauty, generally associated with forms of nature in Zen, is appreciated all the more for being ephemeral and frail.

In an early masterpiece, "Lay Down Your Weary Tune," Dylan sings, "The ocean wild like an organ played,/ The seaweed wove its strands,/ The crashing waves like cymbals clashed/ Against the rocks and sands." As Dylan personifies the music-making of waters, Dogen speaks of the omnipresence of flowing water, and also of the phantasmagoria of the walking of mountains, in his evocative essay, *Shobogenzo* "Sansuikyo" ("The Sutras of Mountains and Waters"). He concludes as follows: "There are mountains hidden in the sky. There are mountains hidden in mountains. There are mountains hidden in hiddenness. This is complete understanding." For Dylan in his song as for Dogen in his philosophical works, the natural elements are not only symbols or mirrors for behavior, but are very much alive as powerful spiritual guides that can enhance or hinder the path.

This recalls a variety of Dylan songs from periods of disillusionment in which he expresses a profound appreciation for nature while acknowledging the pathos of human relations that defies placing it on a pedestal as an eternal godlike image. In "When the Deal Goes Down," Dylan writes, "In this earthly domain, full of disappointment and pain/ You'll never see me frown," and in "Highlands," "Well, my heart's in the Highlands at the break of day/ Over the hills and far away/ There's a way to get there, and I'll figure it out somehow/ But I'm already there in my mind/ And that's good enough for now."

AND THE LOCUSTS SANG

In addition to seeking a mystical vision amid everyday affairs, Zen masters and Dylan are reformers who stand up against the forces of hypocrisy and corruption in society while placing blame at the feet of all those, high or low, who perpetrate morally deficient attitudes. Inauthenticity or the lack of commitment to individual dignity and integrity regardless of the price to be paid was often referred to in the 1960s as the "rising tide of conformity," a phrase used in a famous poster which features a severe-looking Dylan standing alongside the caustic Joan Baez. In the era of Zen's prominence during the medieval period when supernatural beliefs were commonplace, self-deception was equated with the inability to tell a magical shape-shifting fox, which seduces and betrays, from a true Buddha who represents the virtues of detachment and compassion. The fox appears and appeals to wayward souls including adulterous husbands, priests who break their vows, or samurai thinking of betraying their warlord.

For both Dylan and Zen, the goal is to be able to distinguish genuine self-understanding from a clinging to falsity that causes the spiritual path to deteriorate. As Dylan declaims against worldly oppression and cruelty, and calls for justice while warning of the effects of divine retribution, Zen masters also display something of the prophetic in espousing the total awakening of Buddha-nature for all beings, even plants and rocks, arising out of a non-dual awareness actualized through meditative practice.

As an example of taking a stand for integrity against a corrupt social system, idealistic Zen masters debated and sometimes declined the offer of the "purple robe" as a gift from the imperial family, which was the leading civil authority of the time. Similarly, early in his career Dylan walked off the set of the prestigious Ed Sullivan Show because the producers forbade him from singing a controversial song, "Talking John Birch Paranoid Blues," attacking a notorious witch-hunting anticommunist organization. Only with great reluctance did he receive awards from the National Emergency Civil Liberties Committee and Princeton University, and in both cases, he later wrote songs documenting his misgivings, "As I Went Out One Morning" and "Day of the Locusts," respectively.[19] While "the locusts sang off in the distance" and "The man standin' next to me, his head was exploding," Dylan says in the latter song, he "put down my robe, picked up my diploma,/ Took hold of my sweetheart and away we did drive,/ Straight for the hills, the black hills of Dakota,/ Sure was glad to get out of there alive."

An important link between the mystical and social realms for Dylan and Zen is a shared emphasis on making a constant, relentless effort to achieve a genuine sense of self-discovery. As Dylan used to tell Leroy Hoikkala and Monte Edmunson who played in his very first rock band, the Golden Chords, in his hometown of Hibbing, Minnesota, "We don't practice music, we play it."[20] That is, the playing of music is seen not as a means to an end, but as an end in itself. According to a commentator's discussion of the two-decades long Never-Ending Tour, Dylan's main motivation is that he enjoys "playing music to play music."

Similarly, one of Dogen's main doctrines is the "unity of discipline and realization" in that every moment of continuous effort is the key to uplift and self-improvement. Zen masters talk about "just sitting" in meditation, or meditating for the sake of doing it and not because there is a pot at the end of the rainbow, so to speak, since that would suggest an ulterior motive betraying egocentrism and attachment. We can imagine that Dylan's comment to his friend meant that they should simply be in an ongoing state of "just playing," or that a Zen master might say tautologically, "We don't train in order to attain enlightenment, we train to train." For both Dylan and Zen, the ongoing experiential process is the true goal without regard for the outcome or result of any particular activity.

The idea in Zen, and in Japanese culture generally, of taking an artistic form from the fine arts to the martial arts and perfecting it and then making it your own, and by doing so breaking free of the constraints inherent in that form, corresponds to what Dylan does with American folk music. He plays so many different styles in order to capture the essential spirit of the music rather than let any particular genre dominate his overall approach. Dylan has said, "I don't break the rules, because I don't believe there are any to break," an iconoclastic comment that recalls a Zen adage that blasphemes the most sacred object in the Buddhist tradition, Sakyamuni Buddha, who is sometimes called a "bedwetting devil."

Despite significant similarities, the two outlooks are by no means identical. Dylan's approach, from awaiting the fall of the Pharaohs and Goliaths in "When the Ship Comes In" to observing "All the ladies of Washington scrambling to get out of town" in "Thunder on the Mountain," is ever haunted by a sense of the imminence of divine judgment and is rife with apocalyptic warnings. The penultimate verse of "The Ballad of Frankie Lee and Judas Priest" suggests that "Nothing is revealed," as our fate is unknown and unpredictable, even if not necessarily undetermined. The Eastern perspective, on the other hand, tends to accept and go with the flow of the cyclical rotation of the seasons and life cycles. Enlightenment can be attained at each, every, and any moment one realizes it through sustained practice. According to a famous saying associated with Dogen, "Nothing is concealed in the entire universe," since each aspect of reality is an opportunity to realize truth.

However, this distinction is not as sharp as it might seem because Zen rhetoric was developed at the time that medieval East Asian society believed that it was living in an Age of Moral Decline, and was awaiting the coming of a savior Buddha in the future to recover and bring the righteous souls to salvation. Dylan says in "Sugar Baby," "Look up, look up—seek your Maker—'fore Gabriel blows his horn." The Buddhist notion of karma or the inevitable effects of moral causality (good begets good, evil begets evil), would likely agree with the injunction to develop self-reflection and self-criticism through a repentant outlook that anticipates moral judgment.[21]

What Zen recognizes in Dylan is the attitude of quiet yet urgent, back-to-the-wall desperation as expressed in "Things Have Changed": "Standing on the gallows with my head in a noose/ Any minute now I'm expecting all hell to break loose/ People are crazy and times are strange/ I'm locked in tight, I'm out of range/ I used to care, but things have changed." This sense of angst dovetails with the Zen saying about the double-bind quality of decision-making, "It's too late to step back, there are innumerable obstacles in moving forward, and you can't stand still. Now, act!"

THIS BOOK'S STRUCTURE: "DYLAN & ZEN" AND "THE ZEN OF DYLAN"

To better understand and appreciate the role of Buddhism in the broader context of interpreting Dylan's corpus, affinities and connections will be examined in two complementary ways. One way is to look at "Dylan & Zen" by probing affinities between the performer and the unconventional, "wild and extraordinary" rhetorical style of ancient Asian mystical masters. The second and third chapters explore the roots of Dylan's spirituality in relation to Judeo-Christian and other Western intellectual and spiritual sources. This includes discussing how the Blues musical and Beat literary traditions helped to form a cultural bridge linking Dylan to this profoundly mystical/mysterious example of Eastern thought. The unique "Beat Blues" complex of influences led Dylan to embrace Zen-like enigmatic rhetoric regarding the role of detachment and compassion in the spiritual quest. In Chapter 4, Zen literary records expressing transcendental insight into the absurdity of human existence help to explain how Dylan's puzzling words consistently critique the limitations of self amid the failings of social institutions as part of his ongoing quest for spiritual fulfillment.

The second and perhaps more important aspect of interpretation examines "The Zen of Dylan" by evoking the contemplative approach of Zen masters as a powerful hermeneutic tool for tracking the convention-defying nature of Dylan's remarkable zigzag course between the paths of Duality and Non-Duality. He endorses one radical outlook and then veers toward its opposite, while continually crisscrossing back and forth in disparate ideological moves. A characteristically ironic saying in the Zen tradition celebrates the need to see reality from every possible perspective while in the end remaining unbound by any particular viewpoint.

When interpreted in relation to Zen Buddhism's paradoxical meta-physics encompassing all contradictions, Dylan's celebrated indeterminacy can be viewed not so much as an arbitrary or misguided vacillation, but a complicated dialectical process of embracing and renouncing seemingly opposite paths in pursuit of constructive compromise. To see the twin aspects of absurdity and tragedy for what they are and to at once protest and detest human foibles while calmly standing back and distancing oneself is the quality that links Dylan and Zen. In light of this, a detailed dialectical theory that coordinates and integrates the dual elements of change and constancy in Dylan will be laid out in Chapter 5. The remaining chapters in the second part of the book (6 through 9) will further develop and apply this theory to the stages of Dylan's career trajectory, which is divided into four main periods. These range from the protest era of the 1960s, the country era of the 1970s, and the gospel era of the 1980s, to the most recent albums since the 1990s, which form a middle way that encompasses and integrates many of the themes he has previously explored.

Part I

ZEN AND DYLAN

Chapter 2

A Simple Twist of Faith

Dylan's Enigmatic Spiritual Quest

THE WHOLE WORLD'S A STAGE

Bob Dylan is perhaps best known by aficionados and more casual observers alike for his Sphinx-like, about-face quality, whereby little or nothing the ever-changing icon says and does can or should be taken at face value because it may easily be changed or reversed. The mercurial Dylan is commonly thought of as Mr. Variability since the focus of his songwriting has shifted dramatically over the years from social protest in the early 1960s, to love songs in the early 1970s, to born-again religiosity in the 1980s, and to songs of personal anguish and pain beginning in the 1990s.

At the same time, his musical style has changed from acoustic blues interpretation, to folk, to rock, to country, and to gospel, and more recently back to blues-based idioms, along with other variations. Some critics and fans have been puzzled, dismayed, or even outraged at times when they thought that Dylan had turned his back on their concerns while embracing a contrary ideological/theological or musical/stylistic standpoint. Yet, fan reaction has not deterred him from pursuing the paths he has considered appropriate at any given phase or reversing his course abruptly later on.

In defeating labels and deconstructing stereotypes of himself, the legendary performer is known for having been booed while on stage in 1965 at the Newport Folk Festival, where he first introduced the electric guitar, and for being called "Judas" a year later while touring England.

During the Beatles' *Sgt. Pepper's* era of the late 1960s, Dylan surprised his fans by releasing the stripped-down, pedal-steel guitar-sound albums *John Wesley Harding* and *Nashville Skyline*. A decade later in 1979 in San Francisco, Dylan upset his audience again when he began a tour by discarding his usual repertoire for an entirely gospel show.[1] Then, he outdid the "Unplugged" era of the early 1990s with two eclectic collections offering intimate, solo acoustic versions of mostly obscure old folk/blues ballads, *Good As I Been to You* and *World Gone Wrong*.

Dylan has been continuously changing and transforming himself and his image/identity/persona. At times, his whole demeanor including clothes, hairstyle, and decorum seems to be altered along with vocal style and musical genre. As one critic notes, "Bob Dylan is an enigma. A poet, a musician, a philosopher and a sometime rock star, his life and the music he has produced is varied, colourful and ever changing."[2] According to another commentator, "The degree of deception at Bob Dylan's disposal is limitless. He's an irreverent folkie—no wait, a babbling bluesman. Or is he a latent protest singer? Whatever hat he's wearing, or instrument he's playing, Dylan prides himself on being a paradox."[3] In comparing the folk-laden Rolling Thunder Revue in 1975–1976 to the Vegas-style tour that followed a couple of years later at the time of the *Live at Budokan* and *Street-Legal* tours, a reviewer referred to Dylan as an "avatar," who each time materializes in "his latest incarnation."

It is abundantly clear that "Bob Dylan delights in confounding expectations,"[4] and his restless, reinventive spirit cannot be gauged or second-guessed. He expresses the urge to "constantly multiply the confusions and toy with the desire that people have to try and pin him down," according to Todd Haynes, director of the highly innovative and award-winning biopic released in 2007, *I'm Not There*. "The one thing you have to acknowledge about Dylan right off," Haynes said of the film that tries to capture the variety of Dylan personae by showing half a dozen distinct facets of the performer's life—or "many lives"—"is that he's never there when you reach out to claim him. He's already gone, three steps down the road." Indeed, a reviewer of *I'm Not There* asked whether six very different actors, including a prepubescent African–American male playing an early hobo phase called Woody and an adult white female playing an androgynous stage called Jude, are actually enough to show the multiple sides of Bob Dylan. Another critic countered that whether Haynes "went with one Dylan or a dozen, he'd never capture all the qualities of this endlessly self-reinventing soul."[5]

The quixotic nature of Dylan's work is apparent in the way he talked about "masquerading" in his "Bob Dylan mask" (metaphorically speaking) while performing at the 1964 Halloween concert at Carnegie Hall. It is also evident in his donning a Richard Nixon veneer as well as wearing a white-face costume during the first leg of Rolling Thunder Revue tour of fall 1975, which forced people to listen to his words rather than look at his face. Dylan's high regard for masking, literally and metaphorically, was no doubt inspired in large part by the nineteenth-century minstrel tradition whereby white singers wore blackface to take on a new identity either to mock or to reverently emulate the music of African–American slaves and former slaves, who were not allowed to perform publicly until the 1870s. By the turn of the century, blacks themselves were performing in blackface to gain access to a broader audience.[6]

Dylan's whiteface performance inverted American minstrelsy, and was also compared to Japanese Noh Theater's use of masks. His appreciation of minstrelsy is further conveyed by the muse that is featured in his 2003 film, *Masked and Anonymous*, which is the ghost of a mysterious blackface troubadour known as Oscar Vogel, played by Ed Harris. Vogel recounts how he was once considered a troublemaker and was apparently assassinated by authorities who made his death look like a suicide. When the character Jack Fate played by Dylan ends the conversation by saying he must return to the stage (to play a major benefit concert at once endorsed and rejected by the controlling powers of the state), Vogel proclaims

Figure 2.1 Dylan in Rolling Thunder Revue

Figure 2.2   Ed Harris as Oscar Vogel

in ironic, Shakespearean fashion an almost maniacal smirk, "The stage? Ah, yes, the stage. The whole world's a stage." To make another cinematic reference in order to try to get a handle on his intentions, Dylan once described the surrealistic narrative structure of his 1978 quasi-autobio-graphical film *Renaldo and Clara* as "more real than reality." As the main character in Ingmar Bergman's *The Magician* once said, "Nothing is what it seems to be," and just about everything in Dylan's life and works defies real-ity in the conventional sense; it is either more or less so.

Nevertheless, despite the persistent use of guises and disguises, Dylan makes music with a commitment of purpose and dedication of spirit as if his life were at stake in every single note and verse. In "Things Have Changed," Dylan says, "All the truth in the world adds up to one big lie."[7] But it may be the case that linking a pack of lies, so to speak, because they represent partial truths in a relativistic universe, is the way to find the Zen-like nature of fragmented truth. According to Dogen, "A full truth half known is a half truth fully known." Dylan's masquerading is not done for the sake of pretending to be what he is not, but to truly become what he is. However, while masking is a valuable exercise in maintaining sanity in an insane world, there is a flip side to this in an approach that demands transparency. According to "Masters of War," the pursuit of integrity and truth-telling demands saying to those who falsely occupy high places, "I can see through your masks."

ENIGMATIC WORDS AND DEEDS

There are two major aspects of paradoxical, enigmatic Dylan: his words and his deeds. The first aspect involves Dylan's elusive writings, or the cryptic and ever-puzzling quality of particular lyrics and other forms of expression which defy facile interpretation yet are open-ended and subject to incessant discussion and debate. Figuring out a passage in a Dylan song is like trying to hold water in the palm of your hand or to describe the feelings associated with a new aroma, to cite Zen Buddhist sayings about the frustration of depicting enlightenment: As soon as you think you have it mastered, the articulation tends to dissolve and disappear in thin air. The question then arises whether there is a basic meaning that can be grasped despite the apparent meaninglessness.

The second enigmatic aspect involves Dylan's deeds. This refers to the complex and contradictory ways his creative activities have been unfolding throughout an overall career trajectory that has embraced and then reversed and repudiated so many different viewpoints and perspectives. Dylan's personae have included the roles of social activist and country gentleman, blues rocker and gospel singer, withdrawn contemplative and wandering troubadour, and idealistic rebel and entrepreneurial artist. Is there a fundamental continuity beneath the variability and changes?

At every career stage, regardless of other discrepancies, Dylan expresses contemporary angst in the face of changin' times, as well as a timeless sense of moral imperative to overcome the rampant forces of inauthenticity from wherever they stem. As he declares in "It's Alright Ma": "If my thought-dreams could be seen/ They'd probably put my head in a guillotine/ But it's alright Ma, it's life and life only." Dylan has always been a singer–songwriter who probes and moves beyond the limits of any one style or genre when it begins to feel like it is caging him in to pursue a transcendental mystical vision so that "there must be some way out of here," even while "Eden is burning" and "the hour is getting late," as most people are left "expecting rain," to cite references from various songs.

Despite a legacy of wearing many masks and (dis)guises that challenge the way he is perceived by his audience, in concerts on the Never Ending Tour that began in 1988 with around 100 shows a year ever since, Dylan has integrated songs from all phases of his career. These songs have become part of a unified and incredibly dynamic performance of hypnotic, swirling sounds played by guitar, keyboard, harmonica, and vocals. As was said of the remarkable mixture of styles and ideas in *Modern Times* (2006):

> Hardscrabble blues, 19th-century parlor ballads, gospel testimonies, rag-time, Tin Pan Alley tunes, and other songs as old as the hills, and as immovable—Dylan's music has carried these echoes from the start, but never with such a sense of mission as in his recent work. If there is an extra hint of fatigue in his rasp these days, it may be because he's weary from bearing that heavy load. It's not easy being America's living, breathing musical unconscious.[8]

ANY DAY NOW

The sense of integration of his many lives in recent performances and albums highlights that a constant in the variegated Dylan experience has been his continual seeking to reach higher spiritual ground. This extends from awaiting the fall of "Hard Rain" (1963) to finding "High Water (for Charley Patton)" (2001) everywhere, or from trying to remain "Forever Young" (1974) to anticipating that while it is "Not Dark Yet" (1997) "it's getting there." An intense interest in gaining redemption has been crucial to a career marked by an incredible degree of longevity and sustained creativity in an era otherwise famous for the "transient joys," to quote "When the Deal Goes Down," of fifteen minutes of fame and planned obsolescence.

Therefore, Dylan's spiritual searching provides the underlying consistency pervading his variable music-making. It is the most basic dimension of his work extending throughout and helping to clarify underlying connections between different phases of his career. The religious quest is found in songs stemming from all periods ranging from:

- foreseeing that "The Times They Are A-Changin'" (1964) to recognizing that "Things Have Changed" (1999)
- hearing "Chimes of Freedom" (1964) to calling for one and all to "Ring Them Bells" (1989)
- questioning one who acts "Just Like a Woman" (1966) to the anguished praise of "You're a Big Girl Now" (1974)
- contemplating the "Sad-Eyed Lady of the Lowlands" (1966) to trying to occupy the "Highlands" (1997)
- helplessly, hopelessly "Knockin' on Heaven's Door" (1973) to "Tryin' to Get to Heaven" (1997) "before they close the door."

Understanding this continuity in no way reduces, but actually enhances an appreciation of the extent of variability.

The spiritual process that gives much of Dylan's work its compelling, inspirational character is what I call "bargainin' for salvation," as in a line from "Shelter from the Storm" (1975). This song follows by nearly a decade the composition of a lyric about the devastating effects of a storm, "Down in the Flood" (1967), and precedes by a couple of decades two other variations on this theme, "High Water" and "The Levee's Gonna Break" (2006), the latter coming on the heels of Katrina (*Modern Times* was released on the anniversary of the disaster). "Shelter from the Storm" was inspired by a nineteenth-century evangelical hymn, Moody Sankey's "A Shelter in the Time of Storm," and alludes to several Biblical passages including Isaiah's prophecy, the story of Christ's persecution, and Psalm 91.[9]

The song deals with Dylan's relation to his lady, who once "took [his] crown of thorns," thus relieving great struggles and hardships while offering joyful consolation. But, eventually, he tragically alienated her. Now that she is lost to him and he is walking on "a razor's edge," and is unable to retrieve the time "when God and her were born," he longs for, yet experiences insurmountable difficulty, in becoming free from anguish and sorrow in order to gain redemption:

> In a little hilltop village they gambled for my clothes
> I bargained for salvation an' she gave me a lethal dose
> I offered up my innocence, got repaid with scorn
> "Come in," she said, "I'll give ya shelter from the storm."[10]

Dylan's ongoing process of spiritual seeking has been pursued either through introspective self-discovery and self-reliance or via reverence and respect for a salvific power accompanied by eschatological anticipation. Despite his profound desire for salvation, both of these paths have generally resulted in doubt and confusion, or mistrust and disappointment. According to "Shelter from the Storm," Dylan received a Christ-like self-sacrificing treatment in that he was given a "lethal dose" of salvation while suffering scorn in exchange for his innocence.

Thus, Dylan remains all too keenly aware of the barriers to fulfillment and the powers of retribution that make salvation such a difficult goal to attain, as suggested by the following:

- "Inside the museum Infinity goes up on trial/ Voices echo this is what salvation must be like after a while" ("Visions of Johanna," 1966).

- "You can't find no salvation, you have no expectations" ("No Time to Think," 1978).
- "Some trains [to heaven] don't pull no gamblers/ No midnight ramblers, like they did before" ("Tryin' to Get to Heaven," 1997).

In a song derived from a classic blues lyric by Charley Patton, Dylan laments how far removed paradise seems:

- "I been praying for salvation laying 'round in a one room country shack" ("Dirt Road Blues," 1997).

In another recent song, based on a romantic conflict that apparently ended in violence which symbolizes how we all have to face dealing with a lifetime of transgressions, he laments,

- "I can't go back to paradise no more/ I killed a man back there" ("Spirit on the Water," 2006).

On the other hand, during the gospel period of the late 1970s which found him "hangin' to a solid rock . . . and can't let go no more," according to *Saved*, Dylan was confident about the chances of attaining the goal. He also wrote:

- "Oh, the tree of life is growing/ Where the spirit never dies/ And the bright light of salvation shines/ In dark and empty skies" ("Death is Not the End," 1983, released 1988).

This attitude recalls the Buddhist saying that the heavenly paradise of the Pure Land lies 10,000 miles away, but the seeker must walk there wearing only a pair of broken straw sandals. The devotional sect of Buddhism expresses a generosity of spirit and compassion in the saying that if even the good persons gain salvation through the grace of Buddha, how much more so the sinner (who really needs this uplift).

However, a recent Dylan song offers a sardonic comment:

- "Riches and salvation can be waiting behind the next bend in the road" ("The Levee's Gonna Break," 2006).

All of these examples show that Dylan continues to vacillate between rock-solid certainty and profound uncertainty about the chances of reaching salvation, just as Buddhism emphasizes both the value of self-discipline and the need to seek the assistance of the Awakened One.

JUDEO-CHRISTIAN INFLUENCES

During his various career stages, Dylan's spiritual quest has been expressed through different kinds of religious imagery. This includes biblical influences, which pursue apocalyptic visions based on the prophetic view of ethical judgment in which "few are deemed guilty, but all are held responsible" for un-rectified social ills; Judaic thought, which attempts to redeem an existence condemned to incessant adversity and suffering by making a virtue of exile and aimless wandering; and evangelical Christianity, which seeks salvation through divine grace bestowed on a life of righteousness that perfects the path of repentance as an avenue to joyful affirmation.

Raised in a middle-class Jewish family and praised by his elders for his extensive knowledge of Hebrew at the time of his bar mitzvah at the age of thirteen, while also a convert to fundamental Christianity for at least several years in midlife, Dylan sometimes uses allusions to Western esoteric traditions. These include Tarot, Kabbalah, and other occult ideas and imagery that provide symbolic patterns for interpreting the spiritual quest. He makes additional references to classical philosophy, mythology and poetry, which offer ways of grappling with issues of moral responsibility and forces controlling fate versus individual freedom and free will.

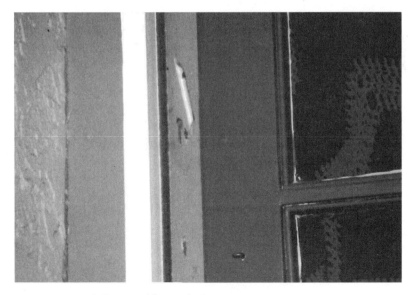

Figure 2.3   Jewish "Mezuzah" at Dylan's Home

Figure 2.4   Hibbing, MN, Synagogue

Furthermore, rather than following a mainstream avenue of faith, Dylan often seems to have found consolation in what could be called secular humanism or natural mysticism unhinged from a particular theological framework. In some songs, he seeks the muse and looks for answers in the immediate environment he occupies instead of an other-worldly realm. Spirituality has been a theme that supports social commentary in "Chimes of Freedom," a mystical awareness of nature in "Mr. Tambourine Man," a hope to attain reconciliation in "The Wicked Messenger," a prayer for renewal in "Forever Young," a hymn of confession in "Every Grain of Sand," an evocation of eternity in "Dark Eyes," an entreaty to overcome conflict in "Ring Them Bells," and a plea for forgiveness in "Tryin' to Get to Heaven."

Other prominent examples in which nature becomes the locus of spiritual release from human travails include "Lay Down Your Weary Tune," "You're Gonna Make Me Lonesome When You Go," and "Highlands." There are also numerous instances of redemption where religion is a by-product of or is eclipsed by idealized womanhood, as in "Love Minus Zero/No Limit," "Sad-Eyed Lady of the Lowlands," "Sara," "Tight Connection to My Heart," and "When the Deal Goes Down." For example, in the latter song he writes, "In this earthly domain, full of disappointment and pain/ You'll never see me frown/ I owe my heart to you, and that's sayin' it true/ And I'll be with you when the deal goes down." Also, Dylan's religiosity is cojoined with the romantic during the gospel period in "Precious Angel," "Covenant Woman," and "Angelina."

Yet, Dylan who once said that the aim of music is to "bring people closer to God" and that "prayer is the highest form of song," has often mocked the hypocritical trappings of traditional religious institutions, recently asserting in a 2007 interview for the fortieth anniversary edition of *Rolling Stone* that "faith is degraded by religion." In "It's Alright, Ma" he associates "flesh-colored Christs that glow in the dark" with "toy guns that spark." In "Highway 61 Revisited," a demonic reading of the story of the sacrifice of Isaac demanded by God of the first patriarch Abraham, an autocratic Old Testament deity instructs his loyal follower here called "Abe" on how to commit infanticide or risk being a victim of homicide. In "Tombstone Blues," the head of the church is conflated with a military leader called the "Commander-in-Chief," who proclaims his disdain for the weak and weary: "'Death to all those who would whimper and cry'/And dropping a bar bell he points to the sky/ Saying, 'The sun's not yellow it's chicken.'"[11] According to this commander's outlook, the meek shall not inherit the earth.

In addition, in "High Water," written three and a half decades after the songs just cited, Dylan is equally scathing in speaking of a Judge and a High Sherriff conspiring to capture Charles Darwin, who is "trapped out there on Highway Five" and is wanted "dead or alive"—the Judge says he does not care which way. Apparently, the traditional religions of the "Englishman, the Italian and the Jew" (representing Protestantism, Catholicism, and Judaism) are threatened by modern scientific theories. In "Ain't Talkin'," Dylan proclaims an alternative path to mainstream institutional religion in that he follows, along with a handful of lonely companions, a long-abandoned faith that has "no altars on this long and lonesome road." Other songs on *Modern Times* locate the sacred on the mountaintop, in the water, or beyond the horizon.

In surveying the many facets of Dylan's religiosity, we come across an important question mark. One cannot help but wonder how the same person who once charged, "It's easy to see without looking too far/ That not much is really sacred," could also make the plea, "When He healed the blind and crippled, did they see? . . . When He rose from the dead, did they believe?" In the heart of mid-1960s disillusionment with authority, Dylan questions, "Now the preacher looked so baffled/ When I asked him why he dressed/ With twenty pounds of headlines/ Stapled to his chest." Even during the midst of the gospel period, he expresses skepticism by saying ambiguously, "the enemy I see wears a cloak of decency, All non-believers and men stealers talkin' in the name of religion."

A few years following his affirmation of faith, Dylan seems to repudiate it in "Man of Peace": "Look out your window, baby, there's a scene you'd like to catch,/ The band is playing 'Dixie,' a man got his hand outstretched./ Could be the Fuhrer/ Could be the local priest./ You know sometimes/ Satan comes as a man of peace." Then, in 1985, he encourages listeners to "Trust Yourself." In 1997 he maintains, "Feel like my soul has turned into steel/ I've still got the scars that the sun (some hear it as "Son") didn't heal" while also declaring in 1999, "If the bible is right, the world will explode," and in 2006, "I'm beginning to believe what the scriptures tell."[12]

Moreover, how is it possible for a songwriter to compose "With God on Our Side," which argues that no single tradition has priority and all are to blame for misappropriating and misusing the supposed power of divine injunction, along with "Are You Ready?" and its unflinching testimony and admonitions regarding Christian belief? The former song has a Tom Paine-like emphasis on a universalism devoid of commitment to any particular ideology, while the latter has a resonance with revival-tent, Bible-thumping, believe-or-be-damned evangelism. Maybe the point is that these seemingly opposite views are oddly enough compatible in their respective ways of pointing the finger at hypocrisy and corruption based on moral outrage.

BIBLICAL ROCK?

As mentioned in the first chapter, much of the current discussion and debate about Dylan's religiosity has focused on the way he fully embraced born-again Christianity with three consecutive albums beginning in the late 1970s (*Slow Train Coming, Saved*, and *Shot of Love*). For a couple of years he gave concerts at which he only performed songs selected from these works (and not his back catalogue). Some observers have seen this phase as an aberration disconnected from the main flow of Dylan's career path. Cynics have simply dismissed its significance or, worse, viewed it as representing the onset of an inevitable decline in his songwriting faculties. They can point out that in the twenty-five years since 1982, Dylan produced a total of only seven albums with completely original material. But in the fifteen years (1963–1978) leading up to the gospel stage he released fifteen such albums (counting *The Basement Tapes* and the soundtrack to *Pat Garrett and Billy the Kid*).

Others have argued the reverse position that Dylan, who sang "Gospel Plow" on his first album and used apocalyptic imagery in early protest songs like "When the Ship Comes In" (1965), was an incipient believer long before he declared this commitment. It has been well documented that the

New Testament's final opus, the book of Revelations, has infused at least several dozen songs in the Dylan canon, and nearly every album contains songs rife with multiple allusions to biblical texts.

Indeed, extensive biblical imagery appears in all stages of his work. Dylan once referred to the album *John Wesley Harding*, with songs evoking St. Augustine, Isaiah's watchtower, and the prophecy of Samuel released ten years before his gospel stage, as the first example of "biblical rock." "Given Dylan's assessment of *John Wesley Harding*," Stephen Webb, author of *Dylan Redeemed*, suggests, "it is hard not to come to the conclusion that he was a Christian for years before he or anyone else knew it."[13]

Webb's standpoint further argues that Dylan never abandoned his Christian piety, for even after he stopped writing explicitly religious songs in the early 1980s, he has continued to perform gospel standards and hymns in concert. An observer of his performances in 2000 noted that one could expect to hear him cover the old-time spiritual "Rock of Ages" as well as "My Back Pages," his own classic statement of detachment from commitment to any ideology that dualistically sees life in terms of black versus white.

A variation on the view that Dylan is a lifelong Christian is the notion that Dylan has always held to an "unshakeable monotheism" regardless of sectarian labels. It has been pointed out, with a grain of salt perhaps, that since Dylan's original foray into electric blues in the mid-1960s was accompanied by guitarist Mike Bloomfield along with Al Kooper on the organ, there were enough Jewish guys hanging around the studio to have a Minyan (minimum number of men needed for a prayer service). More seriously, Dylan who joined one of his sons for a bar mitzvah service at the Western Wall in Jerusalem in the early 1980s has continued to intermittently attend High Holiday services at a synagogue, and has appeared at fundraisers for a Jewish mystical sect (Lubavitcher).

According to Larry Charles, who as director of *Masked and Anonymous* is a Jewish artist with whom Dylan has collaborated on a creative project, Dylan's born-again stage did not jeopardize the faith of his heritage. Rather, it "expanded his feelings about God" without creating any "disconnect between Judaism and Christianity." In support of this interpretation, it is noted that Dylan told Ed Bradley in a *60 Minutes* interview in 2004 at the time of the publication of his autobiographical reflections, *Chronicles: Volume One*, that it was God but not any person who was his "only judge," and that he had made a spiritual bargain to keep writing and singing. When asked with whom he had made the bargain, Dylan said a bit sheepishly that it was with "the Great Commander . . . on this earth and the world we can't see."

DYLAN'S "LEXICON" AND ADDITIONAL SPIRITUAL INFLUENCES

The views discussed above all find Dylan's spirituality rooted in some form of traditional Judeo-Christianity, but tend to disregard other kinds of evidence and perspectives. One concern is that highlighting a pervasive use of biblical citations in an album or a particular song does not necessarily provide conclusive evidence for understanding Dylan's views or guarantee a clear-cut interpretation. For example, "Jokerman" on *Infidels*, the first album in Dylan's post-gospel period, alludes to a dozen passages from the Bible, directly or indirectly, including a reference to the notion that "the Book of Leviticus and Deuteronomy,/ The law of the jungle and the sea are your only teachers." What is the significance of the juxtaposition of biblical and secular/natural sources of inspiration?

The theme of the song is self-praise mixed with self-loathing for one "born with a snake in both of your fists while a hurricane was blowing," and of whom "Michelangelo indeed could've carved out your features." The lyrics' mixed message also states, "You're a man of the mountains, you can walk on the clouds,/ Manipulator of crowds, you're a dream twister," and of an apparent offer from the devil it says, "Oh, Jokerman, you know what he wants,/ Oh, Jokerman, you don't show any response."

Therefore, the biblical allusions are evoked in so many different yet intertwining and perplexing ways that it is difficult to determine what the image in the song's title represents. Is it Christ or Anti-Christ, or Dylan himself, and if so, is he saying he is closer to being a savior or confessing that he feels more akin to the opposing force? Or perhaps the biblical sayings are played off of one another to transmute or defeat a Judeo-Christian standpoint altogether, and Jokerman may refer to an alternative, occult theology by representing a magus.

It can further be asked, must Dylan's outlook be tied to an acceptance of Christianity or Judeo-Christian faith more generally? Or does this belief system serve as a metaphor for an even broader view of spiritual seeking, and do biblical allusions function as a vehicle rather than as the religious content for expressing the spiritual message? When singing a song from one of the gospel albums in the late 1980s, Dylan perhaps ironically referred to this stage as "my religious period," as if it should be understood in this limited context.

My view is that the gospel period along with more general studies of biblical influences on Dylan should neither be dismissed nor exaggerated. Gospel belief is an important link in the chain or a piece of the puzzle, but no more so than other stages in which Dylan seems to repudiate traditional religion. While it is crucial to any discussion of Dylan's spirituality, an exclusively Judeo-Christian approach to hermeneutics tends to ignore alternative factors and forces that may have greatly affected Dylan's approach to music-making. These include the tremendous impact of the Delta Blues musical as well as the Beat poetic/mystical traditions that Dylan embraced in his early years in New York's avant-garde Greenwich Village.

In weighing the merit of a Judeo-Christian interpretation, a devil's advocate (pun intended) view is that Dylan's approach all along was primarily informed not so much by allusions to biblical teachings. Rather, it was influenced by a subtle level of spirituality embedded in the broad tradition of American folk music. This encompasses blues, country and western, gospel, and balladry, along with numerous variations such as bluegrass, rockabilly, jazz, pop, and Tin Pan Alley songwriting styles. The importance of spirituality embedded in folk music was expressed at the outset of his career when Dylan referred to Woody Guthrie, the first great influence he idolized, as "the greatest holiest godliest person in the whole world."

More recently, around the time of the release of *Time Out of Mind* in early fall of 1997, the beginning of a remarkable creative upsurge after he had not released an album of original material for seven years but had two recent recordings consisting only of folk/blues covers, Dylan told reporters for *Newsweek* and the *New York Times* that the old blues and country songs were his major source of inspiration. This was true whether the songs were sung by black bluesmen like Charley Patton, Blind Lemon Jefferson, or Robert Johnson or white country performers like Jimmie Rodgers, Hank Williams, or the Stanley Brothers.

"Those old songs are my lexicon and my prayer book," Dylan said to David Gates of *Newsweek*. "All my beliefs come out of those old songs . . . . I believe in a God of time and space, but if people ask me about that, my impulse is to point them back toward these songs. I believe in Hank Williams singing 'I Saw the Light.'" Dylan further explained the spiritual power of American blues/folk music vis-à-vis mainstream religion:

> Here's the thing with me and the religious thing. This is the flat-out truth: I find the religiosity and philosophy in the music. I don't find it anywhere else. Songs like "Let Me Rest on a Peaceful Mountain" or "I Saw the Light"—that's my religion. I don't adhere to rabbis, preachers, evangelists, all of that. I've learned more from the songs than I've learned from any of this kind of entity. The songs are my lexicon. I believe the songs.

While not denying or negating the role of Judeo-Christian faith, this quote indicates that the main influence on Dylan's spirituality was from another source of inspiration. To give an example of its pervasive impact, consider a key phrase in "The Ballad of Frankie Lee and Judas Priest" from *John Wesley Harding*, Dylan's so-called biblical album. This, the fifth of twelve songs, marks the turning point in the complex narrative structure of an album dealing with symbolic death-resurrection of the narrator's attraction to temptation. The phrase, "He began to make his midnight creep," which refers to seduction, was first used by famed 1920s bluesman Blind Lemon Jefferson and also appears in many other Blues songs.

UNITY OF PRAYER AND PLAY

Dylan apparently admired and emulated the way that Charley Patton and Hanks Williams, among many other performers, freely moved back and forth in their careers between two apparent extremes. These performers were primarily known for playing "devil music," or the "Hellhound Blues" in conveying a sense of distance and disdain while evoking a playful world of turmoil, loss, and betrayal. But the same singers also regularly performed "Holy Blues" or "Preachin' the Blues," the root of what evolved into gospel and soul music. This style repents and longs for relief from disappointment and demoralization through acknowledging and receiving the agency of the Lord.[14]

The link between the Hellhound and Holy Blues involved expressing feelings of regret and remorse for committing transgressions through seeking redemption while expecting retribution. Blues musicians, often loners who lived contradictory lives and sought to convey suffering and sorrow regarding the travails of self and community, were well aware that their singing was comparable to preaching, both in style and in the effect it could have on an audience. For example, Reverend Arnold "Gatemouth" Moore confirmed the tie between the Blues and the church when he was asked about making the shift from popular singer to preacher: "When I came to Christ, I changed the lyrics. I got the same voice, same key, but the words are different. Same music, same everything."[15] Others have pointed out that the spiritual music from a house of worship and the worldly music of the juke joint are not that far apart. This helps to explain why Dylan has both embraced and rejected, while moving back and forth between, sacred and secular, or dualistic and non-dualistic approaches.

In "Gonna Change My Way of Thinking" on his first gospel album, Dylan provides an image that connects the two sides of the Blues by juxtaposing prayer and play: "I got a God-fearing woman,/ One I can easily afford./ She can do the Georgia crawl,/ She can walk in the spirit of the Lord." His "Blind Willie McTell," a tribute to the great but relatively unheralded singer (also known as Georgia Sam as referenced in "Highway 61 Revisited" and the above verse), addresses the relation between Blues and spirituality, especially in the first verse about "martyrs who fell" in land "condemned/ All the way . . . to Jerusalem," and in the last verse suggesting that "power and corruptible greed" prevent us from reaching salvation. Here Dylan speaks of corruption and condemnation, sacrifice and martyrdom, and difficulties in gaining redemption through experiencing "God's heaven" in the midst of concrete worldly affairs involving everyday people and places.

Therefore, according to Dylan's own comments over recent years, these musical sources of inspiration are probably more important and enduring for defining his approach to spirituality than the Western religious traditions he often evokes, but about which he has always held mixed feelings. A key parallel between Dylan, Blues, and Zen is that they all seek to navigate and find a balance between seemingly polar opposite possibilities of human experience as it seeks spiritual release and redemption. This comparison is summed up in the following table, which illustrates that Dylan's ongoing religious quest can best be understood in terms of how it was influenced by the music and lyricism of the great American Blues tradition and the ways it is parallel to the discourse and pathways of Zen Buddhism.

	DUALITY	NON-DUALITY
DYLAN	Judgment	Disillusionment
BLUES	Hellhound	Holy/Gospel
ZEN	Self Power	Other Power

Examining Beat Blues influences as a cultural bridge to a Zen-based interpretation of Dylan which also integrates the role of Judeo-Christian viewpoints is the subject of the next chapter.

Chapter 3

From Beat Blues to Zen

Exploring the Roots of Dylan's Spirituality

BLUES MUSIC AND BEAT LITERATURE AS BRIDGES TO ZEN

The range of traditional and contemporary influences that are received and perpetuated by Dylan's forms of expression is of enormous scope in encompassing diverse styles of music and poetry as well as varieties of sociopolitical ideology and religious belief. A genius can be defined by his or her ability to reflect and yet rise above and remain unique within the context of deeply contrasting cultural components, and this talent is evident in any given example of Dylan's masterful work from all the periods of his career. Dylan has been America's "living, breathing musical unconscious" in that his songs showcase the nation's historical values and concerns. While Dylan is a storehouse of influences absorbed, the movement also goes in the reverse direction in that there is nobody in pop music or popular culture more generally that has not been touched by the impact of the man or his music.

It is, therefore, important to acknowledge that no specific idea or ideal can be sufficient to explain the extent of Dylan's genius, while also recognizing that for the most part he expresses himself through imagery and music lodged within the context of Americana.[1] Dylan responded to a comment regarding the all-American feel of *"Love and Theft"* where "you will find blues, pop, rock, crooning, bebop, Texan swing, country boogie, balladeering, rockabilly and more":[2]

Every one of the records I've made has emanated from entire panorama of what America is to me. America, to me, is a rising tide that lifts all ships, and I've never really sought inspiration from other types of music.[3]

The most important factors of the American context for understanding Dylan's music are the cries of anguish in the songs of the Delta Blues tradition and the philosophical poetry of the Beat movement. The Blues derived from post-slavery southern blacks who worked the cotton fields on the plantations of northwest Mississippi. The powerful lyrics and instrumental sounds of the economically suppressed but spiritually liberated performers influenced so many other modern American musical styles, including jazz, ragtime, gospel, soul, rhythm & blues, and of course, rock & roll. The Beats, rooted in Romantic, Transcendentalist, Existentialist, Modernist, and Dadaist literary and intellectual trends, exemplified the contemporary artistic desire to express interior, subjective truths in unconventional ways rather than to depict external reality.

The Blues and the Beats were two primary elements that greatly affected and shaped Dylan's musical development when he was first gaining attention during the folk revival of the early 1960s in the self-defined and self-contained counter-cultural world of Greenwich Village cafes. Dylan soon became known as the Village "King," before his reputation quickly migrated from that of local underground legend of a subculture to international superstar of mega-proportions rivaling or surpassing Elvis and the Beatles.

Although seemingly quite different cultural traditions, what Beat writers and Blues performers have in common is a commitment to experimenting with innovative means of expressing spirituality that tries to address directly the matter of existential truths regarding love and hate, integrity and betrayal, crime and punishment, and life and death. The approaches of Beat writers and Blues musicians reflect ways of embracing the inconsistency and contradiction of despair regarding the condition of human weakness found in oneself and others. Both Beat literature and Blues music represent styles of plebian art that use unpolished, colloquial syntax which aspires to suggest the heights of transcendental awareness normally conveyed through more elite venues.[4] The dynamic tension between ordinary styles of expression and extraordinary levels of meaning drives the artistry of the Beats and the Blues.

The Beats were no doubt the primary vehicle for introducing Dylan to Zen perspectives, directly and indirectly, which had an impact on his irreverently critical and iconoclastic portrayal of Americana that he viewed as a lost opportunity for utopia or a dystopia tragically in the making. Allen Ginsberg's 1956 prose–poem *Howl*, a surrealistic lament for the loss of the "best minds of my generation" recalls Zen's defiant protest through the use of absurd or surreal metaphors that are wielded as a literary weapon to smash conventional psychological boundaries that limit the attainment of liberation from social and intellectual constraints.

Similarly, the raw liberating power of terse, formulaic twelve-bar AAB-structured lyrics derived from African polyrhythmic ritualism conveys "unflinching subjectivity ... [in that o]nly a man who understands his worth and believes in his freedom sings as if nothing else matters."[5] This sentiment evokes the way pithy Zen sayings express disenchantment with a repressive social order and point to truth located solely within the individual seeker's autonomy. Dylan recognizes an affinity between the Blues and Eastern wisdom in commenting, "Robert Johnson would sing some song and out of nowhere there would be some kind of Confucius saying that would make you go, 'Wow, where did that come from?' It's important to always turn things around in some fashion."[6] In a 1966 comment included in the liner notes to *The Basement Tapes*, Dylan said, "With a certain kind of blues music . . . you can just sit down and play it . . . You may have to lean forward a little."[7] Dylan said one of his goals was to carry himself like Big Joe Williams. This outlook has a resonance with traditional poetry composition in East Asia, for which the writers were instructed to maintain the correct posture of sitting meditation that is conducive to reflecting/producing an artistic state-of-mind.

Therefore, the combined Beat Blues influence forms an important background for connecting Dylan's spirituality with the approaches to rhetoric used in Zen. The next two sections take a closer look at connections between each of the three factors of the Beats, Blues, and Zen in terms of evaluating their collective effect on the development of Dylan's distinctive approach to music-making.

DOWN THE BLUES HIGHWAY

The Delta Blues rose to prominence in American popular culture through recordings first produced in the 1920s and 1930s, the initial heyday of recording industry pioneers such as Columbia, Paramount, and Victor. Itinerant, iconic bluesmen who generally lived hard, loved strong, and all too often died youthful, sometimes tragic deaths left their plantation homes and were thrust into regional or national prominence. Willie Dixon was a famous Blues songwriter, poet, and philosopher who traveled from the Mississippi Delta to Chicago in 1936, where he became a sensation and campaigned for more than fifty years for the recognition of Blues as the root of all American music. According to Dixon, "Everything that's under the sun, that crawls, flies, or swims likes music. But blues is the greatest, because blues is the only one that, along with the rhythm and the music, brings wisdom." Dixon believed that the Delta Blues, also known as Classic, Country, or Deep Blues, represents "the facts of life."[8]

The phrase "having the blues" probably dates back to eighteenth-century England, where the term "blue devils" was slang for melancholia. But it was sorrows that were common among blacks after the Civil War that led to a raw new music depicting work, love, poverty, and the hardships freed men faced in a world barely removed from slavery. Skepticism was interspersed with comic relief regarding the questions of life and death, and good and evil, which were cast not in abstract terms but through very real and down-to-earth narratives of misfortune and redemption. The Blues evoked the uncertainties and instabilities of life's travails experienced along with an awareness of the certainty of death accompanied by fear of a vengeful God.

The origin of the Delta Blues lies in slaves singing a rhythmic "call and response" technique of ritual chant stemming from African fertility rites. These chants were transmuted into work songs and field hollers that became tools for easing the emotional pain of slavery and communicating surreptitiously under the watchful eye of the master. After slavery was ter-minated, the musical tradition continued to evolve during the ensuing era of economic servitude that was perpetuated through the sharecroppers system on Delta plantations.[9] By the end of the 1800s black musicians were allowed to perform publicly for the first time, but their access to a white audience was still severely restricted. Ironically, the breakthrough came when blacks began imitating white minstrels by dressing in blackface and performing in tightly choreographed big band orchestrations reminiscent of John Phillips Sousa's showmanship.

During a period around the turn of the century, black musicians were perfecting their use of string instruments such as guitar, banjo, mandolin, and fiddle, as well as songwriting skills, in part by absorbing a variety of musical influences. Western European immigrants brought the Spanish guitar and Celtic ballad lyricism to the rural southern region, while small groups of Italians, Jews, and Chinese who settled in Delta towns contrib-uted their indigenous musical traditions to the cultural mix. After the annexing of Hawaii in 1895, a fascination on the mainland with Hawaiian-style guitar playing which had probably been affected by Hispanic immi-grants to the islands, led to the development of the slide-guitar techniques created by Charley Patton and Robert Johnson. This was a means of inte-grating a percussive beat into the string performance in order to give the music a multidimensional sound. Patton was also able to throw his voice so that it seemed like more than one singer was performing.

Based on these factors, leading Blues performers were able to "combin[e] phrases, lines, and verses with compatible emotional resonances into associational clusters that reflect the singer's own experiences, feelings, and moods."[10] Through a style of formulaic writing that allows for endless improvisation, the Blues expresses an extraordinary range of emotions encompassing outrage and despair about personal troubles and disappointments in a chaotic world full of natural disasters and social injustices. Although probably best known for making intensely personal statements about love and loss as well as the pursuit of redemption against the background of rural life and urban corruption, the Blues has also been used, especially by Charley Patton, as a vehicle for commenting in an idiosyncratic and ambiguous way on a variety of broader societal issues that later became grist for Dylan's songwriting mill. One main theme was a protest against the oppression of an unfair legal system carried out by biased law enforcers, as expressed in Patton's "Tom Rushen Blues" and "High Sheriff Blues." These songs feature ironic remarks on the problems of racism and classism, but without overlooking the narrator's own foibles and weaknesses as one who provokes the long arm of the law yet also benefits from the corruption of the legal system.

Another topic of social interest expressed in the Blues was the devastating effects of the 1927 flood of the Mississippi River, which broke through the levees and destroyed thousands of acres of farmland in the Delta. This is conveyed in the two-part Patton song "High Water Everywhere" as well as the number "When the Levee Breaks," both of which are rewritten by Dylan. Patton's songwriting in "Bo' Weevil Blues" also dealt with the invasion of the plague of boll weevil infestation that wreaked havoc on the cotton crop in the 1920s. Although these two major natural disasters had a tremendous impact on the economy of the white plantation owners, the greatest hardship was felt by ex-slaves already living a life of poverty and misery in their sharecropper existence. The combined effect of plague and flood created a doomsday, apocalyptic atmosphere seen as retribution for social discord and inequity. This outlook infused Dylan's songs from every period of his career.

The initial epicenter of the Delta Blues was in Clarksdale, Mississippi, located just south of Memphis and east of the river, and several hundred miles north of New Orleans. The town was near the site of the famed "Cross Road" said to be encountered in the 1930s by Robert Johnson and Tommy Johnson (the latter was portrayed in the award-winning Coen brothers' film, *O Brother, Where Art Thou?*). Clarksdale was also not far from the infamous Parchman Farm, also known as the Mississippi State Penitentiary where Patton, Son House, "Bukka" White and other bluesmen were incarcerated for periods of time. It was also down the road from another important intersection frequently highlighted in Blues lore, the location in the town of Moorhead where the Southern Railway crossed another local train line, the Yazoo Delta Railway (better known as the Yellow Dog),[11] which is cited in Dylan's "Nettie Moore."[12]

According to legends, the Cross Road was the place where a novice bluesman could gain expertise in all styles of guitar showmanship by selling his soul to the devil. Influenced by African mythology of how a deity awaits visitors and determines their fate at important pathways, this magical intersection is located where Highway 49 running southeast to northwest crosses the north–south Highway 61. As a cultural image, it conjures the crisis of making crucial choices that give direction to life in the midst of emerging opportunities plagued by inevitable conflicts and insoluble crises. For Blues performers, the Cross Road functions either as an exit/escape and source of hope or as a site that can make one feel helplessly trapped by unfortunate circumstance.

Highway 61, about which countless lyrics were written, including the Mississippi Fred McDowell lines, "Lord, that 61 Highway is the longest road I know . . . Lord, if I have to die, baby, fo' you think my time have come/ I want you to bury my body out on Highway 61," became known as the Blues Highway. Starting at the Gulf of Mexico, it connected the southern United States, with its rich musical heritage of blues, rags, jazz, and hollers in New Orleans and Memphis, to the major cities of St. Louis, Kansas City,

Figure 3.1 Crossroad Near Clarksdale, MS

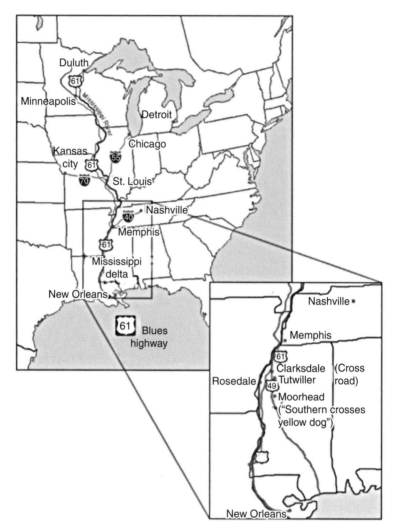

Figure 3.2   Blues Highway

Chicago, Detroit, and other northern locales including Dylan's hometown of Duluth, which was also an important Great Lake port city. In Chicago in the 1940s, the acoustic blues of western Mississippi near the river was electrified by Muddy Waters, Howlin' Wolf, John Lee Hooker, and others who hailed from the Delta. This new musical mix became the basis for the eventual formation and popularity of rhythm & blues, as well as rock & roll that emerged in the late 1950s and 1960s.

Dylan has said, "If I made records for my own pleasure, I would only record Charley Patton songs," and in "Thunder on the Mountain" he praises singer Alicia Keys as a throwback to the old days of the Blues by saying he is "looking for her clear through Tennessee" (home of Memphis). In *Chronicles*, Dylan remarks on the importance of the Blues Highway for his own musical development:

> Highway 61, the main thoroughfare of the country blues, begins about where I came from . . . Duluth to be exact. I always felt like I'd started on it, always had been on it, and could go anywhere from it, even down into the deep Delta country. It was the same road, full of the same contradictions, the same one-horse towns, the same spiritual ancestors.[13]

In the early 1960s, the original country/folk style of the preelectric Delta Blues was being revived as part of the hootenanny boom. In some cases, old-time singers long forgotten since their 1930s heyday were brought straight off the cotton fields of plantations to New York City where they became instant celebrities. This phenomenon occurred just as Dylan was arriving in Greenwich Village and starting to play club dates that were often shared with Blues singers. Like many in the folk revival, Dylan learned his trade by listening attentively to Harry Smith's eclectic six-disc collection, *Anthology of American Folk Music* (released in 1952 but covering recordings from 1927 to 1932). According to many reports, Dylan is said to have permanently "borrowed" a copy of the recording from friend John Pankake in Minneapolis around 1960. In addition, he studied the field recordings of Alan Lomax and his pioneering folklorist father John, and had extensive conversations with Alan in the Village. Dylan befriended and also played on stage and in the studio with Blues singers such as Big Joe Williams and Victoria Spivey.[14]

At the time of Dylan's arrival in New York, folk purists sought the music of "authentic" singers like bluesmen Charley Patton and Blind Lemon Jefferson (even Robert Johnson who followed these singers by a decade was often considered derivative). Dylan's earliest recordings, the unreleased Minnesota tapes recorded in 1961 and his first official album produced a year later, included Blues standards such as Rabbit Brown's "James Alley Blues," along with "Highway 51 Blues," "Freight Train Blues," and songs by Big Joe Williams, Blind Lemon Jefferson, "Bukka" White, and Rev. Gary Davis. Dylan's early records also contained several examples of "Talkin' Blues" compositions, although these were probably based on Woody Guthrie's distinctive hybrid style of songwriting rather than the Delta Blues. In being influenced by both white and black singers, Dylan has long understood just how much give-and-take there was between the Memphis-centered blues and Nashville-centered country traditions, separated by a stretch of only a couple of hundred miles on Route 40 in Tennessee. It was no fluke that *Blonde on Blonde*, in addition to *John Wesley Harding*, *Nashville Skyline*, and parts of *Self Portrait* were recorded in the capital of country music with its leading studio musicians adding flavor to Dylan's work.

A key to Dylan's creativity from the very beginning of his songwriting is his ability to rework many traditional Blues lyrics. To cite just a couple out of dozens of examples, he used the slave song "No More Auction Block" as the basis for "Blowin' in the Wind," "Down on Penny's Farm" by the Bentley Boys for both "Hard Times in New York Town" and "Maggie's Farm," and Lightnin' Hopkins' "Automobile Blues" as a starting point for composing "Leopard-Skin Pill Box Hat." Also, the traditional "Rocks and Gravel," which the youthful Dylan sang in coffee houses in the Village, was transformed into "It Takes a Lot to Laugh, It Takes a Train to Cry," with a nod to Charley Patton's "Poor Me." "Milkcow Blues" by Sleepy John Estes was a basis for "From a Buick 6," and Woody Guthrie's "Taking It Easy" influenced both "Tombstone Blues" and "Subterranean Homesick Blues."

In addition, "Me and My Chauffeur Blues" by Memphis Minnie was an influence on "Pledging My Time," "Temporary Like Achilles," and "Obviously Five Believers," all from *Blonde on Blonde*. "Mother Earth" by Memphis Slim was a basis for "Gotta Serve Somebody" along with Woody Guthrie's "Little Black Train." Charley Patton's "Pony Blues" was the basis for "New Pony," and "Bukka" White's "Po' Boy" was an influence on Dylan's song by that name. In some cases like "Where are You Tonight?," "Tryin' to Get to Heaven," and "Ain't Talkin'," there are multiple Blues songs that can be traced as influences.[15]

As a show of Dylan's great appreciation for the Blues, a picture of a Robert Johnson album graces the front cover of *Bringing It All Back Home*, and a reference to the influence of Sleepy John Estes is included in the liner notes on the back cover. Of course, *Highway 61 Revisited* evokes the famed Blues Highway in the title song as well as several other lyrics. In the 1980s, when asked during an interview what kind of music he was listening to, with the inquirer intending the question to refer to contemporary groups, Dylan dated himself half a century in responding that he was frequently playing records by Memphis Minnie, who was a hit Blues singer in the 1930s.

Following the two blues/folk cover albums of the early 1990s, in *Time Out of Mind* Dylan shows a renewed use of Blues idioms and images, and he has included several Blues numbers on all recent albums. These include the tribute to Patton, "High Water," on *"Love and Theft"*, which followed the reworking of Patton's "Dirt Road Blues" on *Time Out of Mind*, and the rewrites of standards, "Rollin' and Tumblin'" and "The Levee's Gonna Break," on *Modern Times*. In addition to the haunting Oscar Vogel blackface character, the influx of the Blues is highlighted in *Masked and Anonymous* when a guitar said to have been Blind Lemon's original plays an important role in the dramatic action. First presented to Jack Fate, the mysterious performer played by Dylan, as a gift from his friend Bobby Cupid, the guitar is unfortunately—but with significant cultural symbolism—used by Cupid during a fistfight. It becomes a weapon that kills a cynical reporter known as Tom Friend who was harassing Fate's agent called Uncle Sweetheart. This episode ironically evokes the motto, "This machine kills fascists," that was famously scribbled on Woody Guthrie's guitar case. Altogether in his career, Dylan has composed about fifty songs, about 10 percent of his production, in the twelve-bar style, with dozens of others reflecting the influence of at least a passage or image from one or another Blues original. The direct impact of the Blues on Dylan's music, song for song and line for line, is certainly as great as that of the Bible.

EVEN ZEN MASTERS GET THE HIGHWAY BLUES

Dylan would obviously be sold short if he were merely considered an interpreter of traditional folk songs who, like other rock stars from Elvis Presley to Eric Clapton, the Rolling Stones, or Led Zeppelin, gained prominence mainly by appropriating black music for a white audience. He is first and foremost an originator par excellence and a creative force extraordinaire as a master of words and spirit who surpasses any particular influence. In addition to his winning numerous awards for lifetime achievement such as Kennedy Center honors and the Pulitzer Prize as well as the Grammies and Oscars, some of Dylan's songs including "Desolation Row" are included in anthologies of great American poetry while he has been nominated several times for the Nobel Prize for Literature. Dylan has blazed so many new artistic trends and forged cultural pathways that have had an immeasurable impact on innumerable followers in diverse genres, as well as "imitators [who] rob me blind," as he bemoans in an outtake version of "Idiot Wind."

Perhaps more than other 1960s artists, Dylan recognized that the Blues represented the emerging voice of a newly empowered social class and fully incorporated this into his strongly defined yet enigmatic sense of social consciousness. Bluesmen, in part because they had nothing to lose as the ultimate outsiders, were for the first time in the history of American blacks free to tell the truth as they saw it. Yet they could not be direct and

open, so their putdowns were often coded ways—no doubt understood by
their audience who could read between the lines—of saying "no" to a lover
as a means of protesting mistreatment by plantation owners. This critique
of economic suffering and injustice had a significant uplifting crossover
message for white audiences seeking personal freedom yet willing to resign
themselves to harsh reality.

In many ways like the Blues, the Zen Buddhist tradition arose near an
important cultural crossroads at a critical time in the history of Chinese
society during the Song dynasty (eleventh through thirteenth centuries).
Zen temples greatly benefited from their proximity to a major transportation network, the Grand Canal. This waterway linked Hangzhou, the

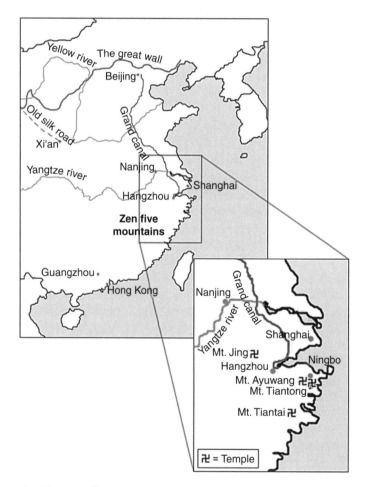

Figure 3.3   Origins of Zen

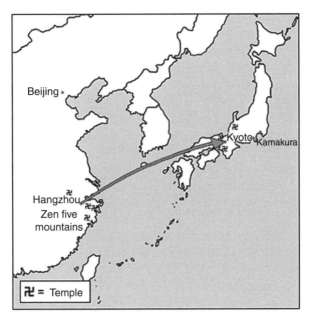

Figure 3.4 Transmission of Zen Buddhism from China to Japan in the Thirteenth Century

then-capital city and major port used by Marco Polo on his return to Europe in the late thirteenth century, which was south of the Yellow River, to the northern urban centers including Beijing near the Great Wall. Ideas and cultural forms, along with goods and economic benefits, flowed on the canal and contributed greatly to the formation of Zen's creative peak. Zen emerged as a social force on the basis of a cultural eclecticism that encompassed Confucian and Taoist, folk religious and shamanic, and literary and other intellectual elements. The rise of Zen as a powerful religious movement was also tied to its ability to help intellectuals resolve inner turmoil that often mirrored conflict and competition within the imperial bureaucracy.

This Chinese tradition was then transmitted in the thirteenth century by Dogen and other dedicated monks to Japan, where it became the dominant religious institution in the thirteenth-century transition from the aristocratic class to a society based on the rule of a warlord or shogun. Zen was used by samurai as a form of military discipline as well as an outlet for artistic self-expression. As with the transmission of folk/blues music by Dylan and some other interpreters that was accomplished in an innovative and trailblazing way, new generations of spiritual masters helped Zen to evolve by adding their own unique interpretations and dynamic contributions to the vast body of literature and training methods they inherited.

Unlike the bluesmen who came from the most impoverished and least educated class of society, however, Zen masters were generally recruited from among the elite sector of scholar-officials in China or warriors in Japan who governed the country. Zen was transmitted by the more traditional and highly accomplished literati who sought to transcend the mainstream cultural trends by taking on the role of the outcast, rebel, misfit, or mischief-maker. Like bluesmen, Zen thinkers and artists were eager to go beyond the conventional boundaries and pursue the truth for its own sake by becoming mystical poets.[16]

For both the Blues and Zen, artistic expression is not mimetic in the sense of trying to depict or represent external reality, but rather it is intensely subjective in conveying mood shifts and states of mind, though implying the sense of its universality. An understanding of abstract truth that is full of contradictions emerges through the use of enigmatic language about a specific representative place or object. For example, Blues songs evoke concrete images such as particular highways and trains, towns and other locations, persons and events in order to heighten awareness of personal and social conflicts. The Robert Johnson catchphrase derived from Kokomo Arnold and made famous by Elmore James, "I believe I'll dust my broom," borrowed by Dylan in "High Water," implies departure by cutting one's losses. This can refer to leaving one's romantic partner behind, departing surreptitiously from the oppressive economic conditions of the plantation, or more spiritually, casting aside troubles and woes by leaving on a journey to find more fertile territory up north in St. Louis, Kansas City, Chicago, or Detroit.

Similarly, records of Zen dialogues share an emphasis on materiality as a crucial factor for expressing transcendental ideas by referencing animals and spirits, sticks and stones, icons and rites. The Zen slogan, "I hung my traveling staff there," can refer to the temple an itinerant monk visited on his last pilgrimage, but it also suggests more broadly what was accomplished by a master as well as his relationships with various teachers, peers, and disciples met during his itinerancy. Like Blues phrasing, it is at once nuanced and filled with multiple levels of meaning.

What Zen and the Blues most have in common is a sense of self-discipline in expressing personal truth by using few words, yet allowing for spontaneity by not letting oneself get boxed into a fixed sense of structure. Both traditions stress artistic self-control coupled with a spirit of intoxicated improvisation that breaks down borders yet rings true because of the charisma and authenticity of the performer or instructor. Truth for Zen and the Blues is often revealed through psychic contests and confrontations that push the rivals or partners in dialogue to break free from ordinary categories and borders. In the Blues, this process is known as "cutting heads," whereby two performers play in close proximity and test each other to see who can draw the bigger crowds. In a similar way, Zen uses the term "cutting the finger" to indicate how a student is forced to abandon all attachments based on the radical teaching techniques of his master. The Zen approach draws from the legend of a novice, who imitated his teacher's style of holding up a finger in response to questions and had his digit sliced off by the master who quickly tired of the mimicry.

An important difference, however, is that the Blues "represents a fusion of music and poetry accomplished at a very high emotional temperature,"[17] whereas Zen tends to be a "cool" form of literature disentangling conflicting emotions and defusing them through aloofness and creative distance. But in some Zen anecdotes, indignity and anger is strongly expressed by masters toward misunderstanding or disrespectful peers or disciples who either break the rules in a misguided way or fail to grasp the significance of following regulations.

For the Blues and Zen, which both derive from cultural traditions where a trading of insults was considered appropriate if done in a ritualized and articulate way, a sense of intense competition and psychic conflict is made widespread through a pervasive and creative use of putdowns. This is done as part of a multilayered exchange of ideas and values in which irreverence is at once pointed yet disingenuous. Zen sayings include "He's adding frost to the snow," "He looked for an eagle and shot a pigeon," and "The shame of his house is exposed to the world," all of which critique one who compounds the error of his ways with more error. Similarly, the Blues standard, "James Alley Blues," contains one of the sharpest of retorts in its final verse: "Sometime I think you're too sweet to die,/ Other times I think you ought to be buried alive." This was emulated yet personalized by Dylan in "Black Crow Blues": "Sometimes I'm thinkin'/ I'm too high to fall./ Other times I'm thinkin' I'm/ So low I don't know/ If I can come up at all."

Zen masters and Blues performers provide spiritually edifying artistic entertainment commenting at least indirectly on political issues and social affairs in ways that have enduring cross-cultural significance extending beyond the community for which it was originally created. For example, a Zen saying, "The green mountains do not move, and the white clouds go on their own," is not merely a commonsense statement. Rather, it is a coded expression that critiques the immobility of the overall despotic sociopolitical system symbolized by the mountains, while holding out hope for the transients and pilgrims represented by the clouds who tenaciously go their own way to find truth.

The twelve-bar, AAB structure of the Blues is highly formulaic in using a storehouse of floating couplets, or pairs of lines that are repeatedly expressed in countless songs. But the Blues is also impulsive, introspective, and minimalist in featuring an innovative third line that adds a new twist by making an incisive and insightful comment on personal feelings or social situations. Robert Palmer stresses that the "Delta Blues is a refined, extremely subtle, and ingeniously systematic musical language."[18] According to Palmer,

> Originality in the blues, then, is not a question of sitting down and making up songs out of thin air . . . . From a lyrical point of view, the art of "writing" blues songs consists of combining phrases, lines, and verses with compatible emotional resonances into associational clusters that reflect the singer's own experiences, feelings, and moods and those of its listeners.[19]

The same method is found in Zen composition and in the process of writing in East Asian poetry generally. This tradition has always prized as an essential form originality, not creating something brand new but rather the use of an "allusive variation" (*honkadori*) of a prominent earlier verse by subtly altering a few key words or phrases. Like the use of floating couplets in typical Delta Blues songs, Zen koan records utilize formulaic rhetoric through a reservoir of catchphrases and stock sayings that are endlessly cited but allow room for an individual to manifest his creativity. Innovation is achieved by completing or supplementing a verse with a unique "capping phrase" (*jakugo*) that comments ironically from the standpoint of a particular thinker's spiritual perspective.

Furthermore, the Blues singers and Zen masters all demonstrate a profound use of "intertextuality" in that the significance of words crosses boundaries of author and text in building multivalent meanings surrounding particular repetitive phrasings. Catchphrases hold a double layer of meaning, with one level of overt significance and another level of covert symbolism. However, the role of ambiguity is featured not to confuse the reader, but to open up a realm of subjective interpretation and appreciation. Dylan employs intertextuality in a masterful way in his references to folk songs as well as biblical passages. Over the course of his career, he also evokes earlier stages of songwriting, such as with the resonances between the critique, "You break just like a little girl" in 1965's "Just Like a Woman" and the reluctant admiration and praise of "You're a Big Girl Now" a decade later. Another example is flood imagery which has implications for an individual person's struggles as well as the challenges facing society at large in "Down in the Flood" in 1967 and "The Levee's Gonna Break" thirty-five years later.

DYLAN'S BEAT BLUES

A striking parallel between Dylan and Zen masters as well as bluesmen is an existential quality in that their artistry deals with all phases of living and dying at the most fundamental level. Dylan comments on the exhilaration experienced when he first heard a Robert Johnson recording and felt that the "stabbing sounds from the guitar could almost break a window."[20] In *Chronicles*, Dylan, who sings in "High Water," "I can write you poems, make a strong man lose his mind," cites a famous Johnson line, "The stuff I got'll bust your brains out," which sounds like the way psychologically explosive Zen koans that inspire instantaneous illumination are often described. Dylan further eulogizes the impact of the famed singer's approach to song-writing on his own musical development by reminiscing how Johnson was impressive in "the construction of his old-style lines and the free association that he used, the sparkling allegories, big-ass truths, wrapped in the hard shell of nonsensical abstractions—themes that flew through the air with the greatest of ease."[21] The effect on Dylan was that "Johnson's words made my nerves quiver like piano wires."

Dylan's appreciation of Robert Johnson recalls Bono's words of praise for his idol. "Bob Dylan," he writes, "is there for you at every stage of your life . . . [he']s got you from the cradle to the grave."[22] Nearly every observer is in enthusiastic agreement regarding the magnitude of the accomplishments attained in the first half-decade of Dylan's creative upsurge and its continuing impact on popular culture. The stunning richness of Dylan's prolific achievements has been acknowledged by his peers. For example, according to George Harrison, who in an interview once quoted Dylan's Zen-like lyric on the limits of intellect, "To understand you know too soon there is no sense in trying," "Dylan is so brilliant. To me, he makes William Shakespeare look like Billy Joel."

Bruce Springsteen, who once referred to Dylan as "the brother I never had," thereby evoking Dylan's eulogy for Lenny Bruce, has said, "The first time I heard Bob Dylan, I was in the car with my mother listening to WMCA, and on came that snare shot that sounded like somebody'd kicked open the door to your mind: 'Like a Rolling Stone'." Moreover, Leonard Cohen has said, "He's Picasso." Paul McCartney echoes this sentiment with the additional inference that, like the painter's genius which went through so many distinct and sometimes contradictory creative periods that often left observers puzzled, all of Dylan's work should be considered worthwhile and not just selections or stages that happen to appeal to a particular fan or critic.[23]

The effect of being so greatly under the sway of the personality of a mentor is conveyed in similar fashion in a multitude of Zen dialogues.

In one example, a disciple of Yuehshan once said of his teacher with deliberately disingenuous self-deprecation,

> For twenty years I studied with Yuehshan. I ate what Yuehshan ate, and shat what Yuehshan shat. But I have not been able to master the way of Yuehshan, and I was only able to raise a neutered water buffalo [symbolic of deficiency].

In other cases, Zen students are struck and ridiculed by demanding teachers, but when the master dies, a key disciple finds that he is able to exert his own sense of authority and lead his followers through a new process of transmission.

FROM DULUTH TO DINKYTOWN AND BEYOND

Considering Dylan's relationship with Zen in light of the Blues is useful for understanding the roots of his spirituality. Michael Gray points out about his formative years, "Dylan's literal journey was east to Greenwich Village. His existential journey was south, down Highway 61 [to discover the Delta Blues]."[24] Yet, as a product of northern, white, middle-class, educated society, Dylan infused and incorporated his approach to the Blues with a variety of other cultural and intellectual elements in order to develop his unique music-making skills.

Therefore, we need to add to Gray's comment that the journey to Greenwich Village was also existentially significant in exposing Dylan both to the Blues and to the Beats. Dylan probably first learned of Beat literature in the hip scene of Minneapolis's bohemian Dinkytown student quarter, located near the University of Minnesota. While enrolled in college, Dylan apparently spent nearly all of his time in Dinkytown for a year and a half before officially dropping out and heading for New York. At the famed Ten O'Clock Scholar coffeehouse, he learned to "go acoustic" after having played electric guitar in high school.[25] Years later, taking license to link the sources of his poetic inspiration with Highway 61, Dylan located avant-garde artistic precursors to the Beats in his birth town down the road from Hibbing by saying in the liner notes to *Planet Waves*: "Duluth! Duluth—where Baudelaire Lived & Goya cashed in his Chips, where Joshua brought the house down! From there, it was straight up."

Similar to the eccentric, truth-seeking lifestyle of bluesmen, rules-breaking Beat generation writers like William Burroughs, Lawrence Ferlinghetti, Jack Kerouac, Michael McClure, and Gary Snyder as well as

Allen Ginsberg used the pursuit of exhilarating, over-the-edge life adventures as an avenue to find a deeper level of spiritual understanding freed from bondage to mainstream society. According to Dylan, "To the Beats, the devil was bourgeois conventionality, social artificiality and the man in the gray flannel suit."[26] Their experiences were gained through exotic travel, intense personal relationships, or experimenting with altered states of consciousness.

The pursuit of authenticity by the Beats based on flashes of illumination as well as sustained self-empowerment, was expressed in distinctive literary styles, such as stream of consciousness prose or what Ginsberg called

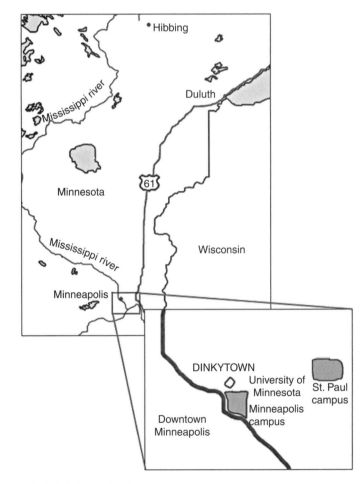

Figure 3.5   Dinkytown, MN

Table 3.1   Beat Blues

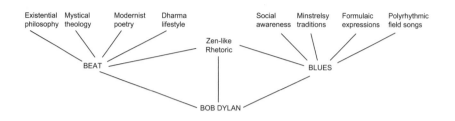

Kerouac's "spontaneous bop prosody," in addition to open-form poetry. Dylan was also influenced by authors who had an impact on the Beats, including the mystical ruminations of Arthur Rimbaud, who made very Buddhistic statements about egolessness like "I is someone else" ("Je est un autre") and "I am thought," in addition to the "nonsense" writing of Lewis Carroll and T. S. Eliot, whose *The Wasteland* is so dense and obscure it requires the author's footnotes.

Allen Ginsberg, whose own works were confiscated by the authorities and who became a spokesman in defending novelists Burroughs against censorship and Kerouac against misguided criticism, has argued that Beat writings cannot be evaluated in relation to standards set for classical literature. The Beats experiment with literary form and style, he points out, because their aim is to convey an interior experience of true insight with the unimpeded spontaneity and immediacy of spiritual writers such as William Blake and Walt Whitman.

A hallmark of the Beats is their explicit embracing of Buddhism. In the novels *The Dharma Bums* and *Satori in Paris*, Kerouac evokes the Zen ideology of living freely in the eternal moment. He epitomizes what Alan Watts has called the "Beat Zen" approach whereby Zen teaching functions as the background for a carefree, itinerant and ever questing lifestyle that is quite different from the traditional Buddhist monastic organization. Other Beats represent "Square Zen," which tries to follow some of the patterns of typical institutional training adapted for modern American society. Snyder, for example, became a confirmed practitioner who studied for a number of years in a monastery in Kyoto where he has long enjoyed an enthusiastic following of readers. Ginsberg, who toured South Asia in the early 1960s, dedicated himself to the practice of meditation and taught for many years at a Buddhist institute in America.[27] Both Snyder and Ginsberg infused their poetry with Buddhist meanings, with the former focusing on nature and environmental themes and the latter on the psychological and cosmic implications of the teachings.

Dylan was especially close to Ginsberg, who became a lifelong companion and collaborator on several projects, especially the Rolling Thunder Revue tour of the mid-1970s. Ginsberg has spoken movingly of the goosebump moment when he first heard "A Hard Rain's A-Gonna Fall" long before he met Dylan, and felt that the "torch had been passed to a new generation." Dylan for his part remarked in the liner notes to *Bringing It All Back Home* in typically irreverent fashion of his respect for the Beat poet, "why allen ginsberg was not chosen t' read poetry at the [presidential] inauguration boggles my mind." Ginsberg frequently spoke of how he encouraged Dylan to consider the path of Buddhist contemplation, and he likely found ways of exposing him to Zen lore and practice, especially given Dylan's predilection toward seeking mystical awareness. Dylan also paid tribute to the Blues and its influences by further commenting, "the fact that the white house is filled with leaders that've never been t' the apollo theater amazes me."

Dylan's complex expression of spirituality is based on his distinctive method of combining outstanding literary achievements in evoking existential angst and the possibilities for transcendence through everyday activities with an appropriation of the rhythmic and lyrical patterns of the Blues. This approach to writing was inspired in large part by the Beats, who introduced the flavor of Zen in concrete imagery, along with other sources of experimental poetry such as the Symbolists, Dadaists, and Modernists. In the mid-1960s, Dylan's "Desolation Row" was influenced by Kerouac's novel *Desolation Angels* in addition to Eliot's *The Wasteland*, and "On the Road Again" was based on *On the Road*, while "It's Alright, Ma" was inspired by Ginsberg's prose–poem *Kaddish* addressed to his ailing mentally ill mother.

But the connections go much deeper than these song titles. The Beat worldview as a source of inspiration is what made Dylan's portrayal of the horrific conceptual landscape of Highway 61 so unique as a living cultural nightmare. For Dylan, the highway is a surreal place of text, taunts, and strange, often grotesque encounters, where all aspects of American society have been plundered or undermined by corruption, confusion, deceit, and betrayal. People's reactions in this scorched realm are typically based on fear rather than faith, concealing the truth rather than revealing it, incestuous rather than genuine relationships, and trying to hide out or escape rather than finding sanctuary.

According to Dylan's postmodern reading of the Blues Highway, Jack the Ripper sits proudly at the "head of the chamber of commerce" and Einstein "with his memories in a trunk" is turned into a blithering idiot. Meanwhile, "roving gamblers who are feeling very bored" plot to start the next world war for fun and profit, while "insurance men" conspire to keep anyone from getting free from the absurdity of this deeply troubled locale. Only the contemplative few are able to attain a symbolic place of serenity and solitude by residing within the innocent "Gates of Eden," hearing the liberating "Chimes of Freedom," or occupying the world-weary detached wisdom of "Desolation Row."

Dylan's twelve-bar Blues lyrics often differ greatly from those of other rock performers in being infused with Beat-style poetics. Songs from different parts of his career, such as "Don't Think Twice, It's All Right," "Maggie's Farm," "Leopard-Skin Pill Box Hat," "Meet Me in the Morning," "Gonna Change My Way of Thinking," "Summer Days," and "The Levee's Gonna Break," are derived from preexisting songs in the vast Blues backlog, and in some cases more than one influence is evident. Yet these songs come alive with compelling contemporary significance largely because the AAB structure is at once captured and enhanced by being transformed into a vehicle for expressing a profound existential quest.

A prime example of the artistic combination connecting the Blues and the Beats that is found in numerous Dylan songs involves the extensive use of railroad imagery. Dylan's interest in train cast as a metaphor for either escaping a troubled situation in order to relocate or an entrapment to a realm of bondage was influenced by Woody Guthrie's boxcar hopping days as celebrated in his memoirs, *Bound for Glory*, in addition to Curtis Mayfield's inspirational song, "People Get Ready" (for the train to salvation), which Dylan covers in *Renaldo and Clara*. In several mid-1960s songs, including "It Takes a Lot to Laugh, It Takes a Train to Cry," "I'll Keep it with Mine," and "Stuck Inside of Mobile with the Memphis Blues Again," railroad imagery conveys a twofold sense of opportunity and loss, travel and fatigue, or eschatological hope and failure.

The image of trains resurfaces in later songs such as the country romance, "Tonight I'll Be Staying Here With You," the excruciating existential anguish of "Where Are You Tonight?," the evangelical finger-pointing of "Slow Train," and the repentant, self-doubt in "Tryin' to Get to Heaven," where it represents the (im)possibility of gaining redemption. According to the latter lyric, anxious people are waiting for the train to arrive at the platform, but Dylan says he "can hear their hearts a-beatin'/ Like pendulums swinging on chains" because they realize that the trains no longer take passengers who have committed transgressions. Railroad imagery also appears in a song of unrequited love, "Nettie Moore," which begins with the lead character sitting forlornly on a train track that helps depict a world "out of whack" with "blues this morning falling down like hail," which is a line borrowed from Robert Johnson.

From a Zen perspective, what is important in these examples of train symbolism is that Dylan, influenced by Beat Blues, is using in diverse, open-ended ways a very specific, concrete, practical, everyday image. The image may at first appear quite superficial, but it functions as a means of commenting on profound states of consciousness and the inner meaning of one's awareness of vulnerability, fear, and sorrow as well as aspiration and longing. As with a Zen pilgrim's itinerancy to a temple on a remote mountain peak or in a hectic urban center, the railway offers reprieve and sanctuary for one who pursues the exhilaration of liberty yet finds that the journey leads nowhere other than within to examine personal troubles and other sources of turmoil. The train ride, like an excursion along the Blues Highway 61 or the Grand Canal in China, takes one not only on an actual journey but into the interior landscape of the soul, including memories, dreams, and desires, which always risk being corrupted and commodified by the social system that cynically sells "roadmaps for the soul/ to the old folks' home and the college."

The right turn just might lead one on the pathway to salvation.

Chapter 4

Masked and Eponymous

Authenticity and Autonomy in Dylan and Zen

ALCHEMY OF WORDS

Zen masters and Bob Dylan are spiritual seekers who perfect the craft of expressing their vision. Perhaps what they share most fundamentally is a common intensity and even passion in their uncompromising quest for Truth, even while questioning assumptions about the very nature of what is true. In differing milieus, they have accomplished a vivid and evocative expression of dedication and commitment to finding the fullness of self-attainment through subdued detachment and sustaining the wholeness of humanity realized through active compassion.

Dylan's writings and sayings are infused with perplexing yet probing and sometimes disturbing expressions couched in inscrutable language that can be difficult to discern and decipher. The lyrics in various songs, as well as passages from other sources including album liner notes, books, films, interview responses, or concert banter, are often intentionally ambiguous and laden with a deliberately cultivated irony. Dylan is a wordsmith whose verbal creations confound the listener, and can be understood—or misunderstood—in numerous ways that are sometimes competing or conflicting.

A recent book published in Japan, which combines an analysis of Dylan's work and its impact on Japanese culture by a variety of musical and social critics with a *manga*-like narrative of his visits to Japan over the years, refers to "Kimi no uta, Wakarinikui yo Bobu Diran," or "Bob Dylan,

Your Songs are Difficult to Understand!"[1] This seems to suggest that the Japanese have a special sense of affinity with his approach. When seen from the perspective of Zen, which specializes in the use of silence, absurdity, and other unconventional rhetorical devices to disclose the paradoxical nature of spiritual insight, Dylan's elusive quality becomes more readily accessible.

This chapter connects the topic of "Zen & Dylan," or identifying affinities in writing and outlook, with "the Zen of Dylan," or interpreting Dylan's trajectory in light of a Zen-based dialectical theory of his attainment of a middle path in recent years. This forms the basis for my analysis of the periods of his career in the second part of the book. The link between these topics involves the ways in which Dylan's enigmatic words and deeds demonstrate attributes and can be illuminated through an understanding of Zen Buddhist literature.

Deconstructive and constructive elements

The writings of Zen masters and Dylan have two complementary aspects. One is a deconstructive side in enabling rhetoric to highlight and criticize the flaws and lacunae of conventional logic and language, or to show the variance between words and the reality they seek to depict. The other aspect is a constructive side in using words creatively and with an almost magical flair to go beyond ordinary reality and express an intuitive grasp of transcendental truth.

One of the most famous examples of Zen deconstruction is the response to the query, "Why did Bodhidharma [the founder of Zen in sixth-century China] come from the West [that is, from India]?" The question is the equivalent of asking a teacher to explain the meaning of doctrinal history in twenty-five words or less. The most famous reply is the non-sequitur, "The oak tree in the garden," and additional possibilities include responding to the inquiry with another query, slapping the disciple, or some other gesture such as sitting silently while holding upright a ceremonial fly whisk. All of these responses seek to disrupt and disturb the complacency of the inquirer. Rather than trying to give a straightforward historical answer, these absurd utterances and mannerisms force the question back on the questioner. This shows that Zen masters are adamant about refusing to explain or simplify their message.

Similarly, Dylan's method is to query an inquirer's assumptions at the root in order to overturn conventional ideas and stereotypical ways of thinking so that, as philosopher Martin Heidegger has said, any question raised is made ever more questionable. In the free-form liner notes to *Bringing It All Back Home*, for example, Dylan writes,

> [I] am standing there writing WHAAT? on my favorite wall when who should pass by in a jet plane but my recording engineer "I'm here t' pick up you and your latest works of art" . . . an' so i answer my recording engineer "yes. well i could use some help in getting this wall in the plane."

In the mid-1960s when Dylan was first forging new ground by making hit singles that were much longer than the typical Top 40, "two minutes and fifty-seven seconds" prepackaged fare, he was pressed to discuss the significance of his songs. He replied in a way that at once irked and amused fans while ridiculing the questioner, "I do know what my songs are about. Some are about four minutes, some are about five, and some, believe it or not, are about eleven or twelve." During that era, a reporter prodded Dylan,

> How many people who labor in the same musical vineyard in which you toil, how many are protest singers? That is, people who use their music, and use the songs to protest the uh, social state in which we live today, the matter of war, the matter of crime, or whatever it might be.

Dylan responded, "Uh, I think there's about uh, 136." When the reporter, apparently oblivious to the fact that many in the room were snickering, next asked, "You say ABOUT 136, or you mean exactly 136?," Dylan shot back, "Uh, it's either 136 or 142."

In an early scene of *Don't Look Back*, which uses *cinema verité* technique to document a tour of England in the summer of 1965, Dylan carries an oversized light bulb to a press conference.[2] He responds to an inquiry about his message for the youth of the day, "Keep a good head and always carry a light bulb." Dylan's comeback line reflects a Dadaist flair for absurdity in trying to upset the expectations of his questioner, or it could be seen as an intriguing symbolic rationale for continuing the quest to attain illumination. Dylan's non-responsiveness can be compared to the use of irony and misdirection in Magritte's painting of a pipe that bears the caption, *Ceci n'est pas une pipe* ("This is not a pipe"), or to the approach of composer John Cage, whose sensational silent composition for piano in the early 1950s titled *4:33* was based on his study of Zen.

The constructive side of their discourse is that Zen masters and Dylan make the most of what Rimbaud in the "Deliriums" section of *A Season in Hell* has called the "alchemy of the word." This refers to constructing special phrasings based on an exceptional illuminative experience that borrows heavily from, yet transforms colloquial and idiomatic expressions in order to convey an ideal image of truth. Rimbaud, a poet who once said he wanted to become a singer, whereas Dylan is a singer who became a poet, uses language neither to depict the external world nor to concoct new phrasings in an arbitrary way. Rather, he enhances ordinary language to reveal truth in terms of an interior state of mind that otherwise is concealed or remains ineffable. In this alchemical world, enigma is by no means an obstacle to understanding but serves as an essential method to plumb the depths of meaning because the true vision is elusive and cannot easily be put in words. A catalog of some prominent examples of Dylan's enigmatic words in the table below reflects a wide variety of rhetorical styles:

Table 4.1   Variety of Dylan's rhetorical styles

Challenging	• Don't steal, don't lift/ Twenty years of schoolin'/And they put you on the day shift • You know, I feel pretty good, but that ain't sayin' much./ I could feel a whole lot better • I will sing it loud and sing it strong/ Let the echo decide if I was right or wrong
Cryptic	• The only thing we knew for sure about Henry Porter is that his name wasn't Henry Porter • I stayed with Aunt Sally, but you know, she's not really my aunt
Defiant	• I used to care, but things have changed • If I catch my opponents ever sleepin'/ I'll just slaughter them where they lie
Elliptical	• John Wesley Harding was a friend to the poor/ He trav'led with a gun in ev'ry hand • aretha/crystal jukebox queen of hymn and him diffused in drunk transfusion wound • I'm beginning to hear voices and there's no one around/ Well, I'm all used up and the fields have turned brown
Mysterious	• The deputy walks on hard nails and the preacher rides a mount • The rifleman's stalking the sick and the lame, preacher man seeks the same, who'll get there first is uncertain
Obtuse	• My fingers are in a knot/ I don't have the strength/ To get up and take another shot • Nothing is revealed; Too much of nothing; Nothing was delivered • In order to deal in this game, you got to make the queen disappear,/ It's done with a flick of the wrist • I've made shoes for everyone, even you, while I still go barefoot
Paradoxical	• [The world] looks like it's a-dyin' an' it's hardly been born • What's good is bad, what's bad is good, you'll find out when you reach the top/ You're on the bottom • Some people still sleepin', some people are wide awake

(Continued)

Perplexingly Allusive	• Ma Rainey and Beethoven once unwrapped their bed roll
	• But Mona Lisa musta had the highway blues,/You can tell by the way she smiles
	• Apache poets searching thru the ruins for a glimpse of Buddha
	• Relationships have all been bad./Mine've been like Verlaine's and Rimbaud
	• Marx has got ya by the throat, Henry Kissinger's got you tied up in knots
	• I'm going where the Southern crosses the Yellow Dog,/ Get away from these demagogues
Probing	• Inside the museums/Infinity goes up on trial
	• I am hanging in the balance of the reality of man
	• Someone showed me a picture and I just laughed;/ Dignity's never been photographed
Puzzling	• Everything I've ever known to be right has proven wrong/I'll be drifting along
	• Since every pleasure's got an edge of pain/Pay for your ticket and don't complain
	• Sometimes it's not enough to know the meaning of things. . . sometimes we have to know what things don't mean as well
Subtle	• She speaks like silence/Without ideals or violence
	• She's delicate and seems like the mirror
	• Your sweet voice/Calls out from some old familiar shrine

Because of their generally opaque yet open-ended quality, Dylan's words, which can be subject to multiple interpretations or resist being interpreted at all, have given rise to the term "Dylanesque." This term suggests a surreal approach to artistic discourse that encompasses highly eccentric and stylized symbolism as well as Blues-based vernacular expressions to convey an aloof attitude. To be Dylanesque means that one evidences an ironic, above-the-fray outlook behind the delivery of enigmatic lyrics that reflect a diversity of cultural and intellectual influences.

One type of Dylanesque technique involves the playful use of double entendre, which has been compared to a suggestive verbal version of the way Elvis the Pelvis introduced sensuality into popular music with his highly controversial body language. In the early days of rock & roll, Elvis complemented his singing style that borrowed heavily from black blues performers in his native Memphis. For example, Dylan makes "garage door" sound like "crotch door," rhymes "don't let the boys in" with "it is not poison," and leaves it vague whether "getting stoned" refers to psychedelic drugs or biblical persecution.

Another method of expressing more than meets the ear is the way Dylan outdoes the techniques of the old Blues singers in using common colloquialisms and street language for rhetorical effect in order to convey a sense of loss and despair. Some of the techniques that appear in Dylan songs from every period include double or triple negatives (as in "ain't got no"), droppin' the final consonant, or slurring syllables in pronouncing certain key words so that "mournin' dove" in "Shelter from the Storm" sounds like "moaning dove." Another strategy is to delete the first person pronoun "I" to give priority to activity rather than the actor—which resembles the impersonal grammatical constructions of East Asian languages—while also diffusing the second person pronoun so that "you" may indicate any of several other people, the Almighty, or a different side of the multifaceted narrator.

Dylan's songs are also known for their innovative use of clichés. Indeed, some of his songs are filled with stock phrases used not in a deadening, mechanical fashion, but in the same manner that Shakespeare's plays are replete with famous quotes. Some prominent examples include the scornful, backhanded praise, "What's a sweetheart like you doin' in a dump like this?"; the reproachful comment on the untimely death in prison of black activist George Jackson, "Some of US are prisoners/ The rest of US are guards"; and the painful admission, "I'm love sick/ I'm sick of it . . . I'm in the thick of it." Other examples are "Going, Going, Gone," which uses a catchphrase to make a bold statement about future directions, and a number of songs from *Red Sky at Morning* which transform seemingly simple nursery rhymes into typically Dylanesque apocalyptic tales.

In some cases, Dylan twists a cliché with irony, such as John Wesley Harding traveling with "a gun in ev'ry hand" or "Highway 61 Revisited's" promoter "who nearly fell off the floor" at the roving gambler's proposal to start the next world war. The subtle adjustment of clichés is perhaps most poignant and evocative in dealing with tales of lost or unrequited love, as in the refrain, "Blame it on a simple twist of fate." In "I Threw It All Away" Dylan comments, holding the vowels seemingly forever as a forlorn expression of loss:

> Love is all there is
> It makes the world go 'round
> Love and only love
> It can't be denied
> No matter what you think about it
> You just won't be able to do without it
> Take a tip from one who's tri-i-i-i-i-e-e-e-e-ed.

At other times, Dylan's writing is almost outrageously original in his use of free-form verse that makes extensive use of historical, mythological, and biblical allusions, often mixing together the real and unreal, or surreal, to reflect inner perception. The more refined and eloquent side of Dylan's expressiveness uses a variety of literary techniques. These include complicated rhyme schemes, allusions to classical and modern literary works, and the frequent use of personification to show how nature either approves or rejects human actions, as when the fishes laugh and the seagulls smile in greeting the Goliath-beating righteous in "When the Ship Comes In."

In "Tombstone Blues," Dylan refers in a mind-altering context to Ma Rainey, the first famous female blues singer of the 1920s, having conjugal relations with the premier classical composer Beethoven, which represents a wedding of the plebian and the elite.

"Nettie Moore" alludes to the intersection of the Southern Railway and the Yellow Dog, an image that refers to the impulse to flee from the repressive sociopolitical forces of southern society by one who is falsely accused or ensnared in complex legal circumstances beyond his control. In these and other phrasings, Dylan evokes iconic images from traditional American music and Western civilization in order to make a forceful

Figure 4.1   Ma Rainey

Figure 4.2   Beethoven

statement and transform perceptions of the contemporary world, its strengths and its foibles, and its ironies and inconsistencies.

In a highly nuanced verse from "Memphis Blues Again," Dylan uses the images of "Texas medicine" and "railroad gin" to represent "two cures" given by "the rain man," which when mixed "strangled up [his] mind." This complex expression comments sardonically on the aspirations and the decline of the American Dream. It epitomizes the interconnections as well as the difficulties of trying to strike it rich on the road while seeking to escape from the turmoil of everyday society. The twofold quality is also expressed in a key line from "Just Like Tom Thumb's Blues": "Up on Housing Project Hill/ It's either fortune or fame/ You must pick up one or the other/ Though neither of them are to be what they claim." Through terse, surrealistic metaphors, Dylan expresses the depths of angst in a world of absurdity and conflict, for which any hope for a balanced perspective quickly dissolves. Temptations lead to pervasive alienation and discord since, as a result of the odd mixture of the two cures, "people just get uglier" and there is "no sense of time," that is, subjective distortions reflecting the defects of a troubled mind are expressionistically projected onto external reality.

Figure 4.3   Southern Crosses the Yellow Dog in Moorhead, MS

DYLAN'S TRAPEZE ARTISTRY AND ZEN KOANS

One of the features of Dylan's compositions that is close to the Zen approach is that just when you think you have figured out a line, you may hear it differently—or he changes words or enunciates in radically different fashion during a concert—so that the prior understanding dissolves and vanishes like morning dew. For example, in some performances he has added to the refrain, "Knockin' on heaven's door," the phrase "just like so many times before" in order to compound the sense of futility and despair. Or, during the gospel stage he enhanced the chorus, "I shall be released" with the words "Don't need no doctor or no priest" to highlight the notion that only a superior power can provide redemption. There are many other examples when a song has been reinvented in performance so that the meaning is dramatically changed.[3] For example, depending on the delivery, the refrain "no, no, no" in "It Ain't Me, Babe"—which some claim was a nihilistic retort to the Beatles' "yeah, yeah, yeah" from "She Loves You" in 1964—can seem to be directed to an individual or to a group, and represent a statement of despondency, a putdown of a forsaken lover, or a proclamation of freedom.

A skeptical concert reviewer has suggested, "Dylan does only what Dylan wants to do. Dylan does not want to play songs even remotely close to the way he recorded them and he definitely does not want to attempt to sing." However, Dylan's aim is not to puzzle or befuddle the audience as an end in itself. Rather, through irreverent yet ingenious free association and inventive wordplay he compels and cajoles—and sometimes, like a Zen master shouting at or slapping his disciple or rival teacher—psychically shocks the listener to deepen his or her understanding of self and society. The cultural violence of going electric at Newport is portrayed in *I'm Not There* with Dylan and his band symbolically firing machine guns at the audience, recalling Guthrie's "fascist-killing" instrument that serves as another prominent image in the film.

The emotionally reclusive Dylan, who may have titillated or irritated followers by comparing his skills to those of a "song and dance man," "ragged clown," or "entertainer" seems loathe to explicate his intentions. In the liner notes to *Highway 61 Revisited*, Dylan says that "the songs on this specific record are not so much songs but rather exercises in tonal breath control."

Despite differences of opinion about the relative merits or meaning of any particular song, followers of Dylan uniformly agree that his comments were disingenuous and he is anything but a mere song and dance man. It has been said that Dylan has introduced more new phraseology into the English language than anyone since Shakespeare, and he was called "his generation's Bard" by B. J. Rolfzen, Dylan's high school English literature teacher who was an early inspirational figure. As is the case with Shakespeare and other great writers, Dylan's inventiveness with words is done for the sake of demanding a greater degree of attentiveness from his audience.

Dylan is an elucidator and evaluator of current social conditions, and an edifier regarding the role of self-realization in an ever changing world. His enigmatic words are remarkably eloquent in evoking depths of emotion unveiled through an introspective process, while he also comments lucidly about the state of the union and the status of world affairs. On the other hand, Dylan was probably sincere when he referred to a song as a "naked person," and compared his craft to that of a "trapeze artist."[4]

It seems that for most listeners, a preconscious glimpse into the meaning of any given Dylan lyric is probably constantly there, lying just beneath the surface level of (mis)understanding. Singer Sophie B. Hawkins said in an interview before her performance of "I Want You" for Dylan's thirtieth Anniversary Concert in Madison Square Garden in 1993, "Each time I sing this song I struggle to grasp what the words are saying." On the right occasion, genuine insight about the Sad-Eyed Lady's "voice like chimes" or the meaning of "sapphire tinted skies" in "Things Have Changed" comes to the fore and is ready to explode by raising awareness of some home truth that is all the clearer in the long run because of the indirectness of the words.

Others have suggested that paying careful attention to Dylan's music is a matter of enhancing the "meaning" of his lyrics by making an association on an unconscious, experiential level that triggers spontaneous insight and wisdom. This process is distinct from finding out the "sense" of the words in terms of logical cognition or analysis. A converse ratio of interpretation, such that the greater the inner meaning based on experience the lesser the outer sense based on logic, has a profound affinity with the religious–literary discourse of Zen Buddhism. According to Zen, the more obscure the words are, the greater the access to ideas through allowing the reader/listener to read between the lines in order to comprehend the context and subtext surrounding the main text. Conversely, the greater the sense of freedom of the spirit, the more cryptic and veiled the rhetoric. In other words, the extent of the quixotic and ambiguous nature of discourse is an indicator of the heights of spiritual attainment.

Zen koans along with brief haiku-like verses ignite a dramatic break-through to a higher level of intuitive awareness. In Zen's notoriously iconoclastic rhetoric—symbolized by the Rorschach test-like cover of a translation of sayings contained in the thirteenth-century text, *The Book of Serenity*—traditional masters confuse and contradict one another, while invariably following the unwritten code to resist analyzing or explicating their words and deeds. In a famous example, when pressed to answer a query about one side of an issue regarding life and death the master responds, "I just won't say," and then he responds the same way when pressed about the opposite side. This double-edged method continually breaks down ordinary logical structures and conceptual boundaries in a way that is strongly reminiscent of Dylan's work.

D. T. Suzuki, the premier twentieth-century advocate of Zen, has said that the aim of a koan is to push the intellect to the limit until it sees that there is a realm of intuitive understanding into which intellect can never enter. The process of resolving the koan results in an experience of Satori, an instantaneous awakening stimulated by the process of deciphering intensely ambiguous or seemingly absurd utterances. Instead of through knowing alone, which after all forms only a part of human nature, the entire person including mind and body, or intuition and ration-ality, must become fully engaged in order to attain a spiritual realization. That moment is like a drop of water put into a full cup which had kept its equilibrium but now, due to the tiny amount of liquid added, is about to spill over. In this approach, which captures yet inverts the sense of frustration felt in a "last straw" experience, meaninglessness becomes the meaning.

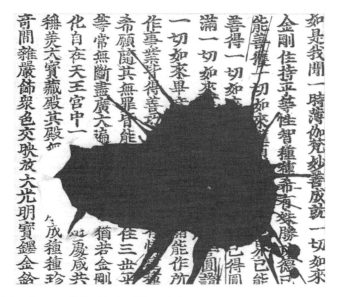

Figure 4.4   Cover of *The Book of Serenity**
*Thomas Cleary. trans. *Book of Serenity: One Hundred Zen Dialogues*. Hudson, NY: Lindisfarne, 1990.
See my reference in Steven Heine. *Zen Skin, Zen Marrow: Will the Real Zen Buddhism Please Stand Up?*
New York: Oxford University Press, 2007.

THERE MUST BE SOME WAY OUT OF HERE

In addition to deciphering his enigmatic words, the primary puzzle encountered by listeners of Dylan's corpus spanning well over 400 original songs
composed during the course of five decades concerns his enigmatic deeds
or complex trajectory. Throughout Dylan's career, rapid, radical transitions
in the message of his lyrics as well overall public persona and musical
style ranging from blues to folk, rock, country, reggae, and gospel, or some
combination thereof in both acoustic and electric formats have either
inspired or shocked different sectors of his fans. For one commentator,
"Dylan . . . has followed the dictates of his songwriting muse . . . [and] has
never remained in one place for very long, moving restlessly from style to
style, generally ahead of the pack, though he has sometimes been placed
in the driver's seat."[5] The breakneck pace of change has no doubt been
greatly affected by the onslaught of mass media and high speed communications that have caused shifts in social paradigms to occur at an ever
increasing rate. Dylan himself once told Allen Ginsberg that "Bob Dylan is
long gone."

At the same time that he continually catapults ahead into future directions, as explained in *Chronicles* Dylan often reflects back on the significance of the Civil War as the pivotal event in the country's history for the way it divided yet helped to connect races and regions. A century later, the core issues that ignited the war, especially with the implications of racism and internal violence, once again became the main factors affecting the social upheaval of the 1960s through the civil rights movement and counter-cultural revolution, and these elements of change are still current today on multiple levels.[6]

There are numerous prominent examples of shifts in Dylan's outlook that convey disdain and distrust for a point of view previously held dear. For example, the period of topical protest songs in the early 1960s expressing a moralistic approach based on inevitable retribution for misbehavior is rejected when Dylan refers in mid-decade in "My Back Pages" to "lies that life is black and white" and in "Positively Fourth Street" to social ills that "are not my problem."

Dylan's endorsement of the joys of love and marriage in the late1960s is dismissed by "Idiot Wind" in 1975 which inveighs, "You're an idiot, babe," and four years later, he proclaims, "You gotta serve somebody/ It may be the devil or it may be the lord." His embracing of fundamental Christian faith in the gospel songs that followed in the late 1970s is, however, questioned by a line in "Tight Connection to My Heart" released in 1985, which ponders ironically, "Never could learn to drink that blood/ And call it wine."

It is difficult to determine whether Dylan is simply being evasive and vacillating or is trying to be comprehensive and expansive in exploring all possible options, including mutually repulsive religious beliefs, while remaining committed to no particular viewpoint. The noncommittal approach represents an ideal found in both Asian mysticism and the philosophy of Nietzsche, who was greatly influenced by Eastern thought and who, Dylan says in the liner notes to *Highway 61 Revisited*, "never wore an umpire's suit." That is, the German philosopher did not pass judgments about right versus wrong based on conventional dualistic standards by virtue of standing, as indicated by one of his book titles, "Beyond Good and Evil."

In either case, Dylan seems to be perennially overturning the assumptions and upsetting the preconceptions and stereotypes, as well as the innate comfort and disposition, of his audience, not just in particular songs but in his entire path of songwriting and performing. A critic observes by using postmodern literary theory concerning the relation between author and reader:

> In an *oeuvre* as extensive, diverse and axiomatically self-contradictory as
> Bob Dylan's, the naïve readerly search for reductive kinds of significance

or "message" has typically been frustrated by a series of playful enigmatic turns which define the authorial intention as provocatively evasive or perverse . . . Dylan's lyrics construct an author–reader relation posited on the model of an irresolvable enigma which is both the incitement to and the perpetual frustration of readerly desire.[7]

This frustration is exemplified by numerous examples ranging from the Newport Folk Festival booing incident in 1965 to the 1979 gospel tour (which Dylan's band referred to as "Newport '79" because they suffered an equal number of rebuffs and catcalls from disappointed fans). Well before Newport '65, Dylan was booed on his very first public performance at Hibbing High School when he banged out a Little Richard piece on the piano and, when booed, had the mike cut off and the curtain pulled by the principal.[8] Over the years, he seems to have acknowledged and accepted, or even savored, perhaps proudly and in some cases almost perversely, the unpredictability to which his followers have been subjected. This has been done in the name of pursuing a worldview based on following a distinctive path, even when this constitutes a radical departure from his previous perspective.

Dylan at times enjoys, perhaps tinged with regret, the role of being misunderstood and misrepresented or symbolically martyred for undertaking an unpopular cause or supporting a principle as a matter of integrity, thus recalling the Beatles' proverbial "Fool on the Hill." He was asked to play "Restless Farewell" at a Frank Sinatra tribute concert because it was the song that most closely resembled the Chairman of the Board's signature "I Did It My Way," frequently referred to as the "new national anthem." This refusal to get pigeonholed by those who only care about themselves is also vigorously conveyed in the line, "You've got a lot of nerve to say you are my friend" from "Positively Fourth Street," and in "I'll burn that bridge before you can cross" from "Ain't Talkin'."

Remorse for being overly distant and alienated is signaled in "It Takes a Lot to Laugh, It Takes a Train to Cry," released in 1965 with the war in Vietnam escalating and the solidarity of the civil rights movement deteriorating. Here, Dylan laments the difficulty of the artist trying to communicate misgivings and forebodings to the larger audience, which is indifferent or conflictive. "Now the wintertime is coming," he writes,

> The windows are filled with frost.
> I went to tell everybody,
> But I could not get across.
> Well, I wanna be your lover, baby,
> I don't wanna be your boss.
> Don't say I never warned you
> When your train gets lost.

In "Tears of Rage," a song recorded on the *Basement Tapes* after his motor-cycle crash, Dylan wonders, "Why must I always be the thief?," that is, why is it that the cloak of responsibility to be "spokesman for a generation" keeps falling on his shoulders and cannot be easily sloughed off. This concern is echoed but from a more affirmative perspective in "Up to Me," which says "No one else could play that tune,/ You know it was up to me."

In reflecting on his sense of self-awareness and self-identity, Dylan has sometimes turned to the image of Jesus, since his "life eerily reflects that of another man who began life as a Jew, adopted Christian beliefs, was belit-tled and persecuted by the establishment, and possessed the ability to move millions with his messages."[9] Dylan's approach has encompassed the dual view of Jesus as role model, or a paradigm to follow for the way he abhorred corruption by storming the temple and casting out profiteers while humbly accepting the punishment of society, and as savior, or a divine entity to be worshipped who offers mankind the only hope for redemption. Both dimensions are integrated in the gospel song "I Believe in You": "And they, they look at me and frown,/ They'd like to drive me from this town,/ They don't want me around/ 'Cause I believe in you." Dylan celebrates being misunderstood since the din of the crowd actually justifies and legitimates an independent outlook based on clinging to faith that rises above the pettiness and shortsightedness of others.

However, the irreverent side of Dylan along with his Beat mentor Allen Ginsberg was demonstrated in an episode where they stood below an image of Christ hanging from a cross, and instructed him to come down off the crucifix before he got hurt. In a tone mocking all the critics of his electric folk-rock sound, Dylan called upon Christ to "play your early stuff, man!," yet as indicated in Chapter 1, he also took the Stations of the Cross very seriously. These examples suggest that gospel imagery has an ongoing reso-nance with Dylan's personal experiences and his feelings of having been thrust into the role of playing martyr. But, it can be asked, to what cause?

WHAT ELSE CAN YOU SHOW ME?

Is Dylan's work complex and contradictory or does it have an underlying sense of consistency and continuity? In exploring this issue in light of Zen, an important theme evident at every stage of Dylan's career regardless of any particular position he is endorsing (or rejecting) is an adamant refusal to whitewash the ills of social institutions or to delimit his pursuit of free-dom from bondage imposed by the chains and shackles of dungeon-like society or self-imposed by ignorance. Some examples include: "I haven't known peace and quiet for so long I can't remember what it's like" in

"Idiot Wind" (1974), and "Standing on the gallows with my head in a noose/ Any minute now I'm expecting all hell to break loose" in "Things Have Changed" (1999).

Dylan frequently expresses the fervent desire to regain true selfhood by achieving authenticity and autonomy, as in: "Let us not talk falsely now" in "All Along the Watchtower" (1968); "In this age of fiberglass I'm searching for a gem" in "Dirge" (1973); "I know all about poison, I know all about fiery darts,/ I don't care how rough the road is, show me where it starts" in "What Can I Do For You?" (1989); and "Every moment of existence seems like some dirty trick/ Happiness can come suddenly and leave just as quick" in "Sugar Baby" (2001). Some other examples include the following:

- "Name me someone who's not a parasite and/ I'll go out and say a prayer for him" ("Visions of Johanna," 1966).
- "The man in me will hide sometimes to keep from bein' seen,/ But that's just because he doesn't want to turn into some machine." ("The Man in Me," 1970)
- "If there's an original thought out there, I could use it right now" ("Brownsville Girl," 1986).
- "Wouldn't know the difference between a real blonde and a fake" ("Highlands," 1997).
- "I'll close my eyes and I wonder/ If everything is as hollow as it seems" ("Tryin' to Get to Heaven," 1997).

The non-parasite, true gem, original thought, and real blonde are all undiscovered items in a world characterized by falsity, hollowness, and dirty tricks. Trying to find each of these genuine items fulfills a vision that conquers the sources of alienation and results in the contemplative state of a Zen-like independence, as expressed by, "Don't send me no more letters no/ Not unless you mail them/ From Desolation Row," as well as the celebration of solitude in "Dirge."

For Dylan, corrupt authority that perpetually stands in the way of this quest and is therefore deserving of disdain and disgust is frequently symbolized by the image of the judge as a negative gatekeeper with ulterior motives who thwarts and defeats the execution of true justice. In "It's Alright, Ma," Dylan lambastes "Old lady judges [who] watch people in pairs/ Limited in sex, they dare/ To push fake morals, insult and stare." According to the social critique in "Jokerman," "False-hearted judges dying in the webs that they spin" try with their deceit to sway us from following the righteous path.

Other examples include the judge who is unfairly indifferent or impotent to deal with the plight of the accused in "Percy's Song" and "The

Drifter's Escape," as well as old folk/blues songs covered by Dylan like "Little Sadie," "Jim Jones," "Frankie and Albert," and "Delia." There is also the racist judge who favors white criminals over persecuted blacks in "Lonesome Death of Hattie Carroll" and "Hurricane," the backward-looking judge in cahoots with the High Sheriff who holds Charles Darwin hostage in "High Water," and the drunken "hangin' judge" of "Lily, Rosemary, and the Jack of Hearts."

The theme of corrupted power sitting in the hands of an almighty figure of legal authority appears in other songs; for example, the image of a blind commissioner who is caught "in a trance" in "Desolation Row," the grudge-holding judge who is "about to fall on you" in "Most Likely You'll Go Your Way," and the judge of retribution who commands respect but is not neces-sarily impartial in "Nettie Moore." Other authority figures criticized in Dylan songs include doctors, lawyers, police, politicians, priests, and teach-ers, as well as intellectuals. These include literary and musical giants (Beethoven, T. S. Eliot, Ezra Pound, Shakespeare), religious icons (John the Baptist, Madonna, St. Augustine), and scientists (Einstein, Galileo), in addi-tion to mythical or quasi-historical figures (Casanova, Mona Lisa, Paul Revere, Quazimodo, Romeo).[10]

Furthermore, Dylan is a scathing and ironic critic of the "masters of war" and other high-class "criminals in their coats and their ties" who profit from and promulgate social inequities and intolerance. The American Dream in the "land of the brave" has become a domain where "Jefferson's turning over in his grave." Dylan asks the corrupted most pointedly, "When you gonna wake up/ And strengthen the things that remain?" His criticism reaches to all who think "death's honesty won't fall upon them naturally."

In responding to deeply ingrained hypocrisy and corruption causing angst and alienation, and to the ever present threat of injustice and unfair treatment of the downtrodden, dispossessed, and underdog, Dylan resem-bles itinerant Zen masters as well as the Beat Blues artists and performers by embracing the standpoint of the Outsider. In Japanese society there is a term for outcasts, muen 無縁, which literally means "unaffiliated or discon-nected," and in Zen the notion of muenbotoke 無縁仏 or "unattached Buddha" has the positive connotation of one who rises above the petty con-cerns of the masses. The Outsider knows the difference between the world of ideal truths and the harshness of the everyday real, and sets his or her sights on attaining a higher moral standard of idealism without losing touch of concrete reality.

Dylan sings songs populated by loners and drifters, outlaws and out-casts, gold diggers and immigrants, moonshiners and gamblers, rebels and misfits, and geeks and clowns cast in the carnival atmosphere of the "cracked bells and washed-out horns" of "I Want You" and of greeting "the blind man at the gate" in "Simple Twist of Fate." For Dylan, the haunted and the hunted constantly suffer betrayal and deceit. The image of Pat Garrett in hot pursuit of the independent Billy in *Pat Garrett and Billy the Kid* epitomizes the conflict between false authority and the longing for authenticity, since Billy learns, "they don't like you to be so free."[11]

Dylan, who also writes "I am a lonesome hobo without family or friends," portrays the outlaw in "John Wesley Harding" as a Robin Hood-like figure who is a "friend to the poor," and a soul seemingly lost yet finding itself through risk-taking for the sake of a higher, just cause.[12] His approach was greatly influenced by John Steinbeck's celebrated character Tom Joad, who is unjustly accused and takes to the road as a mission to help the downtrodden, as well as Woody Guthrie's "Pretty Boy Floyd," which asserts, "You won't never see an outlaw/ Drive a family from their home."

FINDING OUT SOMETHING ONLY DEAD MEN KNOW

Evaluating Dylan's variability in relation to the constancy of his commitment to refuting the forces of corruption must take into account that there are two nearly opposite approaches to upholding the authenticity of a tradition, or helping to carry the past into the present. One way is based on transmission, or faithfully keeping in tact and reproducing the artifacts of a golden period, and the other way is based on transgression, or being innovative and unique by recasting the older forms. According to the transgressive approach, being true to principles is to change and restructure based on interiority rather than to preserve the old guard or status quo by adhering blindly to external standards. Transgression is exemplified by countless tales of Zen monks who are willing to confront their mentors by slapping or cutting them, whether intended literally or figuratively, in order to confirm their independent spirit no matter how extreme an action is required. This involves constantly deconstructing false idols through irreverence or blasphemy, and then deconstructing the deconstructions once they inevitably become reified.

In contrast to the mainstream attitude of the folk music tradition, which has tended to value submerging creativity to ideals of the past by faithfully reproducing older styles without crossing boundaries, authenticity for Dylan is equivalent to individuality.[13] In a 1984 interview Dylan recalled of the early 1960s,

> Folk music was very split up . . . You know, many people didn't want to
> hear it if you couldn't play the song exactly the way that Aunt Molly

Jackson played it. I just kind of blazed my way through all that kind of stuff.[14]

In "11 Outlined Epitaphs" included as liner notes for *The Times They Are A-Changin'*, Dylan comments on his complex views of Woody Guthrie, who he emulated until he realized that this would ultimately entrap and stifle his growth. "Woody Guthrie was my last idol," he writes,

> he was the last idol/ because he was the first idol/ I'd ever met/ that taught me/ face t'face/ that men are men/ shatterin' even himself/ as an idol/ an' that men have reasons/ for what they do/ an' for what they way/ an' every action can be questioned.

Authenticity must continually be earned and renewed.

This accords with the Zen doctrine of the fluidity of self, which is existentially created and recreated at every turn while facing loneliness and despair. Dylan's approach is epitomized in a line in "It's Alright, Ma," "he not busy being born is busy dying."[15] This injunction is followed in the song by the challenge to those who fail to understand him, "False gods, I scuff,/ At pettiness which plays so rough/ Walk upside-down inside handcuffs/ Kick my legs to crash it off/ Say okay, I have had enough/ What else can you show me?" He also writes poignantly of his quest for self-renewal in "Jokerman": "Shedding off one more layer of skin,/ Keeping one step ahead of the persecutor within."

However, pursuing the path of transgression forces one to pay a price by making sacrifices. When the lines between true and false become relative, it is probably not possible to avoid feelings of doubt, self-loathing, and guilt, emotions that characterize the experience of the "dark night of the soul" that can result in nihilism. Dylan's Outsider, who continually struggles to attain individual freedom and dignity despite an oppressive social system that tries to enforce its myths and deceptions, cannot avoid feeling a sense of disobedience and suffer being shunned.

Dylan remarks that it is disturbing to stand on the borderline of reality and illusion in "Visions of Johanna": "We can hear the night watchman click his flashlight/ Ask himself if it's him or them that's really insane." Also, a passage in the liner notes to *Bringing It All Back Home*, "i accept chaos. I am not sure whether it accepts me," does not make it clear whether or not this equivocal state signifies peace of mind. In "Brownsville Girl" he declares, "I've always been the kind of person that doesn't like to trespass but sometimes you just find yourself over the line."

The fierce, fearless pattern of self-reliance recalling Ralph Waldo Emerson's famous essay on this topic is accompanied by the rejection of all manner of authority, whether personal or institutional. Dylan has understood that his calling is to take responsibility, at least rhetorically, through self-sacrifice. This is expressed by "I've made shoes for everyone, even you, while I still go barefoot" in "I and I," and by "My cruel weapons have been put on the shelf/ Come sit down on my knee/ You are dearer to me than myself/ As you yourself can see" in "Working Man Blues #2."

At the conclusion of the 1965 tour documentary *Don't Look Back*, Dylan is visibly distraught when manager Albert Grossman mentions that he is being called an "anarchist" by the media for "not having the answers."[16] Years later in 2004 he told Ed Bradley on *60 Minutes*, "If the common perception of me out there in the public was that I was either a drunk or a sicko or a Zionist or a Buddhist or a Catholic or a Mormon—all of this was better than 'Archbishop of Anarchy!'" On the one hand, Dylan does not want to be expected to have the answers, which is the main reason he once called himself a performer or entertainer. But at the same time, he is constantly seeking answers even while knowing the limitations of any apparent solution.

The next chapter shows how Zen thought helps to clarify the incessant crisscross, zigzag movement of weaving back and forth between unswerving conviction and deep doubt, and dualistic or single and non-dualistic or relative truth claims. It explains why Dylan veers and reverses so drastically and dramatically in different phases of his career, by moving from one extreme standpoint to another view that seems antithetical and repudiates the previous position in pursuit of a middle path.

Part II

THE ZEN OF DYLAN

Chapter 5

Neither Here Nor There

Dialectics of Duality and Non-Duality

TOURS AND DETOURS:
FOUR INTERPRETIVE MODELS

An interpretation that seeks to cover, without partiality or one-sidedness, the full range of Dylan's approaches to bargainin' for salvation must take into account the twofold tendency that lies at the root of his enigmatic words and deeds. This tendency involves, on the one hand, intense variation characterized by strongly held commitments to disparate, often conflicting outlooks. As Dylan once said of himself, "My being a Gemini explains a lot. It forces me to extremes. I'm never really balanced in the middle. I go from one side to the other without staying in either place very long."[1] The other side of the tendency is an underlying consistency in constantly seeking authenticity and autonomy regardless of which path is taken.

The mutability that characterizes Dylan's career trajectory reflects his lifelong experimentation with diverse spiritual paths, while navigating between the wings of the deep certainty of finding a resolution or a specific answer to life's burning questions through prophecy, family life, or the gospel and the profound uncertainty of being disheartened and disillusioned with the quest for truth. Certainty is based on the assertion of a moral imperative to change the world, whereas uncertainty derives from moral relativism and resignation to the notion that the world cannot be changed by a song. From the standpoint of disillusionment, the only conviction is that certitude is an altogether misleading claim based on an awareness of the seeming impossibility of discovering any pat answers. There are many shaded gray areas lying in between these wings. As Dylan said in an ad campaign for a Cadillac SUV, "What's life without taking a detour?"

In addition to the contradiction between the two main wings, there is also another level of antimony within each of the wings. For example, both Dylan's protest songs like "When the Ship Comes In" and gospel songs like "When You Gonna Wake Up?" express a sharp critique of social injustice influenced in large part by a sense of divine judgment and apocalyptic eschatology. Protest music does this in a secular context for which specific theological claims are irrelevant or even counter-productive, whereas gospel music makes an explicit commitment to a particular view of Christian faith. Secular prophecy in some ways seems more in accord with the wing of disillusionment because these approaches expose the hypocrisy and corruption of mainstream social institutions including the church.

How is it possible to do justice to this degree of complexity? There seem to be four possible approaches to interpreting the interaction between and ultimate trajectory of Dylan's distinct career moves. Each method formulates an archeology of knowledge that digs and sifts through the layers of seemingly solid findings while also discovering crevices and lacunae from the singer's past that affect an understanding of the present. The interpretive theories include the following: (1) purposelessness, or the lack of any compelling pattern underlying disconnected events; (2) linearity, or a single connecting theme that links all parts to the whole; (3) circularity, or multiple overlapping and interlocking angles of understanding; and (4) Zen-based dialectics, or oppositions moving gradually toward a constructive middle path (despite Dylan's Gemini-based self-characterization).

The first two approaches will be discussed briefly and together constitute a polarity of unifying vision versus di-vision in interpreting Dylan's overall outlook. The third approach is proffered by Todd Haynes, a former student of semiotics (theory of signs and symbols) and director of *I'm Not There*. This will be analyzed in detail because it is more comprehensive, by showing that in Dylan's weaving back and forth between extremes there emerges a circular yet angular pattern. I argue, however, that Haynes' approach falls short, and that a Zen dialectical methodology is the most thoroughgoing of the possible analytic approaches for understanding Dylan's ongoing spiritual odyssey. It engages the other three views and points the way to a perspective that makes sense out his incessant zigzag course.

While other modern artists from Picasso to John Lennon have been known for changing styles in radical fashion, Dylan has shifted not only artistry but his entire existential being along with the musical genre to express his adherence to a new ideology. He is much like nineteenth-century religious philosopher Soren Kierkegaard, known as the father of the Existentialist movement in philosophy and literature, who published a series of pseudonymous works (with names like Johannes de Silentio, or John the Silent) and then wrote critical reviews about them under a different set of pen names.[2]

First, the view of purposelessness suggests that, although there may be a profound level of significance that can be read between the lines of any particular song or album, in looking at the entire context of his career, there is no clear sense of rhyme or reason. Dylan continually moves freely, but in the end randomly or haphazardly and with vacillation from one persona or set of disguises to another. A number of critics have been "portraying him as a cultivator of irony, hiding behind masks and toying with the vicissitudes of self-identity," or "as an actor who is able to disappear into the characters he plays."[3] Trying to discern a unifying meaning or purpose is like putting a square peg into a round hole.

The second approach to interpreting Dylan's trajectory, which lies at the opposite end of the spectrum from purposelessness, is a linear view endorsed by Stephen Webb in *Dylan Redeemed*, who argues that all along there was an underlying purpose or a method to Dylan's madness. For Webb, starting with a couple of eloquent early songs including important but relatively obscure titles that were not released at the time of their recording, such as "Let Me Die in My Footsteps," to post-gospel period songs such as "Man of Peace," there never were many different Bob Dylans. Rather, there was always the one and the same Christian-oriented Dylan, before and after his actual conversionary experience in 1978, who expressed his beliefs in varying ways, some direct and straightforward and others indirect and allusive. Webb explicitly refutes a natural mystical interpretation of songs like "Lay Down Your Weary Tune," and finds a hidden evangelical meaning.

According to Webb, seeing Dylan as fundamentally a Christian artist causes us to rethink his political affiliations. Based on his protest songs, many would categorize Dylan as a liberal social activist. However, Webb argues, this label is misleading since it does not reflect Dylan's real sense of what changing the world can mean and also what it should not imply. "From the beginning of his career," Webb argues, "Dylan was a visionary in search of a sound that would do justice to his visions of justice and transformation. The justice he preached, however, was not the liberal kind of distributing wealth and leveling the playing field."[4]

Instead of being based on the postmillennialist notion typical of the nineteenth and first half of the twentieth century that "people working for good causes could fundamentally change the world" through intense personal involvement in social projects, Webb argues that Dylan's theology is rooted in premillenialism, which is a very different form of belief. Premillenialism reflects an innate distrust of social institutions and has a knack, very much related to the Blues manner of expression, for conveying a feeling of desperation in song. It believes that "the world is going to get unimaginably worse before God makes it unimaginably better."[5] The standpoint of premillenialism, Webb maintains, is expressed at every stage of Dylan's career, whether or not he was always consciously aware of endorsing this belief.

SIX ACTORS IN SEARCH OF A CHARACTER

The first approach to interpreting Dylan's career based on purposelessness stresses variability at the expense of consistency, and the second approach based on linearity highlights the reverse view that there is a sole constant truth despite the appearance of variation. An alternative to the poles of random indirection and single-minded determination that strives for compromise between extremes is the more complex and nuanced view of circularity tinged with angularity in Dylan's career as expressed in *I'm Not There*. Haynes' film, which in the planning stages bore the postmodern working subtitle, "Suppositions on a Film Concerning Dylan," argues compellingly that the plurality and proliferation of Dylan's personae cannot be reduced to singularity but must be acknowledged and examined in their patterns of interconnectedness as well as disconnectedness.

The unconventional *I'm Not There*, which undermines and turns on its head the typical Hollywood depiction of a celebrity with a nod to iconic 1960s European directors Federico Fellini, Jean-Luc Godard, and Richard Lester, presents six actors playing seven different characters who represent distinct facets of Dylan's career stages without any of them actually being called by that name. The phases range from Dylan's early years when he concocted a fantasy about himself running away and leading the life of a hobo to the times of his celebrity in the 1960s and 1970s, as well as the withdrawal from stardom through retreating to life in the country or embracing evangelism. The film emulates the multilayered structure of an enigmatic Dylan song in deconstructing the stereotypes of his celebrity to present a Zen-like impression of the fluidity and continuing creativity of selfhood.[6]

The character Billy represents the former gunslinger Billy the Kid who lives as a secluded rancher in a frontier town called Riddle, Missouri located in Shadow Valley, which is full of circus folk and archetypal antiheroes who utter lines out of Dylan songs. It seems that Billy must have once escaped sheriff Pat Garrett and years later meets him again when both are much older and Garrett is about to wipe Billy's town, consisting of freaks and misfits for whom every day of the year is Halloween, off the map. Riddle is endangered by an encroaching highway sponsored by Garrett, who is played by the same actor that plays a nasty reporter haunting Jude, who represents the *Don't Look Back*-side of Dylan.

Billy encompasses several stages in Dylan's career, including the post-motorcycle accident period that produced *The Basement Tapes*, with its deep folk roots, and both *John Wesley Harding* and *Self-Portrait*, which draw on the Outsider imagery of drifters, hobos, immigrants, transients, and outlaws. Billy also covers the periods of Dylan's performance in a soundtrack for *Pat Garrett and Billy the Kid* in 1973, as well as the carnival atmosphere of the Rolling Thunder Revue tour in 1975–1976. This character can also be considered to stretch well beyond the mid-1970s into the current Never-Ending Tour which began in 1988, where Dylan generally dons a cowboy hat or wears the outfit of a roving riverboat gambler. During this phase of steadily performing, Dylan has often played smaller venues including minor league baseball parks where he has performed on the same bill with country stars Willie Nelson and Merle Haggard.

This parable is an ingenuous way of capturing some essential ingredients of Dylan's career (although this part of the film seemed to be the least favorite among mostly adoring critical raves). Haynes develops a conceit mixing biography, fantasy, and history that brings to life the main source of Dylan's inspiration, which lies in the great American folk tradition encompassing Blues music along with the pervasive frontier myths of what critic Greil Marcus has called that "old, weird America."

According to a critic's comments on the Billy sequence,

> Living in a dream version of Dylan's country retreat of the Sixties, he visits a town called Riddle that feels like Rimbaud's idea of the Wild West; peopled by carnival costume acts, kids wearing tumbleweed, and stray zoo animals, Riddle seems to be a visualization of the free-associative rambles typical of Dylan's liner notes.[7]

In that Beat Blues cultural context, Billy is challenged to decide whether to return to his early social commitment and sacrifice his identity and happiness in order to serve as a voice for the Outsider and thus remain a somewhat reluctant spokesman for an arcane, authentic Americana. Billy does so by at first wearing a mask, and when he is exposed and captured by corrupt authorities, he escapes on a train.

The film's direction is particularly innovative. Scenes of all the characters are spliced together and interwoven in and out of chronological sequence, sometimes in parallel fashion and sometimes building on each other, creating a kaleidoscopic effect that resembles the alternative

narrative structure of songs on *Blood on the Tracks*. With the older character of Billy who dominates the end of the film and is associated in several
images with the young Woody, whose sequence comes near the beginning,
Haynes presents a fascinating but I think somewhat misleading circular
view of Dylan's career. He shows Dylan striving to juggle the desire for
attaining a state of contemplative serenity with the equally pressing need
for a commitment to a communal cause larger than self-absorption. The
sense of circularity is heightened by the presentation of the 1966 motorcycle accident's death–resurrection symbolism in both the opening and the
concluding scenes of the film.

The limitation of *I'm Not There*, which a critic compared to a ritual
evoking an absent deity, is that while infinitely intriguing for capturing a
sense of unpredictability and reinvention, the portrayal may leave the
viewer with the impression of Dylan as a shape-shifting chameleon.
According to Haynes' theory of what makes him tick, Dylan, who wrote in
"Tangled Up in Blue," "The only thing I knew how to do/ Was to keep on
keepin' on like a bird that flew . . . But me, I'm still on the road/ Headin' for
another joint," cannot escape the fate of being an endless wanderer ridin' a
boxcar to nowhere special and fightin' for a lost cause. If Dylan does indeed
have core convictions, they remain concealed and dispersed.

Although the style of the film is at times reverential in recreating scenes
from various stages of his career, Dylan is shown somewhat cynically to be
a myth-making cipher, a Joseph K.-like figure who has an empty center or
hollow core, with no "there" of the man being there. His sole aim is renewal
and self-transformation from whatever angle seems available or fanciful at
the time as an end in itself, without an underlying note of consistency.
Another commentator said, "*I'm Not There* has six actors playing Bob
Dylan, but the drifter escapes any meaningful definition."[8]

COMEDOWNS, COMEBACKS, CONVERSIONS, AND CASTOFFS

Hinted at yet not fully apparent in *I'm Not There*'s circular view, which
emphasizes the mutability and insubstantiality of self, is Dylan's dedication
to securing authenticity and his aching desire to find salvation. He writes in
"Ain't Talkin'" from 2006 which like "Highlands" from 1997 is based on a
blues tune, "Highway of Regret" by the Stanley Brothers, that he has a "Heart
burnin', still yearnin'," as he journeys "Through the world mysterious and
vague . . . Walking through the cities of the plague."

In contrast to the views of purposelessness, purposefulness, and
cyclicality, my argument is that the key analytic concept that captures the

unfolding of the various stages of Dylan's zigzag career refers to their dialectical nature. The dialectics of change involves a basic contradiction between two main conflicting forces that becomes the determining factor in their continuing interaction, leading eventually toward a balanced unity of opposites.

The primary feature of the pattern of Dylan's incredible variability is the undeniably extreme nature of some of his artistic and spiritual commitments based on, for better or worse, a willingness to dive in all the way to any given alternative. In the sardonic parable included as the liner notes to *John Wesley Harding,* a character named Frank is considered "the key" to the new Bob Dylan album by "three kings" who ask him to "open it up for us." "'And just how far would you like to go in?' [Frank] asked and the three kings all looked at each other. 'Not too far but just far enough so's we can say that we've been there.'" As opposed to these kings, when Dylan pursues a path, he simply goes all out, and there are no halfway measures. He embraces the approach in its ultimate form, not only in terms of music but also dress, mannerisms, and in some cases wholesale image and lifestyle change.[9]

Dylan follows this path as far as it can go in his total being. His pattern has always been to examine all sides of a coin, and then go his own way, while sometimes alienating and disappointing purists of any stripe. Like a typical Zen master, Dylan explores all possible paths encompassing self-reliance and dependence on the power from above without attachment or deception. His pursuit of individuality is not intended as a betrayal of what followers want or expect, but is triggered by an artist who is hell bent on following a particular track and, while willing to make self-sacrifices for the sake of truth-seeking, does not worry about trying to serve as an exemplar or role model.

At the outer edges of pursuing an approach to its extreme level, Dylan insightfully discerns the limitations and, feeling constrained or stereotyped, rebels against its rigidity, then bottoms out from and begins to refute this path. As a continuation of the dialectic process, he leaves the old approach behind—or, rather, discards and casts it aside, as if breaking out of a cage—and turns to its apparent opposite. Or, he makes an abrupt about-face from the previous state to an outlook that could not be more different, at least on the surface. Endorsing a new extreme causes a disdainful rejection of the previous attitude.

The crisscross quality of Dylan's "American Journey" (as in the subtitle of Martin Scorsese's documentary *No Direction Home*) can be associated with a traditional "nine-turn bridge" located in a magnificent garden in downtown Shanghai with modern skyscrapers and towers in the background (similar ones are found in parks throughout East Asia). The "nine

Figure 5.1   Bridge at Shanghai's Yu Yuan Garden

turn bridge"—the number is not literal but indicates multitude—is designed in part to ward off menacing spirits and ghosts who are confused by the corners and also because all the different twists and turns allow the pedestrian to see a variety of vistas and to take in the landscape from diverse, ever-changing perspectives. Therefore, this image conveys a sense of meandering toward a destination in a way that combines purposeless-ness and self-abandonment with purposefulness and self-fulfillment.

Zen training is known for its dramatic, sometimes eccentric personal shifts made for the sake of seeking the truth. For example, a famous modern Japanese Zen teacher, Masao Abe, was raised in the school of Pure Land Buddhism, which practices a path of devotion or Other Power based on faith in the saving powers of the Buddha. However, inspired by the renowned master of ancient Myoshinji temple in Kyoto, Shin'ichi Hisamatsu, Abe was determined to pursue the Zen path of Self Power, and

for a time struggled with reconciling the two seemingly opposite philosophies. According to an account of the erratic quality in Abe's training
following his conversion to Zen:

> The degree of the stress Abe felt was evident in his unusual behavior at
> times. Once he leaped up from his sitting cushions during an intensive
> retreat and rushed toward Hisamatsu as if to attack him. Others tried to
> stop him, but he reached out and grabbed Hisamatsu's robe and screamed,
> "Is that the True Self?" Hisamatsu, unmoved, solemnly replied, "That is
> the True Self." Abe responded, "Thank you," and left the room.[10]

In discussing Dylan's back-and-forth movement it is also important to
recognize the ups and downs in his career—the comedowns as well as the
comebacks, which are often interrelated with conversions. In a strictly
religious sense, there was but one conversion for Dylan to Christianity,
although it is not known whether he ever gave this up. Reports about this
are generally mixed in indicating that he has continued to participate in
Jewish ceremonies and fundraisers, yet he still shows a deep, abiding
sympathy for Christian faith in some aspects of performing but perhaps
prefers to disguise it in order to deflect criticism.

However, the history of radical changes in Dylan's outlook and decorum
suggests that there have been numerous conversionary experiences in
a broader sense of the term that refers to embracing a whole new path,
whether secular or sacred. Conversion in this sense characterizes Dylan's
transition from acoustic folk to electric rock music in the mid-1960s, and
from being the hippest of the hipsters in a town of celebrities to a withdrawn family man in the late 1960s, in addition to the move from rock star
to a performer preaching the gospel in the late 1970s. The term can also
refer to examples of Dylan moving away from what he had converted to, or
perhaps this process can be called "de-conversion."

In some cases, the conversion experience inspired a renewal and
strengthening of Dylan's creativity in that *Highway 61* (electric), *Nashville
Skyline* (country), and *Slow Train Coming* (gospel) were at the time of their
release at the top of the list of Dylan's most highly regarded and commercially successful albums. More than that, each of these albums revolution-
ized the new genre it represented because its innovation and excellence in
music-making broke down conventional boundaries.

Highway 61 Revisited has long been considered one of the premier rock
albums of all time that brought philosophy to the jukebox, in the words of
Allen Ginsberg, and *Nashville Skyline* introduced to country music an
emphasis on imbuing lyrics with intense personal feeling. Also, *Slow Train
Coming*, following on the heels of 1978's film *Renaldo and Clara* and album

Street-Legal, which both got negative reviews, is widely hailed for its sense of urgency and integrity. In putting forth an evangelical message, it was a prime example of a conversion helping to cause Dylan's critical and commercial comeback.

Conversion has not always guaranteed success in that both *Nashville Skyline* and *Slow Train Coming* were followed by releases (*Self Portrait* and *Saved*) that were dismissed by many for having taken the approaches—country and gospel, respectively—too far to an extreme in overdoing what had been previously accomplished with just the right touch. For the most part criticized as rare examples of Dylan's failing to deliver his best product, those albums marked comedowns in Dylan's career in that they led to his comeuppance at the hands of a fickle public which uncharacteristically rejected him. They were quickly followed by the release of "comeback" albums, *New Morning* and *Shot of Love*, which sought to distance themselves from the extreme outlook endorsed just months before in the midst of a conversion and to strike a more balanced chord.

As an example of Dylan's de-conversion leading to a critical–commercial comeback, "Day of the Locusts" on *New Morning* in 1971 was hailed for indicating a renewed commitment to fighting the system following the release of the laid-back *Self Portrait* when Dylan said of a Princeton University ceremony awarding him an honorary degree, "Sure was glad to get out of there alive." However, the album also contained "Sign on the Window" affirming the virtues of family life. In addition, Dylan's mournful celebration on *Shot of Love* in 1981 of the martyrdom of "Lenny" Bruce, who "just showed the wise men of his day to be nothing more than fools" and "was the brother you never had," was praised after the acquiescent *Saved* as an announcement of his departure from the gospel phase, even though the album also contained "Property of Jesus." Songs like "Day of the Locusts" and "Lenny" share a vigorous commitment to pursuing authenticity at all costs regardless of whether they support or conflict with his previous ideology.

Dylan has generally veered and swerved hither and thither between varying worldviews, sometimes at alarming speed, which has often caught his audience off guard—generally to his own delight rather than dismay—and made some skeptics doubt the sincerity of his vision. This process of intensely profound, if somewhat erratic, spiritual exploration whereby Dylan is often willing to abandon a particular worldview as soon as it no longer seems to ring true with his current experience recalls the Zen approach, which demands the discarding or the "casting off" (in the sense of shedding or molting) of all attachments, including being attached to nonattachment as a kind of last temptation. A traditional koan record says of the need to go beyond knowledge in the conventional sense, "The Tao is not subject to knowing or not knowing. Knowing is delusion; not knowing is blankness." Similarly, in the gospel song "When He Returns," Dylan approaches this experience of transcending conventional knowledge from a complementary, devotional angle by asking rhetorically, "Can I cast it aside, all this loyalty and this pride?/ Will I ever learn ...?"

DIALECTICAL THEORY OF DYLAN'S TRAJECTORY

This brings us back to the central question of whether or not there is a basic pattern that connects the dots and gives meaning to the diversity and disparity in Dylan's multifarious approaches. The dialectical theory, which highlights a Zen view of his music despite a pervasive use of Western discourse that seems antithetical in some ways, consists of four main elements: (1) the juxtaposition and interaction of two opposing worldviews; (2) the existence of three major career periods during which the interplay of worldviews is played out; (3) the intervals of gateways to and crossroads between contrary stages; and (4) Dylan's discovery of a middle way in the final phases of his career.

Two opposing worldviews

The first main element of the dialectical theory argues that at different times in his career Dylan embraces two radically different worldviews with distinct variations, which continue to swing like a pendulum through the various stages. The interaction of the two worldviews unfolds over the course of three major periods in the 1960s, 1970s, and 1980s, while key transitions are made by Dylan through traversing personal and cultural crossroads that eventually leads to a constructive compromise in the fourth period beginning in the 1990s.

One worldview, as we have seen, is rooted in blues/spiritual idioms associated with the Holy Blues tradition. This outlook is based on Duality, which refers to an absolute standard for judgment that governs a right-versus-wrong view of all human activity and corresponds to the path of Other Power, the alternative to Zen's path of Self Power. The vehicle of Duality prevalent in the periods of protest (early 1960s), country (late 1960s to early 1970s), and gospel (late 1970s to early 1980s) finds Dylan expressing either moral outrage or uplift in proclaiming a simple, clear, straightforward, take-it-or-leave-it truth that causes retribution for those who fail to live up to the highest ethical standards.

Imagery derived from the prophetic, apocalyptic morality of biblical sources recognizes a clear distinction between the righteous and the vain, as in the protest song "When the Ship Comes In": "Then they'll raise their hands,/ Sayin' we'll meet all your demands,/ But we'll shout from the bow your days are numbered./ And like Pharaoh's tribe,/ They'll be drowned in the tide,/ And like Goliath, they'll be conquered." This is also conveyed in the gospel song "Slow Train," "Can't help but wonder what's happenin' to my companions,/ Are they lost or are they found, have they counted the cost it'll take to bring down/ All their earthly principles they're gonna have to abandon?"

In its extreme form of expression, this approach achieves a "sparkling" degree of Duality in that the commitment to a correct way of action provides Dylan with a remarkable degree of illumination that seems so compellingly irreproachable in a variety of songs which proclaim inevitable punishment for injustice or intolerance, such as "Masters of War" and "When You Gonna Wake Up?" However, enigmatic words are still prevalent in that Dylan finds a way to say what others want to express, but do not know how, because the ultimate truth is never easily disclosed and trying to reveal it demands indirection, ambiguity, and allusiveness.

A possible objection to grouping together these themes under the heading of Duality is that the inspiration for the gospel stage may appear to have a different spiritual orientation based on New Testament forgiveness as opposed to the Old Testament moralism that influences the protest stage. Nevertheless, this category is supported in a compelling way by the dual Jack Rollins–Pastor John roles in *I'm Not There*, in which the same actor plays both a protest singer and a preacher. The prophetic Rollins sings finger-pointing civil rights songs like "The Lonesome Death of Hattie Carroll," but becomes quickly disillusioned and abandons the protest movement, and in a drunken state upsets an upscale white liberal audience in New York which is presenting him with an award. The born-again Christian pastor is passionate about his conversion in singing "Pressing On" before an evangelical audience since he had replaced "the limelight with a different sort of light." This shows an affinity between the two personae based on their dualistic commitment to a higher cause.

Another concern is that it may seem odd to link together under the same banner styles of writing as disparate as protest and gospel apocalypticism with country music's emphasis on family life and withdrawal from social commitment, since the latter approach could be seen as contradicting the moral imperative featured in the other two stages. However, the reason for linking the three outlooks of protest, country, and gospel is that they all point to the need for a single higher truth, which creates a clear, incontestable standard for judging the outcome of human attitudes and actions. "Country Pie," a kind of manifesto for Dylan's belief in the merit of the country stage, has an ironically defiant, "preachy" tone in declaring, "Raspberry, strawberry, lemon and lime/ What do I care?/ Blueberry, apple, cherry, pumpkin and plum/ Call me for dinner, honey, I'll be there."

The second worldview rooted in the "Hellhound Blues" tradition is based on Non-Duality, which means that in the fashion of Zen's Self Power, all oppositions or polarities are blended into an incomprehensible state of non-substantiality—the void or nothingness—for which relativism rules and paradoxes prevail. This worldview is prevalent during three main periods of Dylan's disillusionment, including the mid-1960s as in "Desolation Row," "All these people that you mention/ Yes, I know them, they're quite lame/ I've had to rearrange their faces/ And give them all another name"; the mid-1970's as in "Tangled Up in Blue," "All the people we used to know/ They're an illusion to me now"; and the mid-1980s as in "Brownsville Girl," "The only thing we knew for sure about Henry Porter is that his name wasn't Henry Porter." Non-Duality finds Dylan expressing the illusory quality of conventional categories and distinctions on personal, social, and metaphysical levels.

Non-Duality is characterized by the angst of dealing with a relativistic universe, which does not disclose any particular truth but instead involves accepting the challenge of endless existential turmoil and spiritual pain. Yet it finds comfort in the realization that understanding how the puzzle wrapped in a riddle contained in an enigma is quite frankly all there is. This worldview forms an undercurrent in Dylan's work from the days of "Song to Woody" on his first album, and is especially pronounced in stages when he turns away from seemingly simplistic answers. Dylan becomes disenchanted with any proclamations of truth and finds that he is wandering aimlessly—yet discovering sources of strength in doing so—amid a world of masks and disguises where nothing is ever actually what it claims to be. According to "Just Like Tom Thumb Blues," "Up on Housing Project Hill/ It's either fortune or fame/ You must pick up one or the other/ Although neither of them are to be what they claim."

The non-dual approach has a deep resonance with the Zen adage, "If you see the Buddha on the road, kill the Buddha," symbolizing the need for violence toward false truth claims that must be negated no matter how irreverent the action seems. In its extreme form of expression, this approach achieves a "visionary" degree of Non-Duality in refusing to make any commitment or compromise with a right-versus-wrong viewpoint. Doing so provides Dylan with a greater degree of inspiration in launching an unrelentingly scathing critique of various forms of hypocrisy or "tunnel vision" that seek easy answers to complex problems. The first worldview includes three very different musical styles to communicate what, at the root, is quite similar spiritual content representing Duality. In the case of Non-Duality, on the other hand, there is a basic consistency of folk/ blues/rock genres reflecting disillusionment that occur a decade or two apart.

Three major periods

The second component of the dialectical theory, which is in accord with Zen metaphysics that encompasses the productive interaction of contradictions along the way toward realizing a synthesis, is that the analysis can be applied, step by step, to three main periods of Dylan's career. Extending from the early 1960s through the 1970s to the late 1980s, each of the first three major periods encompasses two seemingly opposite, pro-and-con stages either supporting or refuting an ideological standpoint of Duality or Non-Duality. That is, each period contains a Yang or assertive phase that puts forward a viewpoint favoring Duality which is followed by a Yin or withdrawn phase that tends to unravel and negate the higher truth of dualism from the opposing standpoint of the relative, complementary truths of Non-Duality.

The career trajectory leads finally to the fourth or final main period, the current and ongoing "Modern Era," which is how I refer to the resurgence in the music from the 1990s to the present which integrates the Yin/Yang oppositions that dominated the previous three periods. (See Appendix C

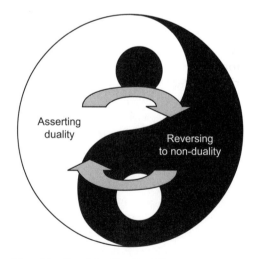

Figure 5.2   Yin–Yang/Duality–NonDuality Diagram

for a pendulum-like diagram illustrating the full flow of Dylan's trajectory.) The first three periods include the following:

Period I: From "Protesting" to "Detesting" (1962–1966). The first very intense outburst of Dylan's creativity is initially dominated by topical protest songs in an acoustic folk style (Duality), and ends with songs of disdainful disillusionment about the capacity of music to change a society filled with hypocrisy and corruption played in the electric, folk-rock style (Non-Duality).

Period II: From "I'll Be Your Baby" to "You're an Idiot, Babe" (1967–1978). Following Dylan's motorcycle accident and marriage in the mid-1960s, the stage of country music affirms a wholehearted commitment to family values over social concerns (Duality), but culminates in a despairing account of being disheartened and disappointed with human relationships in the aftermath of the Vietnam and Watergate era (Non-Duality).

Period III: From "Serving Somebody" to "Letting the Echo Decide" (1979–1988). Following Dylan's divorce and the relative lack of success of several creative ventures, this period begins with gospel music expressing Dylan's conversion to fundamental Christianity (Duality), and concludes with an apparent discouragement about all theological answers and a renewed awareness and openness to accepting relative truths (Non-Duality).

Because transitions are very important in Dylan's music-making, he often provides indicators of his shifting views in the sequence of the albums as well as the way a particular album is constructed, especially with the beginning and closing song. Each stage generally includes a sequence of four albums: an opening album that inaugurates the worldview, a second album that explores this direction more fully, a third album that tries to fulfill the main tendencies of the stage or that represents the worldview's ultimate expression, and then a crossroads album that signals the beginning of a dramatic change toward an alternative, even opposing worldview. (See Appendix B for a discography that clarifies how Dylan's albums are reflected in the various periods).

For example, the last song/side of the original vinyl double-album *Blonde on Blonde* in 1966 is the love song/celebration "Sad-Eyed Lady of the Lowlands," which offers a glimpse of what is to come in the country/ family stage affirming marriage and ideal, almost deified womanhood. Then, the next release, *John Wesley Harding* a year-and-a-half later introduces the new theme by showing, after numerous songs about the unforgiving pain of despair, that the demise of "The Wicked Messenger" in the tenth song gives way to the joy of announcing "Down Along the Cove" and "I'll Be Your Baby, Tonight" as the final two songs.[11] Following this, *Nashville Skyline* consists of all love songs and concludes by affirming that "Tonight I'll Be Staying Here with You," and *Self Portrait* is a double album of country and western tunes delving further into the themes of love and reconciliation.

However, *New Morning* as a crossroads album, while still highlighting romantic themes in the title cut and "If Not For You," includes several songs showing that Dylan is unsettled and not necessarily at peace with his current situation, as in "Day of the Locusts" and "If Dogs Run Free," or is seeking another kind of spirituality in "Three Angels" and "Father of Night." The pattern of cycles of albums is similarly played out in other career stages, such as the gospel period ten years later when *Slow Train Coming* introduces the Christian standpoint, *Saved* fulfills it, *Shot of Love* draws out some of the implications and begins to deconstruct it, while *Infidels* furthers a transition away from this commitment.

Gateways and crossroads

The third element of the dialectical theory is that all the stages in the main periods come to a fulfillment and termination marked by a significant turning point, or a rapid, even drastic transition to the endorsement of an alternative or even opposing worldview. In each period, Dylan either enters what I call a gateway into a new phase or negotiates a crossroads which causes a significant revision of his thinking between the two stages of a main period. During times of alternation, he shifts from Duality to Non-Duality or the reverse, that is, from Non-Duality to Duality. Particular songs and in some cases entire albums reflect a profound degree of change and are therefore especially fruitful for interpretation in the dialectical theory. This includes albums that reflect conversions to Duality, such as *Freewheelin' Bob Dylan* (protest), *John Wesley Harding* (country), and *Slow Train Coming* (gospel), as well as albums that mark shifts or de-conversions away

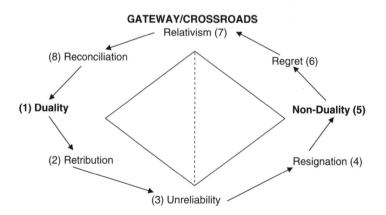

from Duality to Non-Duality, such as *Another Side of Bob Dylan, Blood on the Tracks*, and *Infidels*.

The diagram above illustrates the pattern of transition as each factor of experience, once it is enhanced, is seen as limited and results in the exploration and appropriation of another approach that contradicts it. The moralistic worldview of Duality (1) emphasizes retribution (2) for those who fail to follow the path of morality, but when the standard of judgment becomes questionable and unreliable (3) there is a shift toward relativism based on an awareness of and resignation (4) to the illusory nature of all truth claims. This leads to the detached worldview of Non-Duality (5), but an overemphasis on multiple, relative truths as an end in itself and on staying free from commitment at all costs leads to a sense of guilt and remorse (6) about being withdrawn and self-centered. In turn this drives the crossing of the threshold of being aware of relativity (7) to achieve a state of reconciliation (8) as a gateway to a renewed affirmation of Duality.

Relativism is the crucible that determines the path taken—accepting it leads to the uncertainty of non-dualism, and being repelled by it demands finding an absolute certainty through dualism. In an absolute world determined by a single truth there is no room for error, but in a relativistic worldview there is no possibility of error. The collision course between these two standpoints is what divides most people, but the views are combined within Dylan's remarkably expansive (while occasionally narrow) conceptual framework.

Discovering the middle way

To review the theory thus far, it is shown that when Dylan goes through a new phase, he explores it to the extreme and relinquishes alternative elements, but not in an altogether hard and fast way. While disparaging the previous answer, the new stage may well continue to contain some features that appear to be opposite or part of the reverse cycle. Therefore, what seems like a radical shift may turn out to be quite similar, and on some level incorporates rather than repudiates the previous path.

Comedowns and conversions may lead to a convergence of opposing views, so that there is a forceful protest element in gospel songs and romantic love songs during a time of disillusionment. In stages in which his goal is to clarify and accept a vision of the absurd, Dylan embraces a Zen-like outlook of Non-Duality including attitudes of resignation and detachment. When he seeks a firm resolution of the problems of existence, he endorses an outlook of Duality emphasizing judgment and retribution. Which of the two worldviews is more representative and more meaningful for understanding Dylan's work? Does he seem in the final analysis to give preference to one over the other or, if not, what is the rationale for shifting so frequently between them and how can this interaction best be explained?

A fourth major component of the dialectical theory of Dylan's career trajectory refers to what has been accomplished in the Modern Era beginning in the late 1980s. After a period where Dylan seemed to be struggling with his songwriting and performing, and released what many consider his least popular albums ever in the mid-1980s, *Knocked Out Loaded* and *Down in the Groove*, along with the live album *Dylan and the Dead*, he found rejuvenation with the release of *Oh Mercy*, his work with the *Traveling Wilburys*, and the inception of the Never-Ending Tour. This phase continues with the release of two blues/folk cover albums *Good As I Been to You* and *World Gone Wrong* along with *MTV Unplugged* in the early 1990s. It culminates with the three triumphantly successful albums over a recent decade, *Time Out of Mind*, *"Love and Theft,"* and *Modern Times*, in addition to other recent artistic efforts including several singles, the first volume of his autobiography *Chronicles*, the film *Masked and Anonymous*, the radio show *Theme Time Radio Hour*, and the release of *Tell Tale Signs*.

A Zen interpretive model helps show that in the three most recent albums Dylan has achieved a constructively integrated middle way (MW) that successfully balances Duality (D) and Non-Duality (ND).

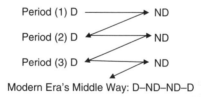

Modern Era's Middle Way: D–ND–ND–D

In Asian Yin/Yang style, pro and con factors complement rather than conflict with one another, and this eventually builds toward an integrated give and take whereby opposites coexist more or less compatibly or even harmoniously. Therefore, in contrast to Haynes' roundabout *I'm Not There*, Dylan does not endorse circularity as an end of itself. Rather, the dynamism of an ongoing dialectical movement betwixt and between extremes, including sub-elements and crossroad flashpoints that are explored yet never fully abandoned, is the goal.

The strength of the Modern Era is that Dylan has brought disparate trends and contradictory tendencies in the rather confusing back-and-forth movement between apparently conflicting positions into a unified presentation, thus capturing a middle way standpoint. The Modern Era represents a sustained phase in which the worldviews of Duality and Non-Duality are endorsed with equal weight. In each collection, and in many cases in a particular song or even a verse, one extreme is juxtaposed and played off its opposite. This interplay is what makes for such a fresh, powerful form of expression that breaks down barriers. Dylan demonstrates a remarkable flexibility and versatility of perspectives which cover a full range of possible variations on the primary standpoints.

Reminiscent of the Zen outlook, Dylan's middle path is based on his years of having explored and fully delved into, rather than suppressed or restricted, a multiplicity of possibilities that emerge from nearly every conceivable angle. His spiritual outlook, striving for a balanced perspective of variability and consistency that does not leave out any of the aspects on either side of the middle ground, recalls the Zen verse "Sandokai," or the "Harmonious Song of Difference and Sameness" about the connections of opposites that complement rather than detract from one another:

> In the light there is darkness, but don't take it as darkness;
> In the dark there is light, but don't see it as light.
> Light and dark oppose one another like the front and back foot in walking.
> Each of the myriad things has its merit according to its function and place.

The role Zen plays in the dialectical theory of Dylan's trajectory is highlighted on two levels. One level involves affinities of Zen's philosophy of relativism with the worldview of Non-Duality, which will be highlighted in the next three chapters. The other level refers to the utility of the Zen approach to the middle way in depicting the overall progression of Dylan's career moves, to be discussed in Chapter 9. The fact that Dylan seems to have arrived at a point of equilibrium and balance suggests a parallel with Zen, which seeks enlightenment through a middle way—or no-particular-view—that navigates between yet remains uncommitted to any and all standpoints.

Note that in the following chapters, I will use several terms to refer to various segments of Dylan's career. The term "period" indicates the three longer sections of time covering the decades of the 1960s, 1970s, and 1980s, each of which encompasses two distinct "stages," with the first emphasizing a focus on dualism and the second non-dualism. Also, each period is introduced via a "gateway," and a "crossroads" represents the transition between stages. The relation between these temporal designations is illustrated in the following figure:

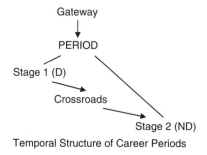

Temporal Structure of Career Periods

Finally, the term "phase" is used in a generic sense to highlight a particular tendency or approach of variable duration.

Chapter 6

Period I (1962–1966)

From "Protesting" to "Detesting"

OVERVIEW: STAGES AND CAGES

The first main period of Dylan's career covers five years and seven albums that display his initial brilliant burst of songwriting and tremendous impact on American culture. The period begins with *Bob Dylan* released in 1962, which consists almost entirely of blues covers, and continues with Dylan emerging as the spokesman for the acoustic-folk protest movement on *Freewheelin' Bob Dylan* in 1963 and *The Times They Are A-Changin'* in 1964. During this phase, Dylan endorses the path of Duality through a series of prominent topical songs which evoke the threat of divine judgment and retribution.

Dylan then abruptly abandons this course, as signaled on *Another Side of Bob Dylan*, and becomes the leader of the electric rock revolution on *Bringing it All Back Home*,[1] *Highway 61 Revisited*, and *Blonde on Blonde*. In these three records released over less than an eighteen-month span in 1965 and 1966, Dylan embraces Non-Duality through an innovative and ground-breaking approach to songwriting that draws on Beat Blues influences and reveals many affinities with Zen.[2] By the end of period I, Dylan's feverishly creative pace leads to severe exhaustion and he nearly disappears from the performing world altogether before launching a new path based on dualism in the late 1960s. The dialectical theory is an important tool for explaining how and why Dylan makes such rapid and thoroughgoing transitions from one extreme view to its apparent opposite.

From interpreter to innovator

Dylan's earliest recordings, which are known for an almost slavish devotion to the folk tradition, help to make traditional music relevant to contemporary society by replicating the style of those who suffered the travails of injustice, yet without trying to infuse new attitudes. According to Robert Shelton's *New York Times* review of an early concert that was included in the liner notes of the first album, Dylan's search for artistic and cultural purity is achieved by transmitting the past. "Mr. Dylan's voice is anything but pretty," Shelton writes. "He is consciously trying to recapture the rude beauty of a Southern field hand musing in melody on his porch. All the 'husk and bark' are left on his notes and searing intensities pervade his songs."

Although at first he functions much more as a preserver than an innovator, once Dylan begins composing his own material, he quickly migrates from being a talented interpreter of classic material to a staggeringly original songwriter.[3] By the time of the release of *Freewheelin'*, it is already clear just how uniquely resourceful Dylan's music-making has become. He almost single-handedly reinvents folk music—or initiates the category of "contemporary folk"—by using his own ongoing quest for authenticity, based on intense personal experience and self-reflection as well as social awareness, as a crucible for writing songs. Still drawing on the old folk/blues for inspiration, his work goes beyond any particular style or label in exploring new paths.[4]

This incredible outpouring of creativity that blazes so many musical and cultural trails during one of the most turbulent decades in American history lasts from the time Dylan writes his first song at the age of twenty until he turns twenty-five. In the first couple of years, he pens two dozen topical protest songs dealing with the themes of racism and other social inequities, including warmongering and fear for humanity's self-destructiveness, set against the dualistic background of expecting punishment for transgressions. During this stage, Dylan is frequently called The Prince of Protest, The Voice of a Generation, The Man with All the Answers, The Unwashed Phenomenon, and Symbol of Peace, among other epithets emphasizing his contributions to the cause of social reform based on adhering to a single higher truth.[5]

However, being pigeonholed as a one-dimensional protest singer suddenly becomes a form of bondage that makes Dylan feel boxed in and claustrophobic, and he begins to break out and establish a new sense of autonomy on *Another Side of Bob Dylan* released in 1964. This record marks the crossroads or turning point from dualistic protesting of various kinds of discrimination and injustice to a non-dualistic sense of detesting the foundations of society's hypocrisy and corruption that causes individuals to experience angst and to act out of bad faith. Years later, Dylan refers to this general condition as a "World Gone Wrong," based on the title of a song he covers by the Delta Blues group, the Mississippi Sheiks, which he says, "goes against cultural policy."

"My Back Pages" is the key song on *Another Side of Bob Dylan* that expresses a de-conversion that repudiates Dylan's previous adherence to a clear standard of right versus wrong, and accepts the frailties and frivolities of uncertainty and moral ambiguity. Disillusioned with his own prior dualistic inclinations in presuming that the answer to complex problems lies in simple verbal formulas and assertions regarding liberty and equality, Dylan starts targeting as objects of criticism not the purveyors of bias and militarism but his former associates in the protest movement. He ferociously attacks unnamed parties who cling to Duality with scathing comments that resemble the kinds of putdowns prevalent in both Zen rhetoric and the Blues. This attack is especially sharp in the single, "Positively Fourth Street," originally an outtake from the sessions that produced *Highway 61 Revisited*, which says,

> You got a lotta nerve
> To say you are my friend
> When I was down
> You just stood there grinning
> You got a lotta nerve
> To say you got a helping hand to lend
> You just want to be on
> The side that's winning.

In the second stage of period I, Dylan departs fully from the topical song mold and delivers more personal, introspective lyrics that continue to draw heavily from Blues influences. In doing so, he becomes known as a kind of postmodern or Dadaist hero (or antihero) who relentlessly explores the implications of relativism and skepticism, as well as nothingness and nihilism in a way that dovetails with Zen thought along with other examples of non-dualistic discourse. The key question is whether this transition marks a drastic break or a logical extension of the previous approach.

According to some doubters, Dylan deserts the civil rights and antiwar causes that he explicitly advocated in the first stage because of self-indulgent and self-destructive tendencies that represent a cop-out to crass commercialism and his newly found celebrity. In the November 1964 issue of *Sing Out!,* one of the two main organs (along with *Broadside*) of the folk revival movement, Irwin Silber writes "An Open Letter to Bob Dylan." He charges,

> Your new songs seem to be all inner-directed now, inner probing, self-conscious—maybe even a little maudlin or a little cruel on occasion. And it's happening on stage, too. You seem to be relating to a handful of cronies behind the scenes now—rather than to the rest of us out front.[6]

While Silber's assessment did capture the concerns of a segment of Dylan's following, in retrospect it was a narrow view that failed to appreciate the dialectical quality of the performer's approach.[7] The alternative interpretation is that Dylan's second-stage songwriting represents an expansion of the earlier protest music in that "Dylan in 1965 was making statements just as disputatious, and far more radical than anything contained in his 'finger-pointing' songs."[8] The newer songs reflect a merging of social consciousness with a deep analysis of the class system in exposing the roots of oppression expressed through a mixture of Beat-influenced free-form poetry and a plumbing of the depths of what bluesmen sang transformed into folk-rock music.

In this music, rather than blaming specific perpetrators of social transgression, Dylan sets his sights on criticizing institutions at their basic structural level that are responsible for fostering racism and imperialism such that individual self-deception is grounded on the ills of society at large. A reviewer in 1965 says of his change, "Dylan used to sound like a lung cancer victim singing Woody Guthrie. Now he sounds like a Rolling Stone singing Immanuel Kant." Allen Ginsberg speaks of Dylan putting philosophy in a jukebox, and another commentator refers to him acting like "Rimbaud with a Rickenbacker."[9]

GATEWAY: THE BASIC BOB TYPOLOGY

A key to understanding Dylan's diverse perspectives and his rapid-fire alternations between accepting and rejecting opposing standpoints is to see that at the dawn of his career, before the labeling became entrenched, there is already a remarkable multiplicity of approaches evident in his work. The gateway to Dylan's songwriting in period I and beyond is what I refer to as "Basic Bob," which includes his earliest recordings of originals and covers, much of which is not officially released until years later.[10] This material reveals his underlying interests and concerns, and provides a roadmap for the different styles and themes he would subsequently develop, sometimes by following a particular pathway to its extreme.

During this primordial phase of music-making, Dylan writes songs about a wide range of social and personal issues that can be grouped into categories of topical protest, social commentary, existential blues, romantic conflict, and spiritual longing. If we consider the fifteen original songs included on *Bob Dylan* and *Freewheelin'*, only four would likely be placed in the category of protesting political affairs, including "Blowin' in the Wind," "Masters of War," "A Hard Rain's A-Gonna Fall," and "Oxford Town." Three songs offer more broad-based condemnation of the absurdity of society ("Talking New York," "Talkin' World War III Blues," and "I Shall Be Free"). Four other songs convey the atmosphere of a loner livin' the blues ("Song to Woody," "Down the Highway" "Bob Dylan Blues," and "Bob Dylan's Dream"), and four reflect on problems and conflicts related to romance ("Girl of the North Country," "Don't Think Twice, It's All Right," "Corrina, Corrina," and "Honey, Just Allow Me One More Chance").

There are variations within each of these categories. For example, protest songs can be further divided into the subcategories of macro-level songs like "Blowin' in the Wind," which deal with the fundamental nature of the problems of unfairness and conflict, and micro-level songs such as "Oxford Town" focusing on transgressions associated with specific events, especially the killings of black civil rights workers or other victims of white supremacy. Moreover, social commentary songs can be grouped into the divisions of those with comical–sarcastic lyrics, such as "Talkin' World War III Blues," and those with serious lyrics that use some ironic humor in order to express devastating disparagement of institutions, an approach that Dylan perfects in later songs like "Gates of Eden." Also, romantic songs suggest either a celebration of an ideal woman as in "Girl from the North Country" or a putdown of a forsaken partner as in "Don't Think Twice, It's All Right."[11]

It is also important to recognize that the earliest recordings reflect Dylan's distinctive approach to bargainin' for salvation. Several songs are multidimensional in that they explore eloquently a longing for spiritual fulfillment in addition to one of the other major themes. For example, "Song to Woody" eulogizes the folk icon of holiness based on his acute social awareness, and the final verse of "Hard Rain" concludes with a compelling line about the role of spirituality in relation to concern for overcoming the challenges of inequity. According to this song,

> And I'll tell it and think it and speak it and breathe it,
> And reflect it from the mountain so all souls can see it,
> Then I'll stand on the ocean until I start sinkin',
> But I'll know my song well before I start singin'.

Although the category of spirituality does not become prominent until a later career phase, an important feature of Basic Bob is the different types of themes regarding the quest for salvation that are expressed in many of the early songs. The following list of "5 r's" contains examples of lyrics that reflect a variety of approaches to religiosity.

Retribution:	"Masters of War"	Duality, Exhortation
Repentance:	"Hard Rain"	
Redemption:	"Song to Woody"	Middle Way, Exaltation
Regret:	"Don't Think Twice"	Non-Duality, Exclamation
Resignation:	"Bob Dylan's Dream"	

These motifs range from an emphasis on dualism in the exhortative responses of retribution and repentance for particular cases of wrongdoing to a standpoint of non-dualism realized in terms of the exclamatory expressions of regret and resignation to a world of relative truths. Another approach highlights the possibility for redemption reached as a compromise or middle way position characterized by the reconciliation and composure of Non-Duality coordinated with the sense of justice characteristic of Duality.

Each of the categories of songs and of spiritual themes that are initiated during the songwriting of the Basic Bob phase will eventually become manifested in full-fledged form in subsequent phases of Dylan's career. In any given stage, one or another of the styles comes to the fore, such as a focus on romance during the country stage and on spirituality during the gospel stage. A key feature of the Modern Era is Dylan's ability to mix and match many of these diverse types in an album or even in a single song or in a specific verse. This shows that an ongoing middle way standpoint is finally achieved in a way that extends naturally from and fulfills the promise of the primordial approach to songwriting.

FIRST STAGE: TOPICAL PROTEST (DUALITY I)

Reflecting just one of the categories of Basic Bob, the first stage of period I is marked by an almost exclusive focus on protest songs supporting the civil rights and antiwar movements with proclamations of judgment and dire apocalyptic warnings of retribution for those who would promulgate war and injustice. This approach based on Duality or a single higher truth is perhaps most unambiguously articulated in "Masters of War": "And I'll watch while you're lowered/ Down to your deathbed/ And I'll stand o'er your grave/ 'Til I'm sure that you're dead."

The answer, my friend

It is helpful to understand how Dylan's affinity and commitment to protest seems to be rooted in his background and formative experiences. Dylan's intense involvement in the protest movement of the early 1960s is forged in part because he is somebody who grew up, intellectually and socially, ever betwixt and between locations and classes, and learned to feel empathy and relate to the problems of the economically depressed and downtrodden. An insider on the beaten path of mainstream cultural trends as a well-educated white northerner, Dylan who grew up Jewish in the WASP-based upper Midwest is also an outsider very much alienated from the main-stream. With an instinct for wandering and exploring alternative view-points, he cultivates an innate capacity to appreciate and appropriate both sides of many issues and remains flexible rather than getting fixated on any one perspective or judgment, or proffering a particular solution.

An important influence on Dylan's political sensibility and sympathy with the worldview of protesting injustice is his background in the Mesabi Iron Range of northeastern Minnesota and his upbringing in Hibbing's unique socioeconomic setting. This teaches him twin lessons of being connected to a larger society yet feeling isolated from sources of power, as well as having privilege yet being subject to forms of victimization. Known as The Town That Moved with the Largest Hole in the World from the Hull Rust Mine located near a Three-Way Continental Divide, the city of Hibbing was a far more significant place than the typical small Midwestern town. Its incredibly rich iron deposits created a tremendous economic boom that lasted for several decades beginning in the 1890s. To mine another vein of ore discovered under the town, the houses were literally picked up by lifts and relocated a mile or two down the road to the "new" Hibbing in the early 1920s.[12]

To compensate the residents for the inconvenience, the politicians at the time were able to persuade the wealthy mining company owners to con-struct several fabulous structures in the new town site, including Hibbing High School.[13] Built with $4 million in 1920 currency of mining company funds, the high school today still features a grand staircase that leads to the medieval castle-like framework of the historic school.[14] It has ornate trim-mings, including a mosaic floor, a mural of American history on the library wall, inspiring paintings throughout, and gold doorknobs in the bathrooms. Unique hand-molded ceilings in the foyer welcome visitors and accent the breathtaking auditorium that holds 1,805 people in velvet seats designed after the Capitol Theatre in New York City. The auditorium is known for its state-of-the-art functions, lavish curtains, and cut glass chandeliers made of crystal imported from Belgium. It boasts a magnificent Barton pipe organ, one of only two that still exist in the United States. It contains over 1,900 pipes and can play any orchestra instrument except the violin. Dylan first performed Little Richard songs on a 1920 grand piano here. Although he was booed, he later said that being on this stage was more of a thrill than playing at Carnegie Hall.

What Dylan no doubt experienced in Hibbing was a great divide between the rich and poor, the mine owners who rose to a fabulously elite status and the miners who were victims of exploitation and often lived lives of poverty and misery. Dylan's father, who suffered from polio, moved from Duluth to join a family-run appliance store. He was probably one of a small group of Jewish merchants in Hibbing who extended credit to help tide over miners who worked on a seasonal basis. Dylan may have been aware or even accompanied his family on visits to repossess items from customers unable to meet payments. Perhaps he felt a strong sense of solidarity with the economically oppressed, as expressed in at least two of the early protest songs "Ballad of Hollis Brown" and "North Country Blues."

By all accounts including interviews with the teachers, Dylan was sensitized to forms of expressing concern for inequities by two influential high school instructors, B. J. Rolfzen and Charles Miller. Rolfzen, who taught literature, made Dylan aware of the power of the word, especially in poetry and mythology, to express—or suppress—human desires and aspirations. In a parallel way, Miller's social studies classes made Dylan aware of issues regarding human rights for striking miners and the discriminated and downtrodden. Both of the teachers remained friends and frequently spoke of the relationship they once had with Dylan over fifty years after he was one of their brightest and most attentive pupils. They also expressed appreciation that they were able to thrive in an atmosphere that encouraged freedom of speech, as supported by the school administration. The teachers demanded that students not just absorb information, but learn to think critically yet constructively about their roles in history and society.[15]

Macro- and micro-protest

Following *Freewheelin' Bob Dylan*, seven of ten songs released on *The Times They Are A-Changin'* fall into the protest category. These include the title cut and "When the Ship Comes In," which are macro-level songs highlighting the inevitability of shifting social tides that will some day punish those who resist social reform. Additional macro-level songs expose the nature of warmongering based on nationalistic trends conflated with or exploiting religious claims in "With God on Our Side," or bemoan the global effects on poverty in a small mining town in "North Country Blues" (very much anticipating current debates about the impact of free-trade agreements).

Several micro-level protest songs comment on specific instances of wrongdoing. "The Lonesome Death of Hattie Carroll" is about the killing of an innocent black maid by a rich white man who receives a ludicrously light sentence as a tap on the knuckles by the system that legitimates discrimination and harassment of minorities. Also, "Ballad of Hollis Brown" is the shocking though probably fictive tale of an impoverished father who murders his own family out of desperation and some of the horrendous social forces that caused this crime.

The micro-level songs are not aimed at targeting individual perpetrators so much as articulating an expansive view of the problems that lie at the root—rather than occupy the branches—of all-pervasive mistreatment of the dispossessed. "Only a Pawn in Their Game" about the gruesome death of black civil rights worker Medgar Evers is perhaps the best instance of this trend. In mid-July of 1963, Dylan makes a trip to Greenwood, Mississippi accompanied by Theodore Bikel (who apparently paid Dylan's way), Pete Seeger, and other northern performers and activists in order to help encourage voter registration and support local volunteers at the height of the civil rights movement.[16] Greenwood is just a short distance down Highway 49 from Clarksdale and the famed Blues Cross Road. This is the same area where Bessie Smith and Emmett Till (about whom Dylan writes one of his first protest songs) once met their tragic fates because of white supremacy. It is also in the vicinity where Son House and numerous other early bluesmen plied their trade in between stints served on a Parchman Farm chain gang.

His multiple self-created legends aside, this is no doubt Dylan's initial actual journey to the Delta. Perhaps while there he deeply realizes the connection between the origins of the Blues music and the social conditions of racism and economic servitude that had long plagued the area yet somehow also inspired creativity in the desire for freedom. During the trip, in "shar[ing] the austerity and fear that made up their daily lives," Dylan learns firsthand of the sharecropper's plight in "the Delta as a place of suffering and disgrace as well as tortured resilience."[17]

On that sweltering summer day in Greenwood, Dylan impresses all observers by singing a highly innovative protest song before an audience of mostly black activists. In reflecting on the tragic death of Medgar Evers at the hands of a racist, whose hideous crime was overlooked and even praised by mainstream society, this song goes beyond finger-pointing. It does not place blame on the individual assassin or even on a group like the Klan which gave him cover and support, but rather shows how insidiously the roots of bias are embedded in and permeate all institutions, large and small, thereby entrapping each and every member of society. Dylan "argued that racist violence was the product of political manipulation and an unjust social system,"[18] and showed that it does not just result from one man's hatred, although the system is pleased to have an individual who becomes a scapegoat while its false sense of integrity goes unchecked.

Zen inklings

The orientation of this stage of music-making is primarily dualistic, but in a couple of ways Dylan's songs evoke Zen-like forms of expression. A quality that early Dylan shares with Zen rhetoric is biting humor that supports a scathing critique of hypocrisy and corruption in society writ large, which is coupled with an attitude of self-deprecation reflecting the detachment of a wise fool. The twin targets of self and other are combined in a Zen saying about self-deception and delusion: "There is little to choose between a man lying in the ditch heavily drunk on rice liquor, and a man heavily drunk on his own 'enlightenment'!"

Dylan points out the absurdity of political institutions and cultural mores while also conveying a sense of detached resignation in several early songs, including "Talking New York," "Talkin' World War III Blues," and "I Shall Be Free." An instance of deadpan humor is the delightfully ironic comment exposing the pomposity of pseudo-liberalism that disguises bias by drawing on the comment that used to be made about white people being willing to live with blacks but drawing the line at marriage. "Now, I'm liberal, but to a degree," Dylan sings, "I want ev'rybody to be free/ But if you think that I 'll let Barry Goldwater/ Move in next door and marry my daughter/ You must think I'm crazy!/ I wouldn't let him do it for all the farms in Cuba." This verse, which is particularly relevant to the times when the civil rights movement is colliding with anticommunism, recalls a Zen master's lampoon of arrogance expressed in the putdown sayings, "The shame of his house is exposed to the world" or "He doesn't even know his shit stinks."

Another affinity is that many of Dylan's early protest songs point out the foundations of responsibility for injustice by adapting an attitude of simple yet probing inquiry. Asking unanswerable questions rather than looking for logical answers is very much in accord with the Zen approach. In "Who Killed Davey Moore?," a micro-protest song based on a true story of a boxer who died in the ring, Dylan says that the referee, the manager, the sportswriter, the gamblers, and the crowd along with the rival boxer all refuse to reply to the lead question, which hauntingly is left hanging in the air. Furthermore, macro-level songs "Blowin' in the Wind" and "A Hard Rain's A-Gonna Fall" raise questions about the foundations of discrimination and supernationalism that lead to destructive consequences, but offer no answers or perhaps only answerless answers. Not having a ready-made solution puts greater emphasis on the questioning process that in a paradoxical way is itself the answer for a world in which there are no solutions but only more questions. This approach resembles the response to the famous Zen query "Does a dog have the Buddha-nature," "Mu," which literally means "no" or negation but also implies universal nothingness as ultimate reality and thus can mean "yes." Or, it can be taken to imply that the question itself is pointless, hence, the message is that one should not ask such questions.

CROSSROADS: FROM DUALITY I TO NON-DUALITY I

The beginning of Dylan's rapid, dialectical transition away from dualism toward its opposite can be seen in that even at the peak of his involvement in the protest movement, three of the ten songs on *The Times They Are A-Changin'* fall into one of the other four Basic Bob categories. One example is "Boots of Spanish Leather," which expresses the theme of romantic conflict that would become more prominent on Dylan's next album. "One Too Many Mornings" is another non-protest song which conveys spiritual longing and contains the relativist assertion, "ev'rything I'm a-sayin'/ You can say it just as good./ You're right from your side,/ I'm right from mine./ We're both just one too many mornings/ An' a thousand miles behind."[19] Finally, "Restless Farewell," the album's concluding song is an example of existential loner blues. Written quickly in the studio just before it was recorded, this lyric marks a de-conversionary moment, in which Dylan "bids farewell" and "point(s) away from the past," in order to "make my stand/ And remain as I am/ . . . and not give a damn."[20]

Dylan apparently considered two other songs as possible finale numbers that in the end were left off the album altogether. One is "Percy's Song," which has protest overtones in lamenting a friend's unjust indictment and pleading his cause before an uncaring judge. The other song is "Lay Down Your Weary Tune," which evokes the beauty of nature as the true judge and teacher beyond any human effort that cannot help but seem hopelessly artificial and superficial by comparison. According to the song's non-dualistic, pantheistic theology, which is very close to Asian mysticism although it has also been given a dualistic biblical interpretation, the natural elements constitute the most glorious musical band of all and play a gorgeously triumphant hymn.

To paraphrase the majestic imagery of "Lay Down Your Weary Tune," the breeze sounds like a bugle and the rain is likened to a trumpet. Furthermore, the dawn seems like drums and the waves are like cymbals, while the river resembles a harp, the branches of a tree are similar to a banjo, and the ocean is likened to an organ. As with "Restless Farewell," this song appears to move sharply away from the protest model, albeit for a very different reason and direction. Both approaches—the Beat existentialism of "Restless Farewell" and the spiritualistic naturalism of "Lay Down Your Weary Tune"—will be pursued vigorously in upcoming career stages as the zigzag trajectory continues.

It is also important to note that after *The Times They Are A-Changin'*, only four songs in Dylan's entire corpus focus explicitly on topical protest themes. These include the antiracism anthems "George Jackson" (1971) and "Hurricane" (1975), as well as the gospel period's attack on political hypocrisy in "When You Gonna Wake Up?" (1979) and corporate greed in "Union Sundown" (1983). Several additional songs could be considered to have significant political implications in a broader sense, although the Dylanesque imagery is often opaque and elusive. This rather short list includes: "I Pity the Poor Immigrant" (1968), "Copper Kettle" (1970), "Lily, Rosemary and the Jack of Hearts" (1975), "Mozambique" (1976) and "Black Diamond Bay" (1976) from period II; "Señor (Tales of Yankee Power)" (1978), "Slow Train" (1979), "Lenny Bruce" (1981), "License to Kill" (1983), "Man of Peace" (1983), and "Clean-Cut Kid" (1985) from period III; and "Political World" (1989), "TV Talkin' Song" (1991), "High Water" (2001), and "Working Man Blues #2" (2006) from the Modern Era.[21]

In negotiating the crossroads leading from dualism to non-dualism, "My Back Pages" on *Another Side of Bob Dylan* stands out as a kind of anti-manifesto that offers a bold statement proclaiming Dylan's departure from the previous stage and the onset of a new path about to be taken.[22] The song makes explicit the transition initiated with "Restless Farewell," in that it features Dylan moving away from embracing Duality I (or the first career engagement with dualism) to abandoning that worldview and instead endorsing the standpoint of Non-Duality I (or the first engagement with non-dualism).

Here, Dylan complains of having accepted "Lies that life is black and white," and for thinking "Good and bad, I define these terms/ Quite clear, no doubt, somehow." He further derides himself for becoming his own worst enemy: "A self-ordained professor's tongue/ Too serious to fool/ Spouted out that liberty/ Is just equality in school/ 'Equality,' I spoke the word/ As if a wedding vow." Dylan's retort to his sense of delusion is, "Ah, but I was so much older then,/ I'm younger than that now," which indicates that dualistic protest is not as effective a tool for dissecting particular social ills as is non-dualistically detesting and resisting their foundational causes.

Complementing the disenchantment and rejection of dualism in "My Back Pages" in a way that resonates with non-dual Buddhist compassion for all beings, "Chimes of Freedom" provides a contemporary prayer for the unfortunate and the dispossessed. The lyric is based on a spontaneous visionary experience which is said to have occurred while the narrator and a companion "ducked into the doorway" of a cathedral during a tremendous summer storm. In unison with the thunder and lightning, majestic church bells are heard—or are imagined—to ring out in solidarity, "For the countless confused, accused, misused, strung-out ones an' worse/ An' for every hung-up person in the whole wide universe."

Although this experience takes place at a traditional sacred site, much like "Lay Down Your Weary Tune" recorded some months before, "Chimes of Freedom" posits nature rather than the religious institution per se as the arbiter of truth and the consoler of the souls of those who are at once oppressed and forgotten by society. Perhaps Dylan's fiercely independent yet naturalistic outlook is influenced by the American Transcendentalism of Emerson and Thoreau. This was also a key influence on Beat literature, which was in turn a response to some of the early translations in the nineteenth century of Asian mystical writings from both Chinese Daoist and Indian Hindu–Buddhist sources.

In another song from *Another Side of Bob Dylan* that is focused more on personal relationships than a communal setting, "All I Really Want to Do" endorses a standpoint of accepting and reconciling to differences while seeking to cast aside conflict or confrontation. According to the lyrics, which are perhaps somewhat fanciful or are intended in tongue-in-cheek fashion toward an erstwhile lover, "I don't want to meet your kin,/ Make you spin or do you in,/ Or select you or dissect you,/ Or inspect you or reject you."

Another Side of Bob Dylan also includes two social commentary songs that recall the stage-one approach by using a primarily comic vein of expression, "I Shall Be Free #10" and "Motorpsycho Nightmare." The latter song is a send-up of the Alfred Hitchcock movie *Psycho* along with Fellini's *La Dolce Vita* in order to highlight cultural differences in the United States with regard to understanding communism in Cuba. This signals a theme of lampooning anticommunist scare tactics that is very similar to what was expressed during the Basic Bob phase in "Talkin' John Birch Paranoid Blues" and "Talkin' World War III Blues." Additional examples of Dylan's sarcastic social commentary will appear in stage-two songs, such as talking blues tunes "Motorpsycho Nightmare," "I Shall Be Free No. 10," and "Bob Dylan's 115th Dream" on *Bringing It All Back Home*.[23] However, in that phase Dylan's approach tends to invert the ratio between humor and deadly serious observations. Comedy becomes a more subtle and ironic comple-ment to the main message, as in the reference in "Tombstone Blues" that Jack the Ripper is serving as the head of the chamber of commerce.

The remaining lyrics on the album deal with romantic conflict. These include two songs on idealized womanhood in "Spanish Harlem Incident" and "To Ramona," and one putdown in "It Ain't Me, Babe" that occupies the other end of the spectrum in terms of dealing with gender. In addition, there are three confessional songs that express the narrator's own sense of per-sonal frailties regarding love in "Black Crow Blues," "I Don't Believe You," and "Ballad in Plain D." The theme of competition and contest in romance is more significantly highlighted in the second stage and it becomes crucial for the thoroughgoing non-dualism of *Blonde on Blonde*. It also is important for the revival of dualism that appears in the first stage of the second period.

SECOND STAGE: SOCIAL DISILLUSIONMENT (NON-DUALITY I)

"The Times They Are A-Changin'" was Dylan's political manifesto during the first stage that became a hit song in 1964, and "Like a Rolling Stone" becomes the epitome of second-stage, folk-rock sound which shoots to number one on the charts just about a year later. The use of paradox is cen-tral to the message in both stages, but there is a shift here away from the vertical, dualistic style of right versus wrong based on a higher source of truth to a horizontal, non-dualistic way of accepting relative truths. As an example of dualism, "The Times They Are A-Changin'" proclaims:

> The line it is drawn
> The curse it is cast
> The slow one now
> Will later be fast
> As the present now
> Will later be past
> The order is
> Rapidly fadin'.
> And the first one now
> Will later be last
> For the times they are a-changin'.

In "Like a Rolling Stone," on the other hand, the use of non-dualistic paradox exposes the inadequacy and hollowness of truth claims, as in the scornful repudiation, "you got nothing to lose/ You're invisible now, you got no secrets to conceal." The second-stage style of paradox is also evident in the topsy-turvy, ironic relativism expressed in "Stuck Inside of Mobile with the Memphis Blues Again": "The ragman draws circles/ Up and down the block./ I'd ask him what the matter was/ But I know that he don't talk."[24]

Both kinds of paradox pass a moral judgment, but the vertical paradox of the first stage implies retribution for transgressions, whereas the horizontal paradox of the second stage reflects a detached acceptance of conditions that cannot be changed. Furthermore, the relation between the two types of paradox can be understood non-dualistically in that Duality and Non-Duality are not wholly separate but interact on various levels. Therefore, within the dualistic stage there exists some degree of non-dualism, and vice versa, as part of the path toward realizing the middle way.

In other words, when seen in light of a Zen perspective, there does not need to be a polarity between the options of dualism and non-dualism, which instead can be seen as complementary, Yin/Yang ways of understanding. A Japanese proverb reads, "The reverse contains its own reversals" (*Ura ni wa ura ga aru* 裏にわ裏がある), which indicates that contradictions are abundant within contradictions so that it is impossible or even irrelevant to try to determine what is conflicting and what is not. This outlook is reinforced by the author of *The Method of Zen*, who writes, "The center of being is *beyond* all opposites just because it dwells within them, and *within* all opposites just because it 'is' beyond them. It is without contradictions and yet full of contradictions."[25]

To put it another way, a spokesman for Zen once said, "Hamlet had it all wrong. It's not 'To be or not to be,' but rather, 'Both to be and not to be.'" Yet this is the case only so long as there is no attachment to the standpoint of either being or of non-being. According to the flexible standpoint of Zen thought that remains uncommitted to either dualism or non-dualism, Dylan's paradoxes may not indicate a change of attitude in that his real interest all along is not politics so much as the matter of justice which plays out on multiple personal and public levels. He is never looking to proclaim answers, but is rather painting pictures of what he sees around him, with an advanced level of insight that outpaces and helps to illumine his contemporaries.

During the second stage, Dylan develops three main approaches that grow directly out of the Basic Bob typology to articulating a Zen-like disillusionment with conventional social values and interpersonal relations accompanied by an attitude of resignation towards relativism. The first approach expresses a devastating, broad-based social criticism in songs

such as "Maggie's Farm" and the eleven-minute long opus "Desolation Row."
The second perspective, especially in blues songs on *Blonde on Blonde* such
as "Temporary Like Achilles," highlights the role of romantic conflict in
evoking pain and despair that creates an appreciation of relativism. The
third approach conveys an Eastern view of karma or moral causality as a
vehicle for understanding the interrelatedness of all phenomena. Since the
three perspectives are all critical for understanding Dylan's view of Non-
Duality in his first main period, I will analyze each of them in some detail.

Down on Maggie's farm

The first approach to non-dualism, which is particularly evident in the
songs on *Bringing It All Back Home* and *Highway 61 Revisited*, involves a
harsh critique of social institutions and forms of behavior based on a
relentless search for individual freedom and the integrity of conscience
outside the constructs that seek order but actually create chaos in society.[26]
In a remarkable series of songs including "Subterranean Homesick Blues,"
"Maggie's Farm," "It's Alright, Ma," "Gates of Eden," "Bob Dylan's 115th
Dream," "Tombstone Blues," "Ballad of a Thin Man," and "Highway 61
Revisited," Dylan skewers the deadly conformism and lethal hypocrisy of
American society. Oppressive "Amerika," to cite the title of a Kafka novel,
seeks to ensure that nobody can think freely for himself or forge his/her
own path in the face of the onslaught of pressure from every angle to tow
the line unquestioningly. With the exception of "Bob Dylan's 115th Dream,"
which is closer to the first-stage style, humor in these songs represents
a dry sense of irony that is submerged to, yet helps to facilitate the delivery
of a deadly serious message.

Although the title of a 1930s book by another Minnesota author, Sinclair
Lewis, proclaims, "It Can't Happen Here"—with "it" referring to a takeover
of the country by undemocratic, fascist elements as in the case of prewar
Germany and Italy—each of Dylan's social commentary songs recognizes
that this country has become hideously corrupt and bereft of its ideals.
This condition causes "the gray flannel dwarf to scream," according to "It's
Alright, Ma." This song also proclaims in a lyric Dylan frequently sang in
concerts during the Nixon impeachment in 1974: "While preachers preach
of evil fates/ Teachers teach that knowledge waits/ Can lead to hundred-
dollar plates/ Goodness hides behind its gates/ But even the president of
the United States/ Sometimes must have/ To stand naked." To paraphrase
images from a number of lyrics that reflect Dylan's relativist vision devoid
of underlying truth, all the senators, diplomats, generals, and other leaders
are no better off than "Napoleon in rags," while the icons of Western reason

and bravery are made to seem ludicrous or tragic, or interchangeable with the likes of Jezebel and Jack the Ripper.

Based on the standpoint of non-dualism, Dylan's aim is to explode any reliance whatsoever on dualistic symbols of authority by, for example, resisting and desisting from working on Maggie's contemptible workplace environment. In this corrupt version of society that is inspired by the Blues standard "Down on Penny's Farm," Maggie and her reprehensible cohorts (brother, ma, and pa) hand you nickels and dimes and then ask blithely, "if you're having a good time." Dylan champions the cause of the Outsider, or outcasts, outlaws, drifters, and other underdogs such as one-eyed midgets and geeks, as well as the misunderstood Good Samaritan and the misfit Hunchback of Notre Dame. All of these figures, along with Ma Rainey and Beethoven, are admirable in that they live in a kind of self-imposed exile, self-removal, or refusal to be involved, and embody resistance and restraint, while at the same mercilessly mocking anything and everything that is tainted.

While suffering the agony of touring before audiences who fail to appreciate his new electric, folk-rock sound in late 1965 and 1966, Dylan's music suggests that only a state of supreme solitude provides equanimity and resolve. In affinity with the demands of Zen, solitary contemplation is needed to reckon with profound disappointment and disillusionment in reaction to the flaws of mainstream society and the tribulations of interpersonal relationships. However, genuine detachment is an exceptionally rare and invaluable experience. There are too many devious, authoritarian nonthinkers like the unnamed object of attack in "Can You Please Crawl Out Your Window?," who is "cursing the dead that can't answer him," but can easily recover and knows, "If he needs a third eye he just grows it."

At this time Dylan is also working on his stream-of-consciousness, prose–poetic novel *Tarantula* (not published until 1971), the title of which evokes a section of *Thus Spoke Zarathustra* called "On the Tarantulas" by Friedrich Nietzsche. Like another nineteenth-century German philosopher, Arthur Schopenhauer, Nietzsche was very much inspired by, although also somewhat wary of what he perceived to be the world-weariness and pessimism of Buddhist thought. According to a key passage that may have influenced Dylan's thinking, "For that man be delivered from revenge, that is for me the bridge to the highest hope, and a rainbow after long storms."

Two prominent songs recorded during the second stage, "Gates of Eden" and "Desolation Row," offer a glimpse of the possibilities for relief from the nexus of oppression and suppression. They both strongly recommend that a contemplative state of mind can only be found in the most reclusive of locales (not necessarily literally, but symbolically), which is reached as the outcome of embracing a standpoint of Non-Duality that accepts a relativistic worldview.

According to "Gates of Eden," life outside the mythical utopia is endlessly plagued by the polarities of war and peace, light and dark, high and low, speech and silence, and reality and illusion. A false hero such as "Aladdin and his lamp/ Sits with Utopian hermit monks/ Side saddle on the Golden Calf," taking all too seriously in a misappropriation of religion, of "their promises of paradise." By contrast, when standing inside the gates "'neath the trees of Eden," from which "no sound ever comes" and towards which "ships with tattooed sails" are heading, one realizes that "there are no truths outside the Gates of Eden." Moreover, as the locus of non-dual experience, "there are no trials inside the Gates of Eden," where "there are no kings" and "there are no sins," and people do not "discuss what's real and what is not/ [as] It doesn't matter inside the Gates of Eden."

Dylan is clearly drawing on explicitly biblical, Judeo-Christian imagery to evoke a site where truth prevails, but here this serves the purpose of countering and defeating the dualism of real versus unreal which derives from falsity and deception. "Desolation Row," which Dylan has referred to as a "minstrel song" inspired by carnivals he saw as a kid and which is also indebted to the poetic works of T. S. Eliot (who is lampooned) as well as the Beats, devises a very different kind of symbolic place for the realization of authentic contemplative solitude. This site of detachment is based on incorporating the worldview of Non-Duality in a way that seems to call to mind the notions of emptiness and nothingness characteristic of Asian mysticism. From the vantage point of Desolation Row, which is located tantalizingly between "the windows of the sea," those who have yet to reach or communicate the same perspective are warned to "send me no more letters, no."

The lyrics feature a complex play of ambiguities that highlight the role of stoic resignation as the only consolation in dealing with the deficiencies of the human condition and how they have infected society at all levels. While "everyone is making love or else expecting rain" in anticipation of the apocalypse, the only way to rise above turmoil and turbulence is to stand back from those who continue to shout out the ultimate dualistic fallacy, "Which Side Are You On?" This represents yet another critique of the folk/protest movement as it struggles to achieve purity in the midst of unmitigated disaster. Instead, Dylan recommends that we take the calm, cool, and collected stance offered by non-dual awareness.

There are several dimensions to the realization of Desolation Row as a conceptual place or state-of-mind representing freedom from bondage to the chains of ignorance that all should hope to reach in order to escape from and transcend social ills. First, although Desolation Row offers much comfort and consolation to the narrator and his Lady who witness the astounding scenarios taking place, it clearly involves great risk as everything is at stake in trying to arrive and to stay there. It is not satisfactory to be content to rest on one's laurels if Desolation Row is glimpsed or reached momentarily. Rather, abiding on Desolation Row requires that you are always looking or leaning your head out far enough to see the sights of corruption and to hear the sounds of repression, as well as to be aware of those calling out for reform.

For example, you can listen to the penny whistles that signal the demise of the "sexless patients," who are imprisoned by Dr. Filth, accompanied by his "loser" nurse, who has led them to the cyanide hole while she "also keeps the cards that read/ 'Have Mercy on His Soul.'" Distasteful or absurd as they may be, these sensations and impressions make you aware of the harsh reality of the drastic forces that compelled you to undertake the path but also try to prevent you from reaching it or maintaining your status.

Second, while it causes the stars and moon to hide and the fortune-teller to take her things inside because of impending doom, the perspective of looking out from Desolation Row sharpens your senses and degree of insight. The full impact of social catastrophes comes clearly into view. These range from the infamous, racist-instigated Duluth Lynchings of June 15, 1920, which were hideously featured on local postcards at the time and are cited in the opening lines of the song's first verse, to the Romeo and Juliet-style turf battles, greed, and buffoonery that helped to lead to the Titanic's sinking in 1912 as evoked in the second and ninth stanzas. These events epitomize the contemptible hypocrisy, corruption, and hubris of modern American society that is out of control and veering off course toward a dangerous path without guidance from wise overseers. Occupying Desolation Row allows you to see vividly the dreadful qualities while also trying to maintain a healthy distance from them.

The third dimension is to be aware of the extent to which the so-called leaders of society who embody authority use their power to try to block those who aspire and to despoil anyone's efforts to reach Desolation Row. This is achieved in a shocking variety of ways, including the restless riot squad led by a corrupt blind commissioner, Dr. Filth's incestuous leather cup, and the Phantom of the Opera's spoon-feeding exercises. Other ways include the superhuman agents sent from the castles with their heart attack machines and the kerosene brought by insurance agents, or the revenge of Nero's Neptune that punishes by splitting and spilling the Titanic.

Fourth, you see that mythical figures or literary archetypes like Cinderella, who sweeps up on Desolation Row after a terrible fight between Romeo and his rivals over her, and the Good Samaritan, who plans to attend a carnival held there for which he is getting dressed, hope to go there amid chaos and confusion. But their attempts are stifled since they can only try to do so as they struggle against violence and loss. Others like Ophelia, who peeks into Desolation Row to escape her sin of lifelessness while wearing an iron vest, are left longing, while Casanova, who is being punished for having gone there, makes a vain effort to stay.

The next dimension is that wise men are hapless and helpless in the face of the continuous onslaught of forces that undercut the realization of authenticity and autonomy. For example, Einstein used to play the electric violin on Desolation Row, but he has been reduced to babbling infancy for pretending to be Robin Hood (although his recitation of the alphabet can also be interpreted as having Kabbalistic mystical power).[27] Also, Ezra Pound and T. S. Eliot are absurd cultural elitists who continue to squabble over the finer points of ideology and literary style instead of genuinely facing and seeking to overcome the reality of decline that takes on apocalyptic proportions.

The sixth dimension is that only those who resist authority like Cain and Abel and the Hunchback of Notre Dame, or who are mystical beings attuned to the simplicity of nature such as calypso singers and fishermen, are free from the dichotomy of being in or out of Desolation Row. The singers and fishermen in the song's penultimate verse may appear as simple down-to-earth people, but because of this they can sit back and laugh or throw flowers, gently mocking the foibles of society. However, while the image of the "windows of the sea" creates a sense of transparency and illumination suggesting holiness, the reference to lovely mermaids flowing in these imaginary locations is actually meant to undermine the sense of the reality or viability of taking the option of living a life of simplicity. According to the implications of this verse, naturalism is close to and resembles, but in the final analysis it is not a realistic alternative and fails to hold the key to attaining the authentic yet desperate spirituality of Desolation Row. Staying stuck on such an artificial or superficial image of apparent freedom that is really an escape threatens to become yet another fantasy and obstacle rather than a vehicle to reach the genuine goal of non-dualism.

This state of mind is also evoked on the surreal liner notes to *Highway 61 Revisited* which depict a ride on "the holy slow train" where "time does not interfere," and discusses the way Nietzsche represents the overcoming of dualities. According to the notes, based on an intriguing wordplay understood by figures as seemingly far apart as Quazimodo and Mozart, the ego and sense of selfhood are displaced and deconstructed:

> I cannot say the word eye any more ... when I speak this word eye, it is as
> if I am speaking of somebody's eye that I faintly remember ... there is no

eye—there is only a series of mouths—long live the mouths—your rooftop—if you don't already know—has been demolished . . .

Similarly, according to Zen, "The essential thing is to become egoless in a radical sense, so that 'egoself' does not exist any more, either as a word or as a feeling, and turns into an unknown quantity."[28] The ego-bound identity must be relinquished in order to reach a transcendental level of selfhood.

Finally, realizing the state of Desolation Row requires the determination to be liberated while remaining against all odds eminently pragmatic. This means that you are no longer content to communicate superficially with anyone who is not on the same level of understanding. False attempts to send messages must be rejected and rebuffed. Moreover, the narrator does not wish to be reminded of old acquaintances because from his new level of insight he realizes that "they're quite lame," and in order to keep things in perspective and remind himself of the new balance of power, he has "had to rearrange their faces/ And give them all another name."

"Desolation Row" indicates that the biblical power of naming and arranging, which represents the ultimate human capacity to control the flow of ignorance or wisdom in encountering the social environment, enables solitude to provide scarce consolation and even a degree of contentment. The image of rejecting by re-naming old, odd faces seems to invert yet complement the concluding verse in "It Takes A Lot to Laugh, It Takes a Train to Cry," which seeks to reach out to warn others of impending doom. The approach of the final verse of "Desolation Row" is opposed to a dualistic outlook which is based on pronouncing and seeking to enforce ways of judging what is perceived as the miscarriage of justice. Instead, the meaning of attaining the state-of-mind of Desolation Row is to withdraw from involvement and refrain from contact lest one fall into the trap of having to render a harsh judgment.

Another way of explaining the final verse of the song according to Aidan Day, is that Dylan seeks to defeat conventional cultural narratives that reinforce the worst in society, and instead rewrite "the received forms of stories in an attempt to demonstrate the essential incoherence of the culture that lives by such stories."[29] Therefore, only "versions scripted . . . from desolation's perspectives" are acceptable, and the "desolating double-bind explored by this lyric is that the rearrangement—the felt necessity to rewrite"[30] is the only viable antidote to social ills.

Thus, the symbolic site of Desolation Row recalls the ideals of reclusion and seclusion endorsed by traditional Zen hermits and wanderers, whether understood in a literal or figurative way. According to a traditional Chinese saying, "Small hermits retreat to the mountains, whereas great hermits stay in the cities." The states of steadiness and fortitude must be enhanced by a continual process of polishing the mind and sharpening the wits through encountering—but without giving in to the foolishness and follies of—ordinary society.

Another Zen-like mystical approach to realizing the non-dual perspective revealed in the final verse of "Mr. Tambourine Man" shows how nature serves as a model or mirror that enhances and purifies human perception gained through enduring suffering and chaos. This song deals with an illuminative experience that transcends the mundane:

> Then take me disappearin' through the smoke rings of my mind,
> Down the foggy ruins of time, far past the frozen leaves,
> The haunted, frightened trees, out to the windy beach,
> Far from the twisted reach of crazy sorrow.
> Yes, to dance beneath the diamond sky with one hand waving free . . .

Here, the narrator tries to stay far removed from the desolate ("foggy," "frozen," "haunted") aspects of nature, which symbolize being trapped between past and future. By making an inward journey that is realized in the eternal present moment as he is "Silhouetted by the sea, circled by the circus sands,/ With all memory and fate driven deep beneath the waves," he can "forget about today until tomorrow." As sky and sea are conjoined, all longing and anticipation are cast aside—but it is the mental outlook realized through hardship and sorrow that is the key to realization, rather than merely an attunement to nature as an end in itself.

Kneelin' 'neath your ceiling

The second approach that expresses Dylan's view of disillusionment and relativism as part of the stage of Non-Duality in his first main career period involves exploring intensely personal, romantic relationships which result in an awareness beyond Duality. In several songs, there are idealized women who represent wisdom and insight that epitomizes a non-dual realization. In others, the evocation of an aloof lover's rebuffs highlights the degree of personal vulnerabilities, frailties, and other troubling syndromes suffered by the narrator—in so many words, this is a matter of singing the blues, indeed, a heavy dose of the Hellhound Blues. The self-awareness of lack and loss typical of Delta songs ironically triggers a realization of the relativism and the hollowness of all values that also, in turn, leads to the supreme experience of non-dualism.

These themes are evident in several songs on *Bringing It All Back Home* and *Highway 61 Revisited*, but they especially infuse *Blonde on*

Blonde. That album includes only one lyric with an exclusive focus on ironic, sharp-edged social commentary that recalls the outlook of the previous two albums, "Stuck Inside of Mobile with the Memphis Blues Again." All of the other thirteen songs deal with various aspects of romantic conflict, although the goal of *Blonde on Blonde* is not so much to focus on romance as it is to facilitate an expression of existential spirituality based on coming to terms with troubled or complex relations with the opposite sex. In the second main career period, there will be a reversal of attitudes in that the image of ideal womanhood becomes revelatory not of non-dualism, but rather of Duality because she embodies a single all-encompassing truth that provides the solution to a world of conflict, as in "Tonight I'll Be Staying Here With You."

An important trend in Dylan's songwriting in the mid-1960s is that the celebration of the sage yet fragile and misunderstood woman hints at enlightenment but in many ways actually heightens the sense of aloneness through confrontation that is felt by the narrator. The pastoral utopian woman who is seen as an antidote to disheartening consumerism seems to represent the value of solitude in embodying just the right balance of expression and action with reticence and detachment. This ideal female image, according to the evocation of non-dualistic paradox in "Love Minus Zero/No Limit," is one who "speaks like silence,/ Without ideals or violence . . . [and] knows too much/ To argue or to judge", or she is with "eyes like smoke and . . . prayers like rhymes . . . and . . . voice like chimes" in "Sad-Eyed Lady of the Lowlands."

According to the "Sad-Eyed Lady of the Lowlands," "With your holy medallion which your fingertips fold,/ And your saintlike face and your ghostlike soul,/ Oh, who among them do you think could destroy you." In "Visions of Johanna," the goddess-like quality of the object of adoration is compared to Mona Lisa and Madonna, and her qualities of caring that rise above and redeem the troubled fray also resemble those of the Buddhist goddess Kannon (also known as Guanyin in Chinese and Avalokitesvara in Sanskrit). Yet, she remains frail like a wounded raven in "Love Minus Zero," with echoes of Edgar Allen Poe, and unapproachable by the narrator who becomes only too aware of his own failings and lack of ability or deservedness in beseeching her.

Some stage-two songs follow the trend established in first-stage numbers such as "Don't Think Twice, It's Alright" and "It Ain't Me, Babe" in bidding adieu to a now rejected romantic partner, including "Farewell, Angelina," "Love is Just a Four-letter Word," and "It's All Over Now, Baby Blue." A fascinating group of songs on *Highway 61 Revisited* and *Blonde on Blonde* very much influenced by the Blues includes "Queen Jane Approximately," "Just Like Tom Thumb's Blues," "I Want You," "Just Like a Woman,"

"Pledging My Time," "Visions of Johanna," "Temporary Like Achilles," and "Obviously Five Believers." These numbers document self-doubt, fear, vulnerability, loneliness, anguish, resentment, desire, and pettiness, along with the emotions of regret, jealousy, disgust, despair, and self-loathing. All of these feelings in their respective ways lead the narrator to a non-dual realization that is parallel but comes from the opposite angle of the songs of celebration.

In "Just Like Tom Thumb's Blues," for example, the narrator says he is left "howling at the moon" due to Sweet Melinda, whom the peasants call "the goddess of gloom." Because of troubles caused by Saint Annie, his "fingers are all in a knot" and he does not "have the strength/ To get up and take another shot." Furthermore, the "cruel" visions of Johanna leave him feeling like "little boy lost," who "brags of his misery," and in "It Takes a Lot to Laugh, It Takes a Train to Cry," Dylan confesses that he "can't buy a thrill." Also, in "I Want You," the narrator is ridiculed and feels stymied and stifled as "The guilty undertaker sighs,/ The lonesome organ grinder cries,/ The silver saxophones say I should refuse you./ The cracked bells and washed-out horns/ Blow into my face with scorn." The only recourse is to take revenge on "the dancing child with his Chinese suit," who lies as he "takes you for a ride."

"Temporary Like Achilles," a honky-tonk blues number with dazzling piano riff complementing a wailing harmonica solo, suggests a buildup of frustrations in trying to negotiate openings and gateways that have been systematically closed off by a remote and unforgiving former or unrequited lover. As in "Just Like a Woman," in which the narrator realizes, "I just can't fit/ Yes, I believe it's time for us to quit," Dylan says he finds himself "standing on your window," "looking at your second door," and "kneeling 'neath your ceiling." He admits to feeling "so harmless" and "helpless, like a rich man's child," or "like a poor fool in his prime." This is because his former or desired lover has him "barred," as a scorpion crawls across her "circus floor, while she sends "no regards."

Meanwhile, the unnamed woman uses Achilles, who is "hungry, like a man in drag," as her "guard." In this and other songs from the stage of Non-Duality I, people of unusual gender orientation become menacing characters, such as the sword swallowers in "Ballad of a Thin Man" and the fifteen jugglers and five believers "all dressed like men" in "Obviously Five Believers." For the narrator in "Temporary Like Achilles," it becomes "all too concise and too clear," to cite a line from "Visions of Johanna," that the longed-for romantic partner is someone with a "heart made out of stone, or is it lime,/ Or is it just solid rock?" The message is that the profound anguish puts one in touch with the depths of non-dual experience.

Ev'rything's been returned

The third approach to conveying the meaning of Non-Duality during stage two is an outgrowth of the Basic Bob category of spiritual longing, and seems to move Dylan's religiosity into territory that closely resembles the Asian notion of karmic causality as an explanation of moral repercussions. To sum it up briefly, the doctrine of karma, or of what goes around comes around in a horizontal, relativist universe determined by the mechanics of causality rather than a higher power, is quite different from the notion of divine judgment and retribution that is characteristic of the standpoint of Duality. Yet both concepts convey a deeply moral view in that there are repercussions for each and every act, whether as a mechanical causal principle or as the result of superior forces determining one's merit.[31]

According to "Visions of Johanna," the process of seeking an unattainable but equally unforgettable woman teaches a moral lesson about the inevitability of cause-and-effect, or the unavoidability of getting a return, whether as rewards and benefits or as punishments and detractions, for every action taken. Here, Dylan, whose first hit song "Blowin' in the Wind" evokes an Eastern sense of fateful yet unpredictable circumstances determining one's life choices, comes close to the Buddhist view of the moral implications of karma.[32]

Just at the point when the narrator becomes all too aware of the disconnect between an idealistic vision of Johanna and the harsh reality of being with his actual lover Louise, and as "Infinity goes up on trial," the song comments that in the final analysis everyone will get what is deserved according to the law of causality. "We see this empty cage now corrode," Dylan writes in a verse that evokes the dualistic icon Madonna, "Where her cape of the stage once had flowed/ The fiddler, he now steps to the road/ He writes ev'rything's been returned which was owed/ On the back of the fish truck that loads/ While my conscience explodes." The phrase about a corroding cage recalls the Buddhist doctrine that all of existence is characterized by ephemerality and impermanence, and the image of an exploding conscience has distinct overtones of a Zen epiphany, or the experience of sudden, eureka-like moment of awakening known as Satori.

The theme of the causal nature of morality in a transient world, which echoes the Eastern view of karmic causality leading to invariable retribution, is carried out in several other compositions from the same period, including "4th Time Around" ("Everybody must give something back/ For something they get") and "Stuck Inside of Mobile with the Memphis Blues Again."[33] In the latter song, after articulating numerous confusions about the impossibility of travel and relationships as well as the transgressions of politicians and preachers that leave him knowing "deep inside my heart" that "I can't escape," Dylan concludes with a forlorn plea. According to the song's final verse "An' here I sit so patiently./ Waiting to find out what price/ You have to pay to get out of/ Going through all these things twice," Endlessly repeating the horrific experiences he has enumerated represents the ultimate karmic punishment. This notion is in accord with Nietzsche's doctrine of the Eternal Recurrence of all activities (indirectly evoked in the *Highway 61 Revisited* liner notes), which in turn was greatly influenced by Eastern thought.

The question that emerges by the end of period I is whether total solitude and infinite patience provide the spiritual resolution. Or, do these states actually stop representing virtues and, if pursued too vigorously, end up having a boomerang effect by indicating that one has arrived at a dead-end or impasse? The next main period begins with Dylan brooding over the significance of nothingness and continuing to explore some of the non-dualistic approaches he has expressed in *Bringing It All Back Home*, *Highway 61 Revisited*, and *Blonde on Blonde* to their outer limit, so to speak.

Based on a combination of circumstances including weariness with touring and a crippling motorcycle accident coupled with the joys of married life, within a year he quickly becomes dissatisfied with this option. The pendulum of Dylan's career path then moves rapidly from Non-Duality to the opposite direction of embracing the path of Duality with full conviction and determination, albeit in a very new style that differs greatly from— and in dialectical fashion is nearly opposite to—the original approach to dualism in the early 1960s.

Chapter 7

Period II (1967–1978)

From "I'll Be Your Baby" to "You're an Idiot, Babe"

OVERVIEW: STAGES AND CAGES

The second main period of Dylan's career lasts for about a decade beginning in the late 1960s. During this phase, Dylan at first fully embraces a dualistic approach in the stage of Duality II by celebrating idealized womanhood and marital bliss as the solution for life's travails. He then rejects this outlook and returns in Non-Duality II to a state of disillusionment with personal relations and resignation to relativism that infuses the "idiot wind" of the non-dual perspective. Therefore, despite many differences in style and substance, in the final analysis Dylan's second career phase is remarkably similar to period I. Both are marked by the successive appearance of two distinct stages and this transition is characterized by a significant, even radical transition from dualism to non-dualism.

Compared to the first period, which evidenced a drastic zigzag quality of change, this period reveals a longer, slower trajectory, yet its roller-coaster-like twists and turns in moving from a deep sense of certainty to profound skepticism and doubt are no less powerful. As discussed in Chapter 1, there are several important examples during the mid-1970s of Dylan expressing an interest in Zen or Asian mysticism, which helps to enhance his distinctive approach to Non-Duality. Yet this period ends with Dylan once again dissatisfied with non-dualism and about to embark on his most extreme approach to dualism in the form of gospel music.

Three years are particularly crucial for the development of period II's approach to music-making. The first year is 1967, during which both

The Basement Tapes and *John Wesley Harding* are recorded. These records deal extensively with the themes of nothingness and of how pessimism and nihilism represent an extreme element of non-dualism that must be avoided. Both works express fatigue with the Dadaism and surrealism of the mid-1960s, and thereby mark a gateway to a joyful affirmation of love and marriage in "I'll Be Your Baby, Tonight," the final song on *John Wesley Harding*, and on the entirety of *Nashville Skyline* two years later.

Then, in 1970, *Self Portrait* and *New Morning* are released back-to-back, and are generally interpreted as extensions of an emphasis on commitment to dualism because they contain songs that affirm family values. *New Morning* is considered to represent a comeback effort to compensate for the dualistic excesses of *Self Portrait*. However, these records are actually much more complicated in their messages. Taken together, the albums indicate the onset of a crossroads that leads Dylan away from Duality I and toward the beginning of another exploration of relativist themes. This culminates a few years later in the stage of Duality II.

Finally, after several years without recording a new album before *Planet Waves* in 1974, the year 1975 sees the release of *Blood on the Tracks* and the recording of *Desire*, including the protest song "Hurricane," which becomes the centerpiece of the momentous Rolling Thunder Revue tour. All of these productions contribute to Dylan reestablishing himself as the master of non-dual expressions of relativism, especially in songs like "Tangled Up in Blue," "Simple Twist of Fate," and "Black Diamond Bay," even as holdovers of romantic songs from the previous stage such as "Sara" are also included on these records.

In the second period, Dylan's achievements reach both the highest heights and the deepest depths of his entire career trajectory. On the positive side, Dylan helps invent the genre of country rock with *Nashville Skyline*, and has three successive chart-topping albums with *Planet Waves*, *Blood on the Tracks*, and *Desire*. *The Basement Tapes* is finally released in 1975 to critical acclaim.[1] There is also a string of hit singles during this phase, several of which are best known for being covered by other performers, including "Quinn the Eskimo (The Mighty Quinn)," "All Along the Watchtower," "Lay Lady Lay," "If Not For You," "Knockin' on Heaven's Door," and "Forever Young." Furthermore, after lighting up the Concert for Bangladesh at the beginning of the decade, "Tour '74" with The Band in which Dylan plays large stadiums to standing room only crowds as well as the Rolling Thunder Revue performances at smaller venues are perhaps his most successful performing engagements.

On the other hand, for the first time, Dylan takes an eight-year hiatus from touring and a three-year break from recording an album of original songs. There are, in addition, the first instances of Dylan works flopping with fans and critics, in the case of the album *Self Portrait* and the film *Renaldo and Clara*. Or, his works gain a mixed reception in the case of the studio album *New Morning*, his first and only full-length movie soundtrack that accompanies his acting in *Pat Garrett and Billy the Kid* in 1973, and the live albums *A Hard Rain's A Gonna Fall* in 1976 and *Live at Budokan* in 1979.

During the first main career period of the 1960s, Dylan was no stranger to controversy or criticism as reflected in booing by fans and scolding of critics received at key turning points, but in the end his genius was generally recognized and effusively praised. In period II, however, he loses universal critical acclaim and instead suffers rebuff and ridicule for the first time in his career, although the reception is almost never one-sided. With the Midas touch at least partially removed, Dylan mounts a series of comebacks to counter the experience of comedowns, both of which are linked to his conversionary experiences.

The two biggest targets of attack are *Self Portrait*, which consists of Dylan performing covers of folk and pop standards along with live songs from the Isle of Wight Festival of 1970, and the four-hour long film *Renaldo and Clara*, which is an unconventional narrative directed by and starring Dylan featuring his soon-to-be ex-wife Sara and Joan Baez who play romantic rivals. These artistic efforts are harshly criticized for nearly opposite reasons—the album for trying to be too slick in its production values and for overdoing its handling of dualism, and the film for seeming altogether unpolished and for taking non-dualism to an extreme.

Nevertheless, when viewed through an interpretive lens based on the dialectical theory, we can better appreciate the considerable merits of both works in their respective efforts to articulate a balance of dualism and non-dualism as part of Dylan's overall path to bargainin' for salvation. Through all the vicissitudes, Dylan continues to pursue whatever path he sees fit in order to attain authenticity and autonomy, and for the most part he lets the detractors be darned as he strives for a middle path, yet sometimes acknowledges that he ends up lurching between extremes.

GATEWAY: FROM JUDAS TO JUDAS PRIEST

The year 1967 is a very good year for Dylan's songwriting, which reflects an artist who is significantly changed from what he appeared to be just a year or so before. Instead of the defiant rocker mocking friend and foe alike as an expression of non-dualism which is reluctantly resigned to the futility of human relationships, the new Dylan is a non-combative empathizer. He wishes to relieve the cultural and personal sense of loss and disillusionment nearly everyone in society seems to be undergoing by conveying the value and comfort of a dualistic adherence to a higher truth.

Apparently "burned out from exhaustion," to cite a line from "Shelter from the Storm," Dylan begins to withdraw from the pop culture scene after completing a series of gigs in the early summer of 1966 in Great Britain. He had gotten a mixed reception that included catcalls of "Judas" from an audience of folk music purists unwilling to accept his new electric sound, which was ironically selling extremely well throughout the world. Following the motorcycle accident later that summer, Dylan does not just speak about solitude, but he becomes notoriously reclusive and does not tour again for nearly a decade, while performing in public only on a couple of occasions. The unseen benefit of the accident was that it gave him an opportunity to step back and reflect before breaking into new creative territory.

After taking a break for over a year, Dylan makes a transition to a different but no less productive phase of music-making. During 1967, he records well over a hundred songs, including several dozen original pieces whose message reinforces the persona he projects of a humble, withdrawn, and repentant family man.[2] This results in *The Basement Tapes* recorded with The Band in late summer/early fall and in *John Wesley Harding* produced in just a couple of days in October and November with Nashville sessions players. It was released shortly before the New Year but without, according to Dylan's instructions to Columbia Records, very much publicity or fanfare. Through these and subsequent works, by the end of the 1960s Dylan finds that he is at the forefront of a very different kind of revolution than the ones he had created earlier as protest singer and as a blues rocker. In this case he generates a counter-revolution by setting himself up as an iconic country gentleman with quotidian yet refined musical tastes. This image serves as a foil for hard-rock sounds and outrageous countercultural images that dominate the airwaves.[3]

Too much of nothing

Dylan starts this phase by continuing to explore the introspective ruminations on nothingness and relativism that had been the focus of the second stage of period I, especially on *Highway 61 Revisited* and *Blonde on Blonde*. Both 1967 albums explore and expose the limits of the worldview of non-dualism, which denies access to any particular truth in order to set the stage for a celebration of the seemingly opposite standpoint of affirming the single truth of love and family. The terms "nothing" and "nowhere" are prominent in several songs produced in 1967, and seem to reflect an experience of the mystical void or abyss. However, Dylan quickly reaches a bottoming out point when he realizes that nothingness can ultimately lead to counter-productive attitudes of despair and antinomianism. Most of the songs on *The Basement Tapes* in addition the first ten songs on *John Wesley Harding* explain Dylan's transition from clinging to non-dualism to embracing dualism, which is celebrated in the last two songs of that album and throughout *Nashville Skyline*.

The music of *The Basement Tapes* is usually examined for the way it marks a return to Dylan's folk/blues roots and is exemplary of the panoramic imagery of the eclectic, offbeat cultural legacy of authentic Americana, or "The Old, Weird America" according to the title of critic Greil Marcus's book which analyzes these recordings.[4] Another way of analyzing this music is to see the lyrics as an extension of the Zen-like theme of how an experience of angst can lead to detachment, which serves as the key to spiritual release but can also lead to the dead-end of loneliness and sorrow.

The Basement Tapes includes several songs expressing the quiet desperation of a troubled vagabond who, while drifting aimlessly in a world where there is no solace or consolation, realizes that relativism and illusion must be reckoned with and endured. The songs in this category include "Yea! Heavy and a Bottle of Bread" and "Clothes Line Saga," both of which convey the futility and frustration of trying to leave home. As with "Tombstone Blues" and the disillusioning depiction of Juarez in "Just Like Tom Thumb's Blues" on *Highway 61 Revisited*, travel to remote, south-of-the-border locations also evoked in "Goin' to Acapulco" and "Santa Fe," may well sound alluring but in the end does not come close to offering respite, and instead only compounds the torment.

The image of being bound to a particular unsatisfying location while longing to escape the Hellhound Blues is reinforced by the upbeat tone of "You Ain't Going Nowhere," which says, "Strap yourself/ To the tree with roots." On the more despairing side, "Please Mrs. Henry" shouts, "I'm down on my knees/ An' I ain't got a dime," while "Long Distance Operator" exclaims, "I believe I'm stranglin' on this telephone wire," and "Lo and Behold!" beseeches, "Get me outa here, my dear man!"

Another theme on *The Basement Tapes* involves a sense of guilt for not being able to live up to the grave responsibilities and high expectations of self and others regarding social commitments. Several of the lyrics are accusatory, including "Down in the Flood," which scolds, "Well, it's sugar for sugar/ And salt for salt,/ If you go down in the flood,/ It's gonna be your own fault," by borrowing passages from one of the Delta standards, "James

Alley Blues" by Rabbit Brown. In "Open the Door, Homer" Dylan returns, in this case bemusedly, to the karmic theme of getting what you deserve, or everything that goes around comes around. "Now, there's a certain thing/ That I learned from my friend, Mouse," he chants ironically, "A fella who always blushes/ And that is that ev'ryone/ Must always flush out his house/ If he don't expect to be/ Goin' 'round housing flushes."

The circularity of causality is further expressed in "This Wheel's on Fire," "If your mem'ry serves you well,/ You'll remember you're the one/ That called on me to call on them/ To get you your favors done." A variation on the theme of dishing out blame for those shirking responsibility is the confessional song, "Tears of Rage," which ponders in the wake of Dylan's withdrawal from political causes the implications of trying to take away others' pain. "Tears of rage," he bemoans, "tears of grief,/ Why must I always be the thief?"

Given the pervasiveness of the feelings of regret and doubt, is there any chance of attaining relief? What does it take to know that "I Shall Be Released," to cite the title of one of Dylan's best known songs from this phase? A couple of songs playfully talk of a secular holy man or healer who can free the soul, including "Tiny Montgomery" and "Quinn the Eskimo." According to the latter song, "Ev'rybody's building the big ships and the boats,/ Some are building monuments,/ Others, jotting down notes,/ Ev'rybody's in despair,/ Ev'ry girl and boy/ But when Quinn the Eskimo gets here,/ Ev'rybody's gonna jump for joy." A more philosophical approach to achieving wholeness is suggested in "Open the Door, Homer," in which Dylan espouses the importance of penitence and compassion: "remember when you're out there/ Tryin' to heal the sick/ That you must always/ First forgive them."

The path to authenticity cannot avoid and, indeed, must embrace an experience of spiritual vacuity. "Nothing Was Delivered," which depicts the void as a neutral, objective realm in which judgments are cast aside, is reminiscent of the Zen notion of ultimate reality as a realization of nothingness (Mu 無 in Japanese). This doctrine ideally encompasses an awareness of, and yet transcends, nihilistic elements by staying beyond the conventional dichotomy of positivity and negativity, or optimism and pessimism. The logic of Mu also recalls the experience of the Abyss (*Abgrund*) or state of Unknowing frequently depicted in medieval Christian mysticism, as well as doctrines of the Hidden Allah in Islamic Sufism, the Concealed Creation in Jewish Kabbalah, Neti Neti (Not This, Not That) in Hinduism, Sunyata (Emptiness) in Buddhism, and Non-Action in Daoism. For many mystical traditions worldwide, a direct experience of nothingness can be a source of joyful liberation in representing the annihilation of ego and the overcoming of attachments.

But in "Too Much of Nothing," Dylan explores the demonic side of facing "oblivion," or a world in which nothing is sacred and no redemption can be found:

> Too much of nothing/ Can turn a man into a liar,
> It can cause one man to sleep on nails/ And another man to eat fire.
> Ev'rybody's doin' somethin',/ I heard it in a dream,
> But when there's too much of nothing,/ It just makes a fella mean.

While nothingness can represent the fullness of unity and caring, it is a double-edged sword and in some cases, it indicates a sense of lack and loss that is devastating and disheartening.

All but straightened out

Nothingness representing what is empty and devoid of meaning, as also expressed in T. S. Eliot's famous verse "The Hollow Men" in which the world ends not with a bang but a whimper, is poignantly evoked in another lyric from this gateway phase, "The Ballad of Frankie Lee and Judas Priest" on *John Wesley Harding*. According to the song's narrative, Frankie falls on hard times and is betrayed by his supposed best friend Judas Priest, who lures him into giving over uncontrollably to temptation at a brothel. Consumed by a passion for sensual pleasure, Frankie Lee dies "of thirst," in a way that recalls the Buddhist notion of selfish craving that lies at the root of human suffering.

According to the song's penultimate verse, everyone jokes about Frankie's demise when he lustfully visits what Judas Priest says "is not a house … it's a home," "except for the little neighbor boy/ Who carried him to rest./ He just walked along, alone,/ With his guilt so well concealed,/ And muttered underneath his breath,/ 'Nothing is revealed.'" Here, nothingness represents not the source of non-dualistic truth, but quite the contrary. It reflects the impenetrable mystery of hidden guilt that has not been redeemed and becomes the main obstacle to attaining spiritual freedom.

The tragic yet humiliating and unheralded death that occurs in "The Ballad of Frankie Lee and Judas Priest" functions as a crucial turning point in the complex narrative structure of *John Wesley Harding*. In the era of the unified themes of rock-opera albums, *John Wesley Harding* outperforms many other efforts by telling the story of one man's spiritual journey encompassing his symbolic death based on the decline and fall of a life of solitude and desolation and his rebirth achieved through an experience of embracing love, wedded bliss, and joyfulness. Through a well-organized set of song-parables, the album depicts the personal odyssey of Dylan who makes a sudden transition from relativism to a single truth. Dylan feels that liberation cannot be reached without abandoning the vestiges of Non-Duality while undertaking a wholehearted conversion to Duality.

Although seeming at first rough and spontaneous (like many Dylan albums, it is recorded in a matter of days), *John Wesley Harding* is incredibly tightly constructed, with every word and note counting and contributing to the overall effect. This stands in contrast to *The Basement Tapes*, which reflect a rambling and ramshackle approach to music-making, as if offering an unguided tour of minstrel-era America, which is probably why Dylan originally thought that it was not ready for prime time. Also distinct from the recording pyrotechnics of *Sgt. Pepper's Lonely Hearts Club Band* released earlier that year, the sparse and austere sound of *John Wesley Harding* greatly enhances the quiet pursuit of authenticity and straightforwardly honest yet cryptic, Dylanesque view of soul-searching that lies at the core of the album's religious message.

The first ten songs performed with Dylan's guitar, harmonica, or piano accompanied only by a rhythm section of drummer and bass are altogether introspective and brooding, opaque and philosophical. They examine and expose some of the many flaws and limitations of a relativist worldview in a way that opens to multiple interpretations. By the conclusion of *John Wesley Harding*, however, Dylan embarks on his country music and family affirmation-based counter-revolution with two songs, "Down Along the Cove" and "I'll Be Your Baby Tonight." Both feature a simple, direct evocation of the power of love, which is accentuated by the sweet sounds of a pedal steel guitar.

John Wesley Harding opens by evoking a topsy-turvy, upside-down carnival-like atmosphere previously visited in "Tombstone Blues," "Desolation Row," and other songs from the second stage of period I. In this world, the Outsider (outlaw, outcast, or drifter) represents the just and righteous, while society's so-called leaders are altogether lacking in integrity or moral standing. The title song celebrates the exploits of a gunfighter from the days of the Wild West cast in the role of a fugitive/desperado like Robin Hood, Billy the Kid, Jesse James, or Pretty Boy Floyd, who is heroic because he refuses to be tracked or chained down. Harding is a criminal who is justified in taking from the rich in that he never hurts an honest man and always lends a helping hand to the needy. Dylan, who may be trying to evoke the Old Testament Yahweh (Jehovah) through the initials of the lead character, takes liberty with the historical record, which indicates that the real Hardin (Dylan adds the final "g," apparently to mock himself for all the times he dropped this letter) was a notorious killer. But he does this in tongue-in-cheek fashion as indicated in the lines about him traveling "with a gun in ev'ry hand" and taking a stand in Chaynee County so that the "situation there/ Was all but straightened out."

The title cut establishes the theme that the true American hero is one who will live free or die even when it means breaking the law. The next two songs, "As I Went Out One Morning" and "I Dreamed I Saw St. Augustine," complete the relativist reversal of values in making it clear that apparently heroic figures such as the secular saint Tom Paine, who once stood for liberty at any price, or St. Augustine, who abandoned secular corruption for faith, seem hopelessly defiled and hypocritical. Paine keeps his captives locked in chains to stifle any hope they have for freedom, and Augustine wears "a coat of solid gold" while pretending to represent the meek and the humble. Since "Absolutely Sweet Marie" from *Blonde on Blonde* says "to live outside the law, you must be honest," the inverse must also be the case, that is, those living inside the law are likely to be dishonest.

What is the real meaning of honesty and authenticity? In "All Along the Watchtower," the anguish of trying to answer the question places one in a face-to-face encounter with relativism and nothingness. The joker is in a state of distress, with no relief in sight, from the confusion caused by those who misunderstand, misappropriate, and exploit his activities. He and the thief (an archetype also evoked in "Positively 4th Street" and "Tears of Rage") approach a castle on horseback in an apocalyptic atmosphere, with the hour getting late as princes look out from the watchtower amid the sounds of a howling wind and a growling wildcat. The thief reassures his partner by counseling him against giving vent to frustration and futility, as "This is not our fate."

In the next song, the forces of disillusionment overtake Frankie Lee, but in the sixth lyric, "Drifter's Escape" (the last cut on Side A on the original vinyl release), relief is suddenly provided when "a bolt of lightning/ Struck the courthouse out of shape." This causes members of the corrupted justice system who falsely accused and tried the drifter to become temporarily repentant and distracted from their watch. Considering the spontaneous nature of the drifter's liberation is not necessarily based on a Zen-like depth of insight since it is facilitated by external circumstances rather than internal awareness, this escape does not provide spiritual satisfaction, as the next group of songs makes clear.[5] According to "I Pity the Poor Immigrant," wanderers in the world of relativism who become deceitful are doomed to feel alone because those who turn their back on their allies will find that their "visions in the final end/ Must shatter like the glass."

John Wesley Harding offers several deceptively easy moral teachings about humility, modesty, and caring as a means of overcoming the travails faced by those who have lost their way, like Tom Paine, St. Augustine, Frankie Lee, and the joker, or have no fixed abode, like the immigrant, wanderer, and hobo. At the end of "The Ballad of Frankie Lee and Judas Priest," Dylan asserts that the key to spiritual fulfillment is to be sympathetic and helpful regarding a neighbor's plight, while at the same time refraining from seeking greener grass on the other side of the fence (i.e., "Don't go mistaking paradise for the home across the road.")

In confessing that "I Am A Lonesome Hobo," Dylan writes mournfully, "Stay free from petty jealousies,/ Live by no man's code,/ And hold your judgment for yourself,/ Lest you wind on this road." Furthermore, he appeals to his "Dear Landlord" to realize that "each of us has his own special gift/ And you know this was meant to be true,/ And if you don't underestimate me,/ I won't underestimate you." Zen-like in simplicity yet also true to biblical teachings, the formula for fulfillment is to accept reality for what it is from the standpoint of constructive compromise and equanimity by eliminating bias or partiality.

Since "nothing is revealed" and the possibilities for escaping from predicaments or overcoming obstacles through showdowns with authority figures is obviated by the pervasive lack of social cohesiveness, Dylan argues in the first nine songs that it is imperative to withhold all judgment-making which is inevitably arbitrary and biased. However, an emphasis on detachment as the means for realizing peace of mind in a troubled world full of loss and decay falls short. Neutrality, while valuable as a kind of spiritual stepping stone, does not guarantee happiness because it lacks the joy and intimacy of home and family, the missing element suggested by the tenth song, "The Wicked Messenger." Non-dualism thus must abruptly give way to an awakening to Duality. As with "The Ballad of Frankie Lee and Judas Priest" and "The Drifter's Escape," which speak of symbolic death and sudden resurrection, the tale of the messenger stresses the need for a spontaneous casting away of deficient attitudes and falsity as the gateway to an experience of true wisdom.

The saints of many traditions, including St. Augustine as well as a number of Zen masters, are said to have attained a great spiritual awakening based on a single seemingly innocuous experience such as hearing a stirring phrase or seeing an inspirational sight. Here, the messenger, who is disgusted with his own empty rhetoric that invariably leads to exaggeration and misleading discourse, repents and converts when the saying, "'If ye cannot bring good news, then don't bring any,'" had an impact that "opened up his heart."

FIRST STAGE: COUNTRY/FAMILY (DUALITY II)

As depicted in the complex narrative of spiritual transformation on *John Wesley Harding*, Dylan suddenly abandons non-dualism in order to embrace the standpoint of dualism through an emphatic affirmation and celebration of idealized womanhood and joyful marriage. The perspective of dualism is conveyed even more vividly through the simple lyrics of *Nashville Skyline* and, to a lesser extent, on *Self Portrait*. All three albums use the instrumentation and vocal style of Grand Ole Opry country music, a conservative musical sound that is integral to the message of compromise and making peace with both personal opponents and cultural obstacles.

I refer to this phase of Dylan's songwriting as Duality II in order to distinguish its approach to articulating dualistic truth based on love and family life from that of the early 1960s protest period, during which Dylan criticized conventional society and called for drastic social change. An aspect of Duality II that is quite different from the previous phase involves the way music is related to the singer–songwriter's public persona. Duality I was known for Dylan's compelling, charismatic public appearances, including both the Newport Folk Festival and the civil rights March on Washington in 1963, a pivotal year in the protest movement. In the second phase of dualism, however, Dylan stays withdrawn and for the most part remains incommunicado and out of the public eye, aside from his recordings, only some of which are released at the time. The hermetic tendency seems to reverse the earlier pattern, and this phase of isolation reflects the way Dylan integrates non-dualistic tendencies in his new approach to dualism.

Dylan's twin emphases in the second stage of period I or Non-Duality I were on the benefits of solitude and seclusion, as expressed in "Chimes of Freedom," "Gates of Eden," and "Desolation Row," and on the pursuit of a woman–goddess, as in "Love Minus Zero/No Limit," "Visions of Johanna," and "Sad-eyed Lady of the Lowlands." Given these trends, it is not nearly as surprising as it seemed to most observers at the time that in the late 1960s Dylan chooses a path of living in isolation in Woodstock, New York, while raising a family and staying as far away from the pop culture scene as he could. Songs elevating his wife to near divine status like "Wedding Song," "'Cept You," and "Sara" could be seen as a logical, even inevitable outgrowth of the Basic Bob category of romance songs including "Girl From the North Country," now taken to the nth degree.

The emphasis in the first stage of period II is on contrition on both personal and social levels. In addition to the effect of raising a family, Dylan's aggressive outlook is greatly tempered by the death in the late 1960s of both his real father Abraham, with whom he had contested over his career choices, and his spiritual patriarch Woody Guthrie, who had inspired him but who was already terribly sick when they met. Dylan is also sending a message to people in the movement who protested at the Democratic Convention in 1968 and/or attended Woodstock in 1969 that finding a way to have peace in Vietnam requires learning to be less confrontational and to reconcile with disparate and even oppositional cultural forces at home.

Oh me, oh my

A crucial factor in Dylan's conversion/counter-revolution is that he now values repentance rather than retribution, acceptance rather than attack, and reconciliation rather than repudiation. He would rather be seen as the glad-handing Tiny Montgomery, liberating Mighty Quinn, or door-opening Homer than adopt the accusatory tone and biting putdown critiques that were a hallmark of his mid-1960s creativity. Indeed, "The Wicked Messenger" represents a double conversion—one is a turning away from relativism/non-dualism, and the other is a rejection of Dylan's original early '60s approach to dualism, a discontent which caused the turn toward Non-Duality I in the first place.

The country-waltz style of the last two songs on *John Wesley Harding* continues on *Nashville Skyline*, released about fifteen months later in the spring of 1969. Except for the opener which is a duet with Johnny Cash of "Girl from the North Country" and the instrumental "Nashville Skyline Rag," each song contains succinct lyrics that make a deliberate use of clichés. The songs, in effect, proclaim that love is all there is (perhaps a complement, meant ironically or not, to the Beatles' 1967 song, "All You Need is Love"). Thus, *Nashville Skyline* has been referred to as a whole album's worth of "I'll Be Your Baby Tonight"-type songs.

True to what the wicked messenger learned about the vices of rhetorical flourish, for the first time in his career Dylan eschews the high-minded poetry that infused all his albums from *Freewheelin'* to *John Wesley Harding* and instead gives priority to sound and atmosphere. In "Talkin' World War III Blues," Dylan said that since the radio does not work so well after the war, "I turned on my player—t was Rock-A-Day, Johnny singin',/ 'Tell Your Ma, Tell Your Pa, Our Loves Are Gonna Grow Ooh-wah, Ooh-wah." During a set at the Newport Folk Festival in 1963, he substituted the name of pop star Fabian for the singer. With *Nashville Skyline*, it seems that Dylan fulfills this once ridiculed role with his new echo-chamber, pop vocal style.

Nevertheless, the songs show Dylan making good use of subtlety and verbal sleight of hand. For example, an irony in "Country Pie," the album's manifesto on preferring the country flavor to any other kind of pie, moderates the song's insistent message when Dylan sings, "I don't need much and that ain't no lie/ Ain't runnin' any race/ Give to me my country pie/ I won't throw it up in anybody's face." He also employs a Zen-like paradox in an otherwise straightforward love song, "Peggy Day," which traverses from "Love to spend the night with Peggy Day" in the first verse to "Love to spend the day with Peggy night" in the second.

CROSSROADS: FROM DUALITY II
TO NON-DUALITY II

With the turn to traditionalism in both *John Wesley Harding* and *Nashville Skyline*, Dylan once again confounds what was anticipated by fans and critics. Yet, he is consistent in staying a step ahead of the lonely crowd and avoiding feeling caged in by any fixed ideology. Nevertheless, it is suspected, and Dylan later confirmed, that after being so prolific for many years, he has his first instance of reaching a creative impasse and suffers from a rather severe case of writer's block.[6] Part of what he needs to learn is how to accomplish consciously with songwriting what he had always been able to achieve unconsciously.

In contrast to 1967, the year 1970 is generally not considered among Dylan's most productive phases even though it sees the release of a double album and a single album, just months apart (June and October). The first of these is considered a major comedown because of an apparent over-commitment to his conversion to Duality, and the second is only a partially successful comeback that is stuck between dualism and non-dualism. When looked at in light of Dylan's ongoing spiritual quest, however, 1970 takes on new meaning because it reveals the artist constructively question-ing his commitment to dualism and searching for ways to integrate the meaning of Non-Duality.

Following the firm commitment to Duality in the initial stage of the second main period, Dylan soon begins negotiating a rather prolonged crossroads or transitional phase in which he struggles mightily with the affirmation of family values embodied in country music. The songs on *Self Portrait* and *New Morning*, in addition to several prominent singles released during these years, have the effect of second-guessing the dualistic stance yet without repudiating it. These works vacillate not only between musical styles, but also in terms of expressing either an avowal of the joys of love or a sense of disappointment and disillusionment with the inadequacy of dualism. This back-and-forth phase lays the groundwork for a sharp shift as Dylan rejects the seemingly simplistic answers he recently admired by reexamining and reaccepting the meaning of non-dualism.

Self-less portrait

Released in the summer of 1970 in the midst of his country music stage, which finds Dylan clinging to the virtues of raising a family, the much-maligned *Self Portrait* at first glance seems to epitomize the *Nashville*

Skyline approach to musical and lyrical simplicity.[7] Since it features so few original songs on a double album and it mixes a country sound with other folk styles, many at the time take this to signal a rapid decline in Dylan's abilities. The record instantly becomes Dylan's first flop with critics—consider Greil Marcus' infamous "What is this shit?" that led off his devastating and lengthy *Rolling Stone* dismissal. Dylan has distanced himself from the product by suggesting in *Chronicles* that he put it out deliberately to throw his followers off track at the time his music is first being bootlegged and his celebrity status causes fans to yearn for every nugget.

The conventional view presumes that with a few notable exceptions, *Self Portrait* is filled with mostly vapid love songs either penned by Dylan in a perfunctory way in a couple of instances or ones that he feebly covers. It sees *Self Portrait* revealing the starkly unoriginal underside of *Nashville Skyline*, although that album was well received, which insists on bombarding the audience with a one-dimensional message that falls far short of addressing the complexity of the times. The problem with this approach is that it focuses on listener expectations, rather than hearing the music for what it is.[8]

Although it might be taken for granted that the message of *Self Portrait* is a triumphal dualistic stance that is antithetical to moral relativism, when seen from a Zen standpoint the album explores the vagaries of non-dualism after just a couple of years of preoccupation with dualism. It marks Dylan's return to the outlook of *The Basement Tapes* and the first ten (rather than the last two) songs on *John Wesley Harding* in celebrating outlaws and outcasts, such as gold miners and moonshiners, hobos and rebels, who were also highlighted on his very first album. Theirs are the stories of an American journey into the world of uncertainty and despair. Thus, *Self Portrait* signals not the enduring length of the stage of Duality II, but rather the beginning of its end and the onset of what would prove to be a four-year long crossroads leading to Non-Duality II.

A Zen interpretation helps to recover the merits and significance of the album which features a guileless performer who communes with and blends into the natural setting or cultural context, as illustrated by the front cover art, which is Dylan's drawing of an unrecognizable clown-like face that is integral with its background. Also, the sleeve includes a photo of Dylan standing in the woods and gazing upward at the sky—not looking at anything in particular, but *just* gazing. The cover art thus recalls the Zen state-of-mind:

> in which nothing definite is thought, planned, striven for, desired or expected, which aims at no particular directions and yet knows itself capable alike of the possible and the impossible, so unswerving is its power—this state, which is at bottom purposeless and egoless, was called by the Master truly "spiritual."[9]

Figure 7.1   Self Portrait Cover

The album opens with the one-line song delivered by a choral group, "All the Tired Horses," in which Dylan does not appear at all in the vocal or instrumental performance (there are also two instrumental-only songs, "Woogie Boogie" and "Wigwam"). This number consists of the lyric, "All the tired horses in the sun/ How'm I supposed to get any 'ridin' done?" (where "'ridin'" sounds like "'ritin'"). It may be a deceptively innocent way of marking a transition away from the family stage which unintentionally stifles creativity that arises from conflict and tension. The sentiment of at least mild discontent and weariness with the absence of an environment that stimulates and inspires art is also subtly expressed in "Time Passes Slowly" on *New Morning* released in October 1970, as well as the single from the following year, "Watching the River Flow." That song says sardonically, "What's the matter with me,/ I don't have much to say,/ Wish I was back in the city/ Instead of this old bank of sand." It concludes by praising the passivity of contemplation, "But I'll sit down on this bank of sand/ And watch the river flow."

Self Portrait features diverse musical styles that range from a kind of deep Nashville sound to folk, blues, pop, rock, hillbilly, and rockabilly, which indicates that Dylan is not wedded to any particular outlook but committed to exploring multiple possibilities, in a way that foreshadows his innovative and integrative approach on *"Love and Theft"* three decades later. In covering traditional songs like "Days of '49," "Alberta," and "Copper Kettle," and in performing tributes to predecessors, peers, and rivals ranging from Rogers and Hart's "Blue Moon" to Paul Simon's "The Boxer" and Gordon Lightfoot's "Early Morning Rain," Dylan is constantly reworking his ever present themes of the loss of love leading to an anguish that is matched only by the inability to fully attain authenticity and autonomy within social constraints.

Dylan's self-portrait does not seek to reveal his inner psyche or to portray himself as someone distinct who stands out from the crowd, since this outlook is what led him to reject and remain in isolation from the world. Instead, he highlights and merges with the background and context of the variegated Americana influences on his work. This synthetic, integrative yet self-effacing approach recalls the saying of Zen master Dogen, "To study the way is to study the self. To study the self is to forget the self. To forget the self is to allow the objective/external world to prevail in and through you (or to be enlightened by others)." In singing a cover of the deceptively innocuous "Take Me as I Am or Let Me Go," Dylan makes it clear that self-forgetfulness does not lead to oblivion but is accompanied by a vigorous insistence on autonomy.

And the locusts sang

Released four months after *Self Portrait* and featuring twelve original songs produced in New York and decoupled from the Grand Ole Opry sound, *New Morning* is hailed as Dylan's second major rebound after *John Wesley Harding*. The last album produced by Bob Johnston, who began working with Dylan on *Highway 61 Revisited* and took him to Nashville studios beginning with *Blonde on Blonde*, *New Morning* mixes the country twang of simple love songs with some of the folk-rock style and mythical lyricism expressing bursts of epiphany and outrage that characterized his 1960s work. Both comebacks demonstrate that after a period of inactivity, either following the motorcycle accident or because of writer's block, Dylan's skills return seemingly undiminished. Whereas the first rebound with *John Wesley Harding* signals the onset of a counter-revolution by deconstructing the counter-cultural revolution of the 1960s, *New Morning*, which features a picture of a younger Dylan standing next to Blues great Victoria Spivey on the back cover, heralds that the end of the country/family stage is in sight.

It is clear that dissatisfaction with dualism first evident on *Self Portrait* is mounting, but Dylan does not leap quickly or move in a straight line into the stage of Non-Duality II. Instead, he tends to veer back and forth between dualism and non-dualism through the release of *Planet Waves* and up until the recording of *Blood on the Tracks*. By that point, his separation and eventual divorce from Sara has a great impact on the despair and sorrow expressed in his music.

Half of the songs on *New Morning* continue an emphasis on idealized romance, with the title cut and "If Not for You" standing out for their joyful exuberance in endorsing family life. "Winterlude" as a waltz and "One More Weekend" as a rocker reinforce the theme, along with the singles from this phase, "I'd Have You Anytime" cowritten with and recorded by George Harrison and "Wallflower" performed on a Doug Sahm album.

"Sign on the Window" seems to be among this group by concluding with a lyric that is powerful in its simple cliché-infused affirmation of the virtues of family life, which recalls the best of *Nashville Skyline*, "Build me a cabin in Utah,/ Marry me a wife, catch rainbow trout,/ Have a bunch of kids who call me 'Pa,'/ That must be what it's all about." But Dylan delivers the lines with such a degree of pathos and uncertainty, as if trying in vain to talk himself into the merits of an abstract formula he knows in his heart he cannot accept, that the impact represents the opposite of a dualistic assertion and suggests the dissolution of traditional family values. According to "The Man in Me," "The man in me will hide sometimes to keep from bein' seen,/ But that's just because he doesn't want to turn into some machine," which may indicate a level of disengagement from the current lifestyle.

Other songs reveal Dylan either trying to reinvigorate his social awareness, as in "Day of the Locusts," along with the single "George Jackson," or to explore alternative spiritual perspectives. "Three Angels" previews a gospel approach in asking, "The whole earth in progression seems to pass by./ But does anyone hear the music they play, Does anyone even try?" "Time Passes Slowly" seems to embrace a natural theology that leans in the direction of non-dualism when Dylan sings, "Like the red rose of summer that blooms in the day,/ Time passes slowly and fades away," although it is difficult to discern whether this implies contentment or restlessness, which is also suggested by the line, "Someday, everything is gonna be smooth like a rhapsody," in a single from this phase, "When I Paint My Masterpiece."

"Father of Night," the final cut on *New Morning*, conveys a spiritual theme when Dylan says we "solemnly praise" a deity, and this is arguably the first recorded prayer in his repertoire, nearly a decade before the gospel period. On the one hand, its presence supports the argument for incipient Christianity. But a close look at the lyrics leaves open the possibility of a Zen-like influence because of the way the Father, whose power encompasses the opposites of night and day, black and white, and cold and heat, is portrayed as a unifier and harmonizer of opposites in Yin/Yang fashion, especially in the first and last two lines of the opening verse: "Father of night, Father of day,/ Father, who taketh the darkness away,/ Father, who teacheth the bird to fly,/ Builder of rainbows up in the sky,/ Father of loneliness and pain,/ Father of love and Father of rain."

The other main product of this phase is the soundtrack to *Pat Garrett and Billy the Kid*, in which Dylan plays a character known as Alias, who accompanies the hunted Billy during some of his travels (and travails) and is so opaque that when asked "Alias what?," he retorts, "Alias anything you please." While much of the album contains compelling instrumental tracks evoking death and loss, the two songs with lyrics celebrate the tragic pursuit of freedom in "Billy," who is "walkin' all alone . . . so far away from home," or accept the fateful interaction of living and dying in "Knockin' on Heaven's Door," which says, "That long black cloud is comin' down/ I feel like I'm knockin' on heaven's door."

As *I'm Not There* shows, there is a conceptual link between the Dylan of *The Basement Tapes*, *Self Portrait*, *Pat Garrett and Billy the Kid*, as well as the subsequent Rolling Thunder Revue in expressing solidarity with the misfits of society. Whereas in the stage of Duality I Dylan was a Rebel With a Cause and in Non-Duality I he was a Rebel Without a Cause, in Non-Duality II he is a Non-Rebel With a Cause, but by the end of the crossroads phase, he is ready to become a rebel once again, with or without a cause.

SECOND STAGE: PERSONAL DISILLUSIONMENT (NON-DUALITY II)

Dylan's fascination with country life and music as a vehicle for dualism does not last more than a few years, and during the second stage of period II he returns to an urban lifestyle and the performing of rock music as an entrée to non-dualism, while also readopting the persona of vagabond or perpetual rolling stone. After a hiatus of over three years following *New Morning*, the next album of original songs, *Planet Waves* released in early 1974 to accompany Dylan's first tour with The Band since 1966, helps bring to fruition the transition and marks the beginning of the phase of non-dualism. In many of the songs, *Planet Waves* expresses a dualistic message that harks back to the country/family stage, but several lyrics also forcefully question dualism and signal a new direction of turning to disillusionment. This is accomplished by focusing on the experience of loss and departure in the "world of illusion," a term used here that becomes important in songs on *Blood on the Tracks*.

On a night like this

As part of the transitional aspect of the album, seven of the eleven *Planet Waves* numbers are love songs, including "On a Night Like This," "Hazel," "Something There is About You," "You Angel You," "Never Say Goodbye," and "Wedding Song." The last of these is especially forceful in proclaiming the Duality II ideology of love conquering all and eclipsing the significance of social commitment:

> It's never been my duty to remake the world at large,
> Nor is it my intention to sound a battle charge,
> 'Cause I love you more than all of that with a love that doesn't bend,
> And if there is eternity I'd love you there again.

An outlook of reverence for an ideal woman envisioned as a goddess who provides all the necessary spiritual sustenance is reinforced by the outtake "Nobody 'Cept You": "There's nothing 'round here I believe in/ 'Cept you, yeah you/ And there's nothing to me that's sacred/ 'Cept you, yeah you."

However, an exploration of Non-Duality is compellingly conveyed in the remaining four songs. First, "Forever Young" is a joyful hymn that offers a positive, uplifting message about ongoing renewal and redemption based on accepting the flux of existence: "May your hands always be busy,/ May your feet always be swift,/ May you have a strong foundation/ When the winds of changes shift." This is expressed in a way that recalls Buddhist teachings of impermanence at a time when Dylan is also making his first references to Asian mysticism, including the album's liner notes.

The other songs investigate a darker, more introspective side of human experience, in which loneliness and despair become touchstones for an awareness of nothingness and relativism. "Dirge" valorizes solitude, which overcomes fixations with celebrity and status: "I went out on Lower Broadway and I felt that place within,/ That hollow place where martyrs weep and angels play with sin." Furthermore, "Tough Mama," which celebrates a raunchy female image similar to the "junkyard angel" in "From a Buick 6" on *Highway 61 Revisited*, expresses the need to throw off the shackles of responsibility for social commitment while at the same time gaining liberation through insight into the delusory nature of conventional values:

> I'm crestfallen
> The world of illusion is at my door,
> I ain't a-haulin' any of my lambs to the marketplace anymore.
> The prison walls are crumblin', there is no end in sight,
> I've gained some recognition but I lost my appetite.

Finally, in "Going, Going, Gone," Dylan proclaims that he is ready and pre-pared for a new direction: "I'm closin' the book/ On the pages and the text/ And I don't really care/ What happens next./ I'm just going,/ I'm going,/ I'm gone." In retrospect, this can be interpreted to mean he is leaving dualism and moving to non-dualism. What would it take for him to get where he is going? The formula encompasses the unfortunate breakup of Dylan's marriage and heretofore serene family lifestyle, leading to a deep sense of disillusionment and shame regarding personal relationships as well as social affairs in a broader sense.

A new way of seeing

Released just a year after *Planet Waves* and indicating a burst of creative energy, *Blood on the Tracks* instantly introduces Dylan's audience to the stage of Duality II with a fury and a vengeance realized through impecca-ble lyrics and haunting melodies not seen in Dylan's works for years. It is often ranked at the top of fans' lists of all-time favorite albums, although it is hard to imagine anything surpassing the mid-1960s records from the stage of Duality I or the more recent albums from the Modern Era. The greatness of *Blood on the Tracks* is that it integrates the very best elements of the disciplined approach to spiritual storytelling of *John Wesley Harding* with the wildly innovative use of surreal narrative pastiches in *Highway 61 Revisited* and *Blonde on Blonde*.

The songs on this record excel in connecting issues of personal discon-tent with the larger context of American society suffering from a loss of idealism and momentum for reform in the aftermath of the twin fates of the Vietnam War and the Watergate Scandal. In other words, Dylan uses the end of his marriage as a metaphor for the turmoil of the whole society, and/ or vice versa, in the traumatic American landscape of the post-Nixon era.

The opening lines of "You're a Big Girl Now" set the tone for how Dylan suddenly finds himself in the realm of troubles or the Hellhound Blues, which is where he touches base with non-dualism by proclaiming, "I'm back in the rain." The appearance of rain is reinforced on *Blood on the Tracks* by the lyrics "rain fallin' on my shoes" in "Tangled Up in Blue," "lightning that might strike" in "Idiot Wind," feeling "the hail fall from above" in "Meet Me in the Morning," "the sky was overcast and black" in "Lily, Rosemary and the Jack of Hearts," "Buckets of rain/ Buckets of tears" in the opening verse of "Buckets of Rain," as well as "the road was full of mud" and "buried in the hail" in "Shelter from the Storm." Moonlight is another important image on *Blood on the Tracks*, as in "Sundown, yellow moon" in "If You See Her, Say Hello" and "buckets of moonbeams in my hand" in "Buckets of Rain."

What is the significance of these two natural images? From a Freudian perspective they suggest entering a dreamlike realm of the subconscious. Another line of interpretation notes that just a few years earlier, Dylan sang, "If not for you/ My sky would fall,/ Rain would gather too," as a way of emphasizing that an affirmation of dualism could fend off the suffering symbolized by excessively harsh precipitation. Here, the combined impact of the imagery evokes the mixed-up confusion of non-dualism by recalling the prominent early modern collection of Japanese folklore, "Tales of Rain and Moonlight" (*Ugetsu monogatari*), which was made into a famous movie in the 1950s by director Kenji Mizoguchi. These Japanese folk tales deal with the haunted and hunted, deception and delusion, seduction and betrayal. These are the themes that Dylan conjures as well, as he falls from the grace of the simple verities of holding to a single, higher truth, and is helplessly yet resolutely tossed and turned anew amid the travails of non-dualism, which he must learn to accept … at least for now.

While acknowledging the merits of other albums from period II, including *Nashville Skyline, New Morning,* and *Planet Waves,* many observers have wondered how Dylan is able to make such a spectacular comeback in songwriting. According to his own account, the key to recapturing his talents is the rediscovery of what he has called "that wellspring of creativity," inspired by painting teacher and self-styled guru, Norman Raeban. In 1974, Raeban teaches Dylan much more than painting. He opens up an innovative manner of perception that leads to a novel way of understanding the artist's relation to the world that seems to dovetail with Dylan's budding interest and explicit references to Zen-style meditative insight.

Raeban, who was not at all familiar with Dylan's celebrity and may have even thought he was a homeless outcast because of his scruffy appearance, uses a Zen-like sink-or-swim style of instruction, more than once calling Dylan and classmates an "idiot." By challenging his students to draw based on their recollection of an image (a process Dylan later alludes to in an ironic episode in "Highlands" when he tells a waitress standing before him, "I don't do sketches from memory"), Raeban instructs Dylan that "real perception … was a matter not just of looking but of *seeing*."[10] This technique, which recalls Leonardo da Vinci's notion of *saper vedere* or "knowing how to see" because sight alone conveys the facts of experience immediately, correctly, and with certainty, so motivates Dylan to tap into his deep reserve of inner resources that he calls the teacher "more powerful than any magician."

Dylan said,

> [Raeban] didn't teach you how to paint so much. He didn't teach you how to draw. He didn't teach you any of those things. He taught you putting your heart and your mind and your eye together … He looked into you

and told you what you were. He taught me how to see in a way that
allowed me to do so consciously what I unconsciously felt.

The notion of true seeing without blinders and free from the defects
of tunnel vision (i.e., partiality, limitation, and bias) is a theme that is
frequently repeated in Zen discourse, which shares the goal of uniting
the conscious and unconscious, or the deliberate with the spontaneous.
In Zen one seeks to function with eyes that see and ears that hear, as well as
paradoxically speaking with "eyes that hear and with ears that see."[11]

The renewed way of seeing helps to overcome the last vestiges of
Dylan's early 1970s writer's block and unleashes his pent-up artistic imagination by enabling him to live fully in the present and utilize a holistic
vision with the ability to view the whole in parts and the entirety through
particular details. This triggers a novel approach to multi-perspectival
narrative formation that is particularly evident in "Tangled Up in Blue,"
which features dramatic shifts in temporality (from present to past, and the
reverse), location (from here to there, and back), and viewpoint (from first
to third person, and return). These techniques are useful in "allowing
[Dylan] to reveal underlying truths about the song's characters while
letting them remain shadowy, secretive figures."[12] Dylan thus combines
postmodern literary motifs that echo Zen attitudes with traditional methods of storytelling.

In renouncing Duality for the second time in his career, the songs on
Blood on the Tracks mark a return to a classic folk-rock sound heavily influenced by twelve-bar blues and accompanied by guitar picking and harmonica riffs reminiscent of Dylan's best work in the mid-1960s. As opposed
to the proclamations of a single truth in stage one, such as "Love is all there
is, it makes the world go 'round,/ Love and only love, it can't be denied" as
well as the affirmation that "I'll Be Your Baby Tonight," non-dualism is
expressed in pronouncements that signal a profound resignation to deception and delusion. "Tangled Up in Blue" epitomizes this trend by declaring,
"All the people we used to know/ They're an illusion to me now," and the
world of multiple truths is also evoked in many of the other songs.

The stage of Non-Duality II is very similar to what was expressed during
Non-Duality I ten years earlier. Both phases which focus on the realization
of relativism demonstrate a scornful mockery of those who cannot escape
illusion because they "never turned around to see the frowns on the
jugglers and the clowns/ When they all come down and did tricks for you,"
according to "Like a Rolling Stone." A harsh critique of the bad faith that is
typically adhered to by the dazed and deluded is articulated in "Idiot Wind."
This song suggests that a foul breeze is "blowing every time you move your
mouth,/ Blowing down the backroads headin' south./ Idiot wind, blowing

every time you move your teeth,/ You're an idiot, babe./ It's a wonder that you still know how to breathe."

The stage of Non-Duality I for the most part placed emphasis on social commentary, with romantic conflict functioning as a subordinate theme or as a metaphor for external affairs. In Non-Duality II, the emphasis is reversed. These songs explore a more personal, interior world depicted against the backdrop of the turmoil and social upheavals of the times. They also reveal an artist eagerly in pursuit of reconciliation rather than finger-pointing, as in the final assertion in "Idiot Wind" that "We are idiots, babe," and in "Tangled Up in Blue" that "We always did feel the same,/ We just saw it from a different point of view."[13]

"Idiot Wind" further shows that Non-Duality II differs from Non-Duality I in that Dylan has learned from his confessional phase experienced during Duality II. The final verse of the song was rewritten between its first recording in New York in September 1973 and the recording in December which became the official version in order to reflect the attitude of repentance and reconciliation as central to salvation. According to the outtake version's scornful conclusion, "I been double-crossed too much, at times I think I've almost lost my mind . . . / You can have the best there is, but it's gonna cost you all your love/ You won't get it for money." The rewritten verse transforms this accusatory rejection into a statement of acceptance and hopeful resignation toward all opponents and obstacles: "I been double-crossed now for the very last time and now I'm finally free,/ I kissed goodbye the howling beast on the borderline which separated you from me./ You'll never know the hurt I suffered nor the pain I rise above,/ And I'll never know the same about you, your holiness or your kind of love,/ And it makes me feel so sorry."

Heading for another joint

Like *Blonde on Blonde* in which all but one of the fourteen numbers deal with romance, the songs on *Blood on the Tracks* treat the topic of women either in an intimate, confessional way by referring to them as "you" or "she" or from the distance of impersonal narration. In any case, the women, whether idealized or demonized, are more than mere mortals. They are seen as a bridge to the realm in which salvation is bargained for and can only be gained through a struggle with the forces of self-deception and ignorance, yet they remain ever elusive and out of reach. This suggests that the single truth of dualism cannot be found and that each one of us has no choice but to come to terms with the relativism of Non-Duality. In the midst of the pain this causes, Dylan tries to "turn back the clock to when

God and her were born," while realizing that "Everything about you is bringing me/ Misery."

It is interesting to see that the various approaches taken in the songs on *Blood on the Tracks* toward the valorized or stigmatized female reflect Basic Bob categories. Several songs explore the theme of womanhood from the standpoint of romantic conflict involving a still respected though departed partner. This leads to heartache and an unending sense of sorrow and loss, which feels "Like a corkscrew to my heart/ Ever since we've been apart" in "You're a Big Girl Now," and causes self-doubt in "If You See Her, Say Hello": "Oh, whatever makes her happy, I won't stand in the way/ Though the bitter taste still lingers on from the night I tried to make her stay." "Simple Twist of Fate," on the other hand, concludes in a more philosophical vein by pointing not just to the lack of dualistic truth, but to the need to accept non-dualism and unpredictable karmic causality: "She was born in spring, but I was born too late/ Blame it on a simple twist of fate."

Two other songs dealing with unfulfilled love are expressions of the loner blues category, including the classic twelve-bar-style refrain of anguish in "Meet Me in the Morning," and the innovative narrative style of "Tangled Up in Blue." The latter number is the album's opener and its best example of implementing Raeban's approach to perception to the art of personal, introspective storytelling framed against the broad background of social history and cultural concerns. The first two verses evoke the beginning and the end of an intense relationship, and the remaining lyrics weave backward and forward in terms of both temporal conditions and human understanding with flashpoints of instantaneous insight or Satori appearing in every verse. For example, in referring to medieval Italian poetry in the fifth of the song's seven stanzas Dylan evokes poignancy and sorrow by declaring, "And every one of them words rang true/ And glowed like burnin' coal/ Pourin' off of every page/ Like it was written in my soul from me to you." The atmosphere is reminiscent of the traditional Japanese aesthetic ideal featured in the *Tale of Genji* and other sources of *mono no aware*, or sadness at the passing of things (relationships and circumstances). The next verse captures the rise and fall of the culture wars: "There was music in the cafes at night/ And revolution in the air./ Then he started into dealing with slaves/ And something inside of him died./ She had to sell everything she owned/ And froze up inside."

The song, which concludes with Dylan firmly ensconced in the relativism and emptiness of Non-Duality II as he is "headin' for another joint," occupies the same realm of solitude as the concluding, "don't send me no more letters," in "Desolation Row." The earlier song's opening stanza which refers to, "As Lady and I look out tonight," implies a cool confidence and self-assuredness about what is being observed. However, "Tangled Up in

Blue" shows a new approach to Non-Duality based on the intensely personal and self-doubting experience of separation.

Blood on the Tracks' two longest songs approach the issue of women from the standpoint of social commentary. "Lily, Rosemary and the Jack of Hearts" is the least personal song on the record and tells a complex tale of intrigue in the Wild West. The mysterious Jack of Hearts enters a cabaret in a town without pity and manages, without suffering any harm to himself, to weaken the corrupt but seemingly invincible Big Jim and to help cause his demise. The murder is for better or worse blamed on Rosemary, who is executed by a drunken, contemptible hangin' judge and is mourned by Lily, who also has had an entangled relationship with Jim. Meanwhile, Jack's troupe manages a major swindle and he is free to escape with the loot. Thus, in the post-*John Wesley Harding* era of confession and reconciliation, Dylan seems intent to expose not only the detestable deceit of authority figures but his own opportunism as one who has reaped economic benefits from his involvement in social causes and conflicts.

The theme of self-doubt and self-criticism also appears in the opening verses of "Idiot Wind" when Dylan says blithely of his windfall profits from Tour '74, "I can't help it if I'm lucky." The song argues, however, that this concern should not distract from the real matter at hand, which is widespread disappointment and disenchantment caused by deception and betrayal at all levels of the social fabric. One of the towering achievements of "Idiot Wind" is the way it deliberately blurs the line between accusations against an anonymous "her," or unfaithful lover, and an amorphous "them." This encompasses disloyal companions, as well as society at large, that have consistently failed to live up to its ideals, in addition to Dylan's own failings.

The major weakness Dylan identifies lies in the simplistic either/or answers of the dualistic worldview, and he shows how this source of misconception becomes all too easily jaded and overturned when it faces an encounter with relativism. "Now everything's a little upside down, as a matter of fact the wheels have stopped," he sings, "What's good is bad, what's bad is good, you'll find out when you reach the top/ You're on the bottom." Herein lies an echo of the "first will be last" paradoxical logic of "The Times They Are A-Changin.'"

Finally, three of the songs on *Blood on the Tracks* examine love affairs from the standpoint of spiritual longing. "You're Gonna Make Me Lonesome When You Go," in which the narrator regrets not realizing the temporal goal. "I could be with you forever and never realize the time," ironically delivers an upbeat message that "I'll see you in the sky above,/ In the tall grass, in the ones I love." However, "Buckets of Rain" ponders the inevitability of flux in lamenting, "[I] seen pretty people disappear like smoke./ Friends will arrive, friends will disappear."

"Shelter from the Storm" contains ten verses that express the high and low points of a spiritual attachment to an ideal woman. The first half of the song celebrates how she kept the narrator "always safe and warm," after "She walked up to me so gracefully and took my crown of thorns." However, the last five verses reveal a topsy-turvy world where all values are reversed and nothing is what it is expected to be or is even relevant in the grand scheme which anticipates the apocalypse leveling all disparities: "Well, the deputy walks on hard nails and the preacher rides a mount/ But nothing really matters much, it's doom alone that counts/ And the one-eyed undertaker, he blows a futile horn." In evoking a sense of self-identity through a comparison with Jesus and in comparing the ideal but lost woman to God, the last two verses indicate that, although seemingly ensconced in Non-Duality II and far removed from its opposite viewpoint, "Shelter from the Storm" contains the seeds of spiritual longing for an absolute other that will become the mainstay of Duality III.

Seeing double

Another interesting element in Non-Duality II is its explicit examination of various manifestations of dualism, especially on *Desire* and in *Renaldo and Clara*. These include the phenomena of seeing double, the role of twins, brother–sister relations, alter egos or dual personae, and the image of darkness versus light, as well as traditional blackface reversed into whiteface.

Desire is released on the heels of *Blood on the Tracks*, indicating that the two-year stretch from fall 1973 when *Planet Waves* is recorded to fall 1975 when the tracks for *Desire* are laid is one of Dylan's most prolific periods, although he does not produce another record of original songs until *Street-Legal* in the summer of 1978. The only Basic Bob category missing on *Blood on the Tracks* was topical protest, which is manifested in the single "Hurricane," the lead track on *Desire* about the plight of the falsely accused boxer, Rubin Carter.[14]

However, "Hurricane," which like all but two of the nine songs on *Desire* is cowritten with Jacques Levy, does not turn out to signal a new commitment to the protest movement. Instead, juxtaposed with "Joey," a lengthy song about real-life Mafioso Joey Gallo who was shot down during a New York turf battle, it fits into the album's pattern of telling stories of Outsiders, including drifters and gypsies. Other numbers include "Isis," "One More Cup of Coffee (Valley Below)," "Romance in Durango," and "Black Diamond Bay." As with the characters in *Blood on the Tracks*, these travelers are often victims of the elements, such as the "devilish cold" in "Isis" and the "blistering sun" in "Romance in Durango."

With the exception of the final song "Sara," which reveals intimate details about his marriage and drug-taking, the narrative viewpoint on *Desire* is far less personal than *Blood on the Tracks*, but suggests a cool distance of withdrawnness characteristic of Non-Duality. Indeed, the problem with non-dualism that is exposed in the final verse of "Black Diamond Bay" is that resignation and acceptance of fate can easily lead to aloof indifference and lack of involvement. The narrator says that in watching the destruction of a remote island he quickly bores of the news and turns off the TV to go "grab another beer," while reflecting, "Seems like every time you turn around/ There's another hard-luck story that you're gonna hear/ And there's really nothin' anyone can say."

In fact, some of the productions of this career phase convey a sense of Dylan feeling rather drained and desperately in need of a new source of release and consolation. This seems to explain his fascination with the double in that he explores various aspects of polarity as if looking to find a sense of wholeness or some other dimension that would complete and heal him. One of the first such examples, perhaps imitating (or some would say, parodying) Simon and Garfunkel, is Dylan's dual voices in covering "The Boxer," which at once compete and complement one another. Then, in "When I Paint My Masterpiece" he refers to "seeing double" while traveling in Rome, and in "Simple Twist of Fate," while referring to one partner as "a parrot that talks," he comments on the loss of a lover: "People tell me it's a sin/ To know and feel too much within./ I still believe she was my twin, but I lost the ring."

The image of the lost or missing twin is also explored in *Desire*'s "Oh, Sister" (parodied by Joan Baez in "Oh, Brother"), which says, "We grew up together/ From the cradle to the grave/ We died and were reborn/ And then mysteriously saved . . . Oh, sister, when I come to knock on your door,/ Don't turn away, you'll create sorrow./ Time is an ocean but it ends at the shore/ You may not see me tomorrow."[15] Issues of finding the double are also investigated in various ways in *Renaldo and Clara*, in which Dylan appears in concert wearing a mask or in whiteface. In this very innovative but underappreciated film, both of the main characters have a twofold aspect. Bob Dylan appears in the guise of guitar-strumming Renaldo while Ronnie Hawkins plays an egotistical rock star known as Bob Dylan, and Clara played by his real wife Sara is foiled by her seductive counterpart, the mysterious Woman in White played by Joan Baez. The Woman offers Renaldo "the real thing," but is criticized for being "cold" by Clara, who admits that the two are "like sisters."

All of these examples indicate that by the end of the second period, Dylan senses that salvation cannot come by holding to a strictly non-dual position. Rather, he must find paradise through a relationship with another person, force, or power, so he is intent on looking for a sense of totality with self or other, male or female, human or divine. In *Renaldo and Clara*, Dylan seems to think he is like Jesus, as a persecuted martyr, and also believes he needs to rely on Jesus who is coming again on the holy slow train, as both dimensions are evoked in his compelling rendition of Curtis Mayfield's "People Get Ready." Soon, this issue would be resolved, at least for a temporary stage.

Chapter 8

Period III (1979–1988)

From "Serving Somebody" to "Letting the Echo Decide"

OVERVIEW: CH-CH-CH-CH-CHANGES . . .

As with the previous two periods, the third main period of Dylan's career, which lasts for about ten years beginning near the end of the 1970s, encompasses two distinct but consecutive stages. The first stage, or Duality III, features Dylan's abrupt reversal and turning away from non-dualism based on his conversion to fundamental Christianity on *Slow Train Coming* released in 1979, the first of two born-again albums followed by *Saved* a year later. The explicit religious message of Duality III is reinforced by the use of a gospel sound recorded at Muscle Shoals Sound Studios in Alabama.[1] On these two recordings, Dylan switches from singing the Hellhound Blues to the Holy Blues, but without altogether losing the flavor of the former, especially on songs like "Gonna Change My Way of Thinking" on *Slow Train Coming*.

The process of Dylan totally altering his musical style to suit a new ideology that seems counter to all his prior beliefs and values is comparable to what he went through in previous stages of dualism. The protest message of Duality I used folk music recorded in New York with musicians recruited from Greenwich Village cafes as Dylan donned the image of wandering troubadour, while the family message of Duality II highlighted country music recorded in Nashville with Grand Ole Opry sessions players when Dylan became a country gentleman.

In all three phases of dualism, the creative use of a distinctive musical sound has served as an essential model and vehicle for Dylan to express his unique vision of a single higher truth. Therefore, according to one commentator's view of Duality III as seen in light of the innovative spirit that characterizes his overall career trajectory,

> Gospel was more than a way to do penance to his new found God. He used it as a medium in which he could explore his beliefs and grapple with the process of becoming a person of faith. As with his embrace of ballads, blues, and country, Dylan did not just parrot the original practitioners of the style but adapted it to fit his needs.[2]

The approach to dualism in the gospel stage may appear to have more in common with the social commitment of the stage of Duality I than with the country music stage's withdrawal from an association with political causes. At the same time, the gospel and country stages are quite similar because both represent Dylan the radical protestor moving into what seems like very conservative cultural and political territory that flies in the face of what his audience expects him to represent. Duality III, during which Dylan is frequently booed by his followers, also resembles the stage of electric rock in Non-Duality I in terms of the degree of resistance by fans to Dylan's new style of songwriting.

Christian faith so preoccupies Dylan for a couple of years that he performs only his new, born-again material in concerts featuring a gospel choir as an opening act, without any of his older songs being included in the repertoire. As with the country stage, however, after reaching an impasse with this outlook Dylan once again rather quickly begins a process of de-converting and reverting to the standpoint of non-dualism as signaled by the crossroads album, *Shot of Love* released in 1981.

The second stage of this period, or Non-Duality III, is marked by a return to relativism and disillusionment with all truth claims on *Infidels* in 1983 and *Empire Burlesque* in 1985. The recording of *Infidels* features classic folk-rock that was also used in both Non-Duality I and Non-Duality II. In contrast to the diverse styles utilized in the various stages of dualism, it seems that the non-dual phases rely on a more consistent musical sound.[3] Non-Duality III concludes with *Knocked Out Loaded* released in 1986 and *Down in the Groove* in 1988. These albums have been criticized as being of slipshod quality because the uneven style of writing and of recording covers fails to either entertain or edify. Yet, while a grab bag assortment, each record does contain at least one major original song— "Brownsville Girl" and "Silvio," respectively (both coauthored)—that is crucial for understanding Dylan's post-gospel relativist perspective.

A key aspect of period III involves issues of public perception and the reception of Dylan's music-making. After the nearly universal acclaim attained throughout period I despite some objections to the use of electric music by some folk-purists, in period II Dylan for the first time had a couple of clunkers in terms of commercial and/or critical reaction, but for the most part, his fame and celebrity were perpetuated and enhanced. Period III, however, turns out to be a phase of seemingly steady decline.[4]

The third represents Dylan's most controversial period due to the particularly rapid and extreme nature of the zigzag pattern. Following a tour in 1978 in which he characterizes himself as an "entertainer" and dresses like he is trying to mimic Neil Diamond doing a Vegas show, in 1979 he does an about-face and joins the evangelical Vineyard Fellowship, with which he actively participates in bible study groups. He becomes so enthusiastic about his faith that during the recording of *Slow Train Coming*, he tries to harangue and convert producer Jerry Wexler, who fends off the advances with a light touch by saying he is a "sixty-two year-old confirmed Jewish atheist," who just wants to make a record.

Dylan's direct involvement with religion and his explicitly theological message becomes a kind of last-straw turn-off for many hard-core fans. In the earlier stages of dualism, spirituality helped to form a backdrop either to the theme of protesting war and civil rights through warning of divine retribution in Duality I, or to an affirmation of love and family by equating the bride with goddess in Duality II. But religion per se was not necessarily a prominent feature of these phases.

Just a couple years after the gospel stage, Dylan is pictured wearing the Judaic prayer implements of a *yarmulke* and *tefillin* while praying at the Western Wall for his son's bar mitzvah, and he records "Neighborhood Bully" as a defense of victimized Israel for *Infidels*, which features a picture of Jerusalem on the back cover.[5] These twists and turns are remarkably rapid and drastic, even according to Dylan's increasingly haphazard patterns. Is he, or is he not, still born-again, or a rehabilitated Jew, or something else altogether? It seems that only his most recent pastor/guru/rabbi knows for sure.

Many observers wonder whether Dylan is so lost in a crisis of religious identity that he reaches a creative roadblock that might never let up, and thus loses a grip on quality control of his artistry. Instead of spirituality and art complementing and enhancing one another, for the first time a focus on the former overwhelms the latter. Although he had endured dead-end phases in the early 1970s, critics are putting more emphasis on Dylan's own indecisiveness and poor judgment rather than placing blame on the producer, manager, record company, or some other external factor.[6] There are complaints about seemingly incomprehensible decisions regarding production, including the homegrown quality of *Street-Legal*, which is recorded in a garage studio, and the hollow disco atmosphere of *Empire Burlesque*

Figure 8.1   Dylan at the Western Wall in Jerusalem

provided by producer Arthur Baker. A highly praised album like *Infidels*, which is seen as a valiant comeback after deterioration in songwriting caused by the excesses of the born-again orientation, is condemned for leaving the outtakes "Blind Willie McTell" and "Foot of Pride" off of the official release.[7]

The typical critics' view of this phase is expressed by Clinton Heylin in *Bob Dylan: The Recording Sessions 1960–1994*:

> The years from 1984 to 1987 represent the nadir of Dylan's studio career. The albums he came up with in those years became ever more slight, nay superficial . . . . The way that Dylan compiled *Empire Burlesque* and *Knocked Out Loaded*, the dearth of inspiration they appear to represent, and the modern sheen they share makes them two volumes with the same depressing story to tell.[8]

Recent assessments, particularly of the gospel phase, have been much more generous in constructively situating the material in historical/ biographical context.[9] From the standpoint of tracking Dylan's pathway to bargainin' for salvation, there is clearly much that is valuable in the later phases of the third period. Although the overall album production is erratic and may not live up to Dylan's high standards, intensely introspective songs like "Every Grain of Sand" and "Jokerman" point to a post-evangelical outlook that assimilates Zen-like non-dual elements and paves the way for the middle way approach achieved in the Modern Era.

GATEWAY: FROM DYLAN-AS-JESUS TO DYLAN LOVES JESUS

Following quickly on the heels of Non-Duality II, an outlook of disillusionment still infuses the gateway album *Street-Legal* released in 1978 as it starts pointing to a new, nearly opposite direction. *Street-Legal* is similar to period II's *The Basement Tapes* in returning to Blues roots for inspiration to explore the outer limits and the need to turn away from the excessive attitudes including the deep despair of non-dualism. Dylan says in a 1978 interview that *Street-Legal* captures the "thin, wild mercury sound" of *Blonde on Blonde*, generally considered his towering achievement. As on *Blonde on Blonde*, nearly half the songs either directly ("New Pony" and "Baby Stop Crying") or indirectly ("Love in Vain" and "Where Are You Tonight?") emulate Blues classics by Charley Patton, Robert Johnson, or Son House, while the other half feature Dylanesque Beat imagery at its finest, particularly on "Changing of the Guards," "Señor (Tales of Yankee Power)," and "No Time to Think."

Street-Legal may be the single most underappreciated and overlooked record in the catalogue. This is true not only for fans and critics but for Dylan, who has generally included only "Señor" in his performance repertoire over the years. Part of the problem has to do with the album's production values. The unevenly structured big band sound featuring sax solos (rather than harmonica) and distaff singers along with a back cover photo that shows Dylan wearing an Elvis-style jumpsuit (a year after The King's untimely demise) leaves critics scratching their heads. As Nigel Williamson comments, "The album can be summed up in one simple phrase—fine songs ruined by poor recording, production and mixing."[10]

Another factor affecting reception is that *Street-Legal's* release is sandwiched between the sparse folk style of *Renaldo and Clara* first shown six months before and the Vegas approach featured on *Live at Budokan* released in early 1979. With *Slow Train Coming's* gospel sound debuting later that year, these very diverse and diffused styles send mixed messages to an audience already jaded from years of watching his zigzag path about where Dylan's music-making stands on issues of private life and public persona in relation to an engagement with social affairs.

With the sound quality vastly improved by a 2003 remastered rerelease, looking back after three decades the main question from the standpoint of dialectical theory regarding *Street-Legal* is where to place its role in the unfolding of Dylan's ongoing spiritual quest. Originally distributed just a few months before his conversion took place rather abruptly in fall 1978, critics wonder about how the album fits in with the preceding phase of disillusionment and the succeeding phase of evangelism.[11] Does *Street-Legal* represent an extension or perhaps an afterthought to the stage of Non-Duality II, and thus a follow-up to the relativist worldview articulated in the songs on *Blood on the Tracks* and *Desire*? Supporting the non-dual reading is the use of complex mythical themes couched in surreal imagery featuring double-edged wordplay that depicts the angst of personal relationships and the futility of trying to reform society.

Or, are the songs on *Street-Legal* a foreshadowing or a preview or the beginning of the stage of Duality III? This reading is supported by the presence of backup vocalists—used sparingly in Duality II albums *Self-Portrait* and *New Morning*—which gives a gospel feel to a record filled with apocalyptic imagery in addition to the extensive use of biblical allusions, especially from the Four Gospels. The Hellhound Blues song "New Pony" adds the gospel chant, "How much longer?" a device widely used by bluesmen to sanctify their otherwise irreverent music.

In *Song and Dance Man III*, Michael Gray strongly recommends a Christian interpretation of the album by arguing, "The truly central album is "Street Legal" (1978)—on which every song deals with love's betrayal, deals with Dylan's being betrayed like Christ, and deals head-on with Dylan's need to abandon woman's love." Furthermore, Gray maintains:

> "Street Legal" is one of Dylan's most important cohesive and complex albums—and it warns us, as pointedly as art ever should, of what is to come. It prepares us for Dylan's conversion to Christianity just as plainly as the end of "John Wesley Harding" prepares us for the country music of "Nashville Skyline" ... "Street Legal" brings it all together—Dylan the consistent moralist, Dylan the writer who draws heavily on the Bible, Dylan caught in the struggle between the flesh and the spirit, Dylan ending his relationship with Sara, Dylan the betrayed victim both of what he sees as Sara's love-in-vain and of all of us.[12]

According to Gray's analysis, *Street-Legal* marks a dramatic transition from Dylan's final disappointment in viewing love for ex-wife Sara (divorce proceedings were completed in 1977) as the key to redemption to his new-found devotion to Jesus as the one true source of salvation. Gray sees the album's role as being parallel to that of *John Wesley Harding*, which gives an account of Dylan's conversion to dualism, rather than, as I have suggested, to *The Basement Tapes*, which plays a more preliminary and tentative role in this process of shifting viewpoints from non-dualism to dualism.

I fully concur with Gray's recovery of the neglected importance of *Street-Legal*, which eloquently depicts deceit and betrayal in a world of conflict and illusion. I argue, however, that seeing it as the first Christian album is a premature conclusion. The shift to evangelism occurs soon, of course, but not yet on this album. Instead, *Street-Legal* should be viewed as a powerful expression by someone who experiences the depths of the void and emerges with an overwhelming need to forsake non-dualism because it has led to the dead-end and distress of profound uncertainty and regret. But this gateway album fails to reach a conclusive goal of attaining salvation, and claiming this might well seem forced or hypocritical in the context of the album's honesty about the meaning of angst.

Betrayed by a kiss

Like "Shelter from the Storm," *Street-Legal* finds Dylan occupying the "wilderness" of being dismayed and disillusioned. This is consistent with a subtheme of Duality II which suggests that he is Christ-like in his suffering as one who wears "a crown of thorns" while others are gambling for his clothes in "a little hilltop village." This motif is reinforced in "No Time to Think," which says Dylan is "betrayed by a kiss." On both *Blood on the Tracks* and *Street-Legal*, Dylan is looking for redemption within the realm of humanity through self-discovery, love, or social awareness rather than by means of a higher power, and it will take a significant leap of faith to bring his quest to the gates of worshipping Jesus, or to transition from the angelic to the evangelic.

In the opening song on *Street-Legal*, "Changing of the Guards," Dylan's perpetual concerns with reforming social affairs and resolving romantic entanglements are very much intertwined. A lover inspires the narrator to embark on a protest campaign against the devastating effects of "destruction in the ditches" that are manipulated by "renegade priests and treacherous young witches." These nefarious forces must either brace for "elimination" or muster the courage to accept inevitable change. The final verse of the song promises that "Peace will come/ With tranquility and splendor on the wheels of fire/But will bring us no reward when her false idols fall," however, this seems to be meant with irony.

In several love songs on the album, Dylan declares that he is weary and regretful and suffers from a "low-down feeling," and in engaging an estranged romantic partner who is "two-faced" and "double-dealing" he realizes that reconciliation will likely never happen, much "Like the sound of one hand clappin.'" The mood of *Street-Legal* reflects feeling disheartened by oppression and violence, which leads Dylan to "the brink" on

"No Time to Think," perhaps either of destruction or radical alteration. Feeling stranded and abandoned, Dylan wishes that nobody would try to intrude upon the darkness of his solitude, which provides at least some degree of consolation, unless they can "understand my pain." This emphasis on the value of reclusion is a prototypical non-dual image that recalls the declaration of isolation in the final verses of both "Desolation Row" and "Tangled Up in Blue," as well as Zen Buddhist eremitic traditions. Yet it is apparent that Dylan does not want to feel alone and isolated any longer, and is crying out for more constructive relationships.

The concluding stanza of "Changing of the Guards" seems to offer a promise of attaining "tranquility and splendor on the wheels of fire," an apocalyptic image that recalls Daniel 7.9 and Ezekiel 10.6,[13] but the effort is left incomplete and confused. This is more the case in the south-of-the border conspiratorial atmosphere of "Señor," where experiencing "the real thing" of hostility and deception makes one wish it were all but a dream. This song, which asks, "Señor do you know where we're headin'?/ Lincoln County Road or Armageddon?," seems to signal that a shift from Non-Duality to a new form of Duality is about to take place. The lead query hints that "Only a God can save us," as modern philosopher Martin Heidegger, who was known for his non-theological existentialist thought, said in an interview shortly before his death.

In contrast to an important subtheme of the stage of Non-Duality II whereby Dylan sought to find refuge in a complementary double or twofold image in a way that stretched the boundaries of non-dualism, "Where Are You Tonight?," highlights impasse and disappointment by saying, "I fought with my twin, that enemy within, 'til both of us fell by the way." In evoking Robert Johnson lyrics Dylan further complains, "Horseplay and disease is killing me by degrees while the law looks the other way." This song ends with the bittersweet verse that sums up the outlook of *Street-Legal*:

> There's a new day at dawn and I've finally arrived.
> If I'm there in the morning baby, you'll know I've survived.
> I can't believe it, I can't believe I'm alive,
> But without you it doesn't seem right.
> Oh, where are you tonight?

Recognizing the failure of love to provide a fulfillment of the spirit or to offer salvation and finally giving up clinging to that pathway compels Dylan to face the need to find a higher truth, beyond the realm of humanity. I agree in part with Gray's analysis of this passage, which emphasizes that the last verse of the song—and of the album—announces Dylan's final arrival at rebirth. "He has made it at last," Gray states, and "There is no end-ing on any note of glee or superiority. There is only a gladness which Dylan admits to, while admitting also that it is lessened by the final loss of love."[14] Again, however, I disagree with Gray's conclusion that "'Street Legal' [is] … surely a charting of Dylan's move to embracing Christ,"[15] because in "We Better Talk This Over" he proclaims, "I'm exiled and you can't convert me." There is as yet no clear path articulated.

Struggling to transcend feeling lost in the midst of betrayal and despair, through which kind of ideological vehicle might one expect Dylan to find himself? As discussed in Chapter 1, a crucial turning point regarding the respective roles of Eastern and Western religious influences is soon to occur. Over a decade of Dylan's flirting with Asian mysticism as a source of inspiration will suddenly come to an end in the wake of his conversion to fundamental Christianity.[16] In this context, I appreciate Gray's insightful analysis of the religious and cultural significance of a seemingly innocuous lyric in the final verse of "True Love Tends to Forget" on *Street-Legal*: "You belong to me baby without a doubt/ Don't forsake me baby, don't sell me out/ Don't keep me knockin' about/ From Mexico to Tibet." According to Gray:

> Dylan is here using the Mexico–Tibet see-saw to stand for two choices he can no longer accept: the warm, southern world of the sensuous and a cold, eastern, religious asceticism. Dylan knows he must reject, and soon, both his lover and the fashionable Zen-maintenance so popular as a ref-uge for displaced rich Americans, neither of which offers a way forward to the saving of his soul.[17]

FIRST STAGE: GOSPEL/EVANGELICAL (DUALITY III)

In the first stage of period III, *Slow Train Coming* resembles *John Wesley Harding* in providing narratives that tell the story of Dylan's (re-)conver-sion to dualism, and *Saved* is close to *Nashville Skyline* in carrying a com-mitment to evangelism to an extreme form of expression. "Precious Angel," the second song on *Slow Train Coming*, completes the rejection of Buddhism indicated on *Street-Legal*, and also dismisses all views stemming from other theological or indigenous ritual orientations. A necessary corollary of fundamentalism is an exclusivist outlook which foregoes any commitment to non-Christian belief.

Because of this one-dimensional focus, evangelical Christianity might seem the unlikeliest of ideologies by which Dylan, the wandering Jewish troubadour and postmodern rock icon who once said "When you got nothing, you got nothing to lose" and "Nietzsche never wore an umpire's suit," would find solace. Therefore, it is easy to see why the shock of learning of this remarkable development, which may seem like the ultimate flip-flop, leaves some fans deeply disappointed with Dylan's incessant zigzag course.

In coming to terms with the various meanings of Christian teachings in Dylan's career, it is important to recognize that Jesus' life and teachings were cited in Duality I protests songs, "With God on Our Side," "Masters of War," and "The Times They Are A-Changin'," as a mirror of justice and model for righteous behavior. However, just four years before *Slow Train Coming*, in the *Blood on the Tracks* outtake "Up to Me" Dylan equated the Sermon on the Mount with what a broken glass reflects, putting the teachings of Jesus on the level of earthly discourse in Zen-like fashion. But in the gospel stage, Christian doctrines are seen as the literal embodiment of absolute truth as Dylan elevates biblical sayings to the status of divine revelation, which alone provides the route to salvation, by asking rhetorically: "Will I ever learn that there'll be no peace, that the war won't cease/ Until He returns?"

In retrospect, Dylan's temporary sojourn in the realm of born-again faith makes a great deal of sense for the way it contributes to the dialectical movement of his overall approach to spirituality. Nobody ever expected to see him grinning like a country gentleman on the cover of *Nashville Skyline*, another radical reversal of cultural roles prompted by a dualistic conversion exactly ten years before. Similarly, the gospel stage is an important way for Dylan to find a way of making peace with what would appear to be his natural "other" by experiencing dualism in its most extreme form in order to reject it and continue the process of finding a middle path.

Holy slow train

The gospel-stage music is a very rich phase of creativity in that, over the course of just a couple of years, Dylan composes more than three dozen songs, including a number of important tunes that were later or never released. There are several areas of continuity and discontinuity between Dylan's evangelism and the spiritual approach evident in earlier phases. One element of consistency involves the variety of styles used in his gospel music, which is by no means monolithic or one-sided. To cite a few examples from *Slow Train Coming* and *Saved*, these lyrics fall into a few different groupings that are more or less in accord with the typology of Basic Bob, especially when we consider that there is a significant overlap of social commentary with topical protest themes:

- Social—"Gotta Serve Somebody," "Slow Train," "When You Gonna Wake Up?"
- Spiritual—"When He Returns," "What Can I Do for You?," "In the Garden"
- Blues—"Gonna Change My Way of Thinking," "Solid Rock," "Pressing On"
- Romance—"Precious Angel," "I Believe in You," "Covenant Woman"

The diverse styles indicate that although Dylan's message reflects a single-minded commitment to faith, he expresses a renewed interest and appreciation for the moral foundations of both sociopolitical issues and personal affairs. In borrowing heavily from Woody Guthrie's "Little Black Train" for both the opening song on *Slow Train Coming*, "Gotta Serve Somebody," and the title cut, for example, Dylan shows how he is able to integrate a variety of traditional folk influences into his approach to gospel music.

A second area of compatibility between Dylan's born-again mentality and his previous attitudes involves the way he views himself as a misunderstood hero (or antihero). In "I Believe in You" Dylan expresses concern for his outcast status, and "Property of Jesus" on *Shot of Love* he bemoans, "He's the property of Jesus/ Resent him to the bone/ You got something better/ You've got a heart of stone." Although a parallel point about feeling estranged was made much earlier in "It Ain't Me, Babe" and "Positively Fourth Street," nothing distanced Dylan from his fan/critic base more than evangelism. Yet he relishes the sense of heroism through martyrdom this alienation creates. As a card-carrying loner, so to speak, Dylan wants to "stop being influenced by fools" and to be sure that he "Ain't Gonna Go to Hell for Nobody," as in the title of an outtake song, even if taking this stance seems to enhance a sense of Dylan-as-Jesus more than of Dylan worshipping Jesus.

A third point of continuity is Dylan's extensive use throughout the gospel stage of the ideal female image as a model to be celebrated for serving as a vehicle that at once facilitates and inspires his religious conversion. According to "Precious Angel," no doubt addressed to an African–American romantic partner with whom he feels solidarity since both his ancestors and hers suffered but were eventually released from slavery:

> You're the queen of my flesh, girl, you're my woman, you're my delight,
> You're the lamp of my soul, girl, and you torch up the night.
> But there's violence in the eyes, girl, so let us not be enticed
> On the way out of Egypt, through Ethiopia, to the judgment hall of Christ.

Furthermore, in the tradition of *Song of Songs* and other religious poetry which mixes the rhetoric of romantic passion with the biblical notion of *agape* or divine love, "Covenant Woman" says,

> I've been broken, shattered like an empty cup.
> I'm just waiting on the Lord to rebuild and fill me up
> And I know He will do it 'cause He's faithful and He's true,
> He must have loved me so much to send me someone as fine as you.

This represents a new outlook that alters the approach, evident during a prolonged cycle that encompassed Non-Duality I ("Visions of Johanna" and "Sad-Eyed Lady of the Lowlands"), Duality II ("Wedding Song"), and Non-Duality II ("Shelter from the Storm"), which saw spiritual belief as a by-product of the "worship" of a human goddess with salvific powers. In that context, the female image reflects the power and is in some sense considered equal to the divine, but in the gospel stage she is a conduit for receiving blessing and is clearly separate from the heavenly being.

A fourth type of inner consistency is Dylan's focus on apocalyptic moral judgment, probably first expressed in "A Hard Rain's A-Gonna Fall" and "When the Ship Comes In," and continued during period two in "Three Angels" and "Black Diamond Bay." *Slow Train Coming* in particular brings out Dylan's dark, brooding reflections which suggest that only divine retribution is able to overcome the chaos and confusion of social transgressions. It is particularly interesting that the gospel phase affords Dylan a new vantage point on political issues, and in several songs on *Slow Train Coming* he unleashes a devastating critique of a vast array of forces of hypocrisy and corruption in society at large. This linkage is highlighted in *I'm Not There* when the same actor plays in both the protest phase and gospel phase by singing both "The Lonesome Death of Hattie Carroll" before black civil rights protesters at a small rally in Mississippi and "Pressing On" in front of a small church assembly of mostly white evangelicals in Los Angeles.

Dylan's linked protest-gospel phases show that every type of person and societal force including seemingly opposite aspects, like the rich and powerful along with the poor and disenfranchised, are encompassed by the same moral principles. Also included in divine judgment are "Sheiks walkin' around like kings," who control foreign oil that dominates America, and domestic "masters of the proposition," who rob Americans blind through the legal system (in the era of California's Proposition 13 tax revolt), along with the false ideology of Karl Marx and the manipulative diplomacy of Henry Kissinger. Dylan reflects that "Jefferson [is] turning over in his grave" because of the decline of "brotherly love," and declares that "All non-believers and men stealers talkin' in the name of religion" will ultimately pay the price for having contributed to his "loved ones turning into puppets." Corrupt politicians and preachers, as well as all those who do not reform must invariably be held accountable for their transgressions.

His gospel music reminds us that Dylan probably never shared the utopian vision of many of those who were inspired by him in the 1960s, especially the pacifists or millenarians of the peace movement. According to the prayer-like "When He Returns": "He unleashed His power at an unknown hour that no one knew," and "like a thief in the night, He'll replace wrong with right/ When He returns." Rather than trying to analyze the variable ups and downs that occupy the ordinary level of sociopolitical interaction, Dylan evokes God's judgment based on an eternal ethical standard that will inevitably lead to an *Endzeit*, either in a literal or metaphorical sense (which of course could be an important distinction).

In seeking to transcend differences based on political leanings by pointing to their spiritual foundations, as mentioned in Chapter 3, Dylan frequently uses the image of the train as a metaphor rich in historical and cultural symbolism for the route to salvation. The train is one of the most powerful images in Blues songs where it represents both freedom and constraint and is at once disquieting and comforting through "images of light, darkness, motion, and loneliness."[18] It was evoked by the *Highway 61 Revisited* liner notes reference to the "holy slow train" and the title of *Blood on the Tracks*, which highlights the bloody train of personal and national historical conflicts that leaves its dark residue on the tracks of time. The "slow train comin' up round the bend" holds a double-edged quality of signaling the possibility for redemption as well as the inevitability of retribution. While neither of these aspects is directly linked to a particular ideological viewpoint or policy position, for Dylan reckoning with the interlocking quality of these aspects is crucial for an understanding of eschatology. The image of the train that can lead to the religious goal, but only for those who have earned it and are deserving of the reward, will resurface in *Time Out of Mind*'s "Tryin' to Get to Heaven."

Lost or found?

While the tone of moralistic social protest that infuses *Slow Train Coming* recalls the early phase of Duality I and is also not so distant from Non-Duality I, the gospel stage is distinct in its emphasis on the full-scale repudiation of false beliefs other than Christian faith. Finding truth in fundamental Christianity belittles all other outlooks as unrighteous, so that Dylan condemns "counterfeit philosophies [that] have polluted all of your thoughts," in addition to the trend to heed "Spiritual advisors and gurus to guide your every move,/ Instant inner peace and every step you take has got to be approved."

In Dylan's view of the gospel, which is based on bible study fellowships in southern California, "Truth is an arrow and the gate is narrow that it passes through," and negotiating this path requires a strict adherence to dualism because:

- "it may be the devil or it may be the Lord/ But you're gonna have to serve somebody" ("Gotta Serve Somebody").
- "Ya either got faith or ya got unbelief and there ain't no neutral ground" ("Precious Angel").
- "Sometimes I feel so low-down and disgusted/ Can't help but wonder what's happenin' to my companions,/ Are they lost or are they found, have they counted the cost it'll take to bring down/ All their earthly principles they're gonna have to abandon?" ("Slow Train").
- "Jesus said, 'Be ready,/ For you know not the hour in which I come.'/ He said, 'He who is not for Me is against Me,'/ Just so you know where He's coming from" ("Gonna Change My Way of Thinking").
- "God don't make no promises that He don't keep./ You got some big dreams, baby, but in order to dream you gotta still be asleep" ("When You Gonna Wake Up?").

Therefore, the most notable feature of the evangelical stage representing a departure from Dylan's earlier dualistic phases is the degree of the strictness of the Either/Or worldview for which there are a number of irresolvable polarities:

Condemnation	vs.	**Salvation**
Devil		Lord
Unbelief		Faith
Lost		Found
Unprepared		Ready
Unremorseful		Repentant
Asleep		Awake

The exclusive and divided Either/Or worldview in which one side of the equation is antithetical and repugnant to the other side that is valorized and celebrated seems averse to Zen's inclusive and holistic Neither/Nor worldview which encompasses all oppositions in an incomprehensible unity. Modern Japanese Buddhist philosopher Nishida Kitaro has referred to ultimate reality or the "logic of Nothingness" as the "self-identity of absolute contradictions." An important implication is that the conventional polarities that support Christian faith like time and eternity, sin and grace, or human and divine do not obtain because they dissolve into inseparability and oneness.

However, the difference between one worldview based on distinction and another based on non-distinction is not so clear-cut for several reasons. Zen Buddhism traditionally has argued that there are two levels of reality. One is the everyday standpoint, in which dichotomies between truth and untruth, transcendence and the mundane, theory and practice do, indeed, apply. The second level is for those who have realized the truth and can therefore discard all of these distinctions, like the way a traveler to a distant shore does away with the vehicle that carried him across the river to the new destination; the raft was an essential tool that becomes a burden once the new locale is reached.

The Zen approach is comparable to the mystical branch of Christian thought, which seems to influence Dylan's view that also emphasizes making a distinction between those who have gained true knowledge of reality, or gnosis, and those who are incapable of that level of insight. A key passage is Matthew 13.13, in which Jesus responds to a question about why he teaches in a different way to disciples and non-disciples: "Therefore I speak to [non-disciples] in parables; because while seeing they do not see, and while hearing they do not hear, nor do they understand." Dylan alludes to this passage, which is echoed in Luke and Mark, in "When He Returns": "For all those who have eyes and all those who have ears/ It is only He who can reduce me to tears./ Don't you cry and don't you die and don't you burn." He then suggests that this special level of knowledge is the primary inspiration for his own spiritual renewal: "How long can I listen to the lies of prejudice?/ How long can I stay drunk on fear out in the wilderness?/ Can I cast it aside, all this loyalty and this pride?"

Although in some ways the experience described here based on Duality seems to have a theological basis that is worlds apart from the Zen meditative standpoint, the result of "casting aside" one's weaknesses and limitations to achieve a higher mystical vision is quite similar to the goal of Zen. According to Zen master Dogen, the basis of enlightenment is precisely that of "casting off" the trials and tribulations that plague body and mind. The Japanese word for this process, *datsuraku* 脱落, is the term that is also used for the natural acts of a snake shedding its skin, a caterpillar's metamorphosis to a butterfly, or a tree dropping its withered leaves during the autumn. It signals a crucial turning point to a new form of being, and in a religious context highlights the meeting point of self-created and other-powered spiritual transformation. Thus, within the heart of the dualistic gospel stage, there is much in Dylan's outlook that has an affinity with non-dualistic Zen thought.

Saved or not

The two born-again albums *Slow Train Coming* and *Saved*, which are parallel to the relation in the stage of Duality II between *John Wesley Harding*'s moral parables and *Nashville Skyline*'s simple affirmation, are sometimes treated as a package. Released just about nine months apart, many of the songs on these records were written and first performed live at around the same time before and during the concert series of fall 1979. One difference is that *Slow Training Coming* has an Old Testament feel in emphasizing the wrath of an unforgiving divine law, whereas *Saved* provides a New Testament atmosphere in emphasizing forgiveness and compassion, although there are crossover songs on both albums.

Nashville Skyline quickly gained acceptance and generated one of Dylan's biggest hit singles with "Lay, Lady, Lay," despite or perhaps because of the shock value of using a duet version of "Girl from the North Country" performed with Johnny Cash as the opening number. On *Saved*, the lead song covering "A Satisfied Mind" does not work nearly as well, and this album proves to be one of Dylan's duds both commercially and critically. This precipitates a long cycle of disappointing sales and reviews that continue throughout this decade and the next. Seen in light of the dialectical theory, however, *Saved* is valuable because of its bold, unabashed commitment to dualism expressed in several compelling songs. These include "Solid Rock," with its core wordplay linking religion and contemporary music through a dynamic rhythm; the poignant lyricism of a true devotee expressed in "What Can I Do for You?" and "Covenant Woman"; the simple yet forceful proclamations of faith in "Pressing On" and "In the Garden"; and the Judgment Day exhortations of "Are You Ready?," the second song on the album whose title reflects an inquiry.

Although much of the criticism of *Saved* is surely unwarranted, there is no doubt that a lesson is to be learned from the fact that two of the first three—and with *Shot of Love*, three of the first four—albums of period III are generally considered unsuccessful. Dylan fans and critics expect ambiguity and obscurity in his lyrics, but also prefer to find an underlying thematic coherence and consistency on his albums. Pitfalls occur when the viewpoint is expressed in an overly vague and unclear manner as in the case of *Street-Legal*, which is ambivalent and is not quite able to project a message of self-transformation, or in an overly clear-cut and obvious manner as with the overt didacticism of *Saved*. On the latter album, Dylan demonstrates that he is spiritually satisfied but the music's limitation is its uncharacteristic one-sidedness. According to Michael Gray, Dylan tends "to assert and argue and declaim but he has hardly bothered anywhere . . . to fulfill the more important tasks of the artist: he has not created worlds here, he has only argued about them."[19]

CROSSROADS: FROM DUALITY III TO NON-DUALITY III

The key issue from the perspective of analyzing Dylan's religiosity is whether and to what extent he could ever return to an appropriate amount of Dylanesque material, in which his spiritual strivings and passions are cogent and compelling but his underlying motives and commitments are cryptic and puzzling enough to stimulate listeners to read between the lines. To be Dylanesque means to inspire but not to instruct, to be discerning but not dogmatic, and to explore but without ever expecting exactitude. Dylan's best work is like an ongoing Rorschach test that allows the audience to interpret it as they see fit.

One commentator has characterized Dylan's songs as "a kaleidoscope of observations and impressions about life," while also noting that "Dylan knew how to go knockin' on heaven's door, and in general, there was a certain God-consciousness in the underpinnings of his songs that were full of Biblical imagery."[20] Furthermore:

> The [songs] spoke about keeping to your true North and what happens when you don't, aligning with your vision and your dreams, and about being real with yourself and your feelings. . . . Dylan seemed to operate from the inside out, instead of the outside in. He had an artistic integrity that made him follow his inspiration wherever it took him. It didn't mean that he never admitted to getting confused, which he did quite often in his lyrics. But he saw the confusion and the clarity and the hope and the despair as all part of some very big picture, and he accepted it all and tried to squeeze all of it into his songs.

Would Dylan ever be able to recapture this open-ended, expansive approach to spirituality that allows room for accepting chaos and confusion, while also building on and integrating the stronger suits of the gospel stage, such as the courage and conviction of moral rectitude?

There were considerable differences in the way the crossroads took place in the first two periods. In the case of the very compressed time frame of period I, the transition from Duality I to Non-Duality I transpired practically overnight. The release of *Another Side of Bob Dylan* was sandwiched between *The Times They Are A-Changin'*, which consisted almost entirely of topical protest music based on divine retribution, and *Bringing It All Back Home*, which contained social commentary evoking relativism without a specific political focus. In the case of period II, the process of shifting took a much longer time, stretching from *New Morning*, which hinted at abandoning family life as the single truth, through *Planet Waves* released over three years later, which continued the process of change by embracing non-dualism in a way that was made more emphatic on *Blood on the Tracks*. Period III resembles the second period in that the transition away from gospel belief is not such a quick or clearly marked path. It involves fits and starts, and internal zigzags, as Dylan moves back and forth between a lingering acceptance and distancing from Christian faith while pursuing a broader vision of spiritual fulfillment.

The function of *Shot of Love* as a crossroads album is akin to that of *Another Side of Bob Dylan* in period I and to *New Morning* and *Planet Waves* in period II. However, the single main song that represents the quintessential statement of retreat from evangelism and shows Dylan saying he is "not buying it" to the rigid dualism of the gospel stage comes a couple of years after the beginning of the transition. "Tight Connection to My Heart" is originally recorded as "Someone's Got a Hold of My Heart" in April 1983 with a video shot in Tokyo for *Infidels* but is released two years later on *Empire Burlesque*. It plays a role comparable to that of "My Back Pages" in enunciating in its final verse a casting aside of the born-again ideology: "What looks large from a distance,/ Close up ain't never that big/ Never could learn to drink that blood/ And call it wine." "Trust Yourself," which delivers a strong affirmation of the path of Self Power, is also included on this album.

It is important to note that after the declaration of his departure from dualism, explicit Christian imagery by no means disappears and, in fact, biblical citations remain a viable factor in Dylan's songwriting. Furthermore, the evangelical song, "Death is Not the End," also recorded for *Infidels* in 1983, is not released until *Down in the Groove* five years later, thus giving the impression that Dylan does not lose interest in delivering an evangelical message. This gets reinforced by concert performances of "In the Garden" and other gospel songs, some of which are covers of Holy Blues standards. Nevertheless, the exclusivist commitment to fundamental Christianity and the unambiguous style of expression on *Saved* is no longer in vogue.

For many reviewers, *Shot of Love* is considered the third and final album in the born-again series, since at least six of its ten songs continue the gospel theme, including the title cut, "Property of Jesus," "Watered Down

Love," "The Groom's Still Waiting at the Altar," "Dead Man, Dead Man," and "Summertime." In that sense, the cup is more than half full with evangelism. But given that many of these lyrics mark a return to constructive ambiguity and mythical imagery, along with the presence of four non-gospel songs, "Heart of Mine," "Trouble," "Lenny Bruce," and "Every Grain of Sand," I am designating *Shot of Love* as representing the crossroads of period III. In addition, two prominent outtake songs play an intermediary role in delivering an essentially non-dual message with dualistic allusions, "Caribbean Wind" and "Angelina." According to the latter song, the narrator who repudiates "the crowd/ Worshipping a god with the body of a woman well endowed/ And the head of a hyena" is left "Begging God for mercy and weepin' in unholy places."

Shot of Love is crucial for the transition from dualism to non-dualism because it points the way toward the relativistic universe that is vividly depicted on *Infidels*. Several of what are considered gospel songs seem to reveal a moderately post-evangelical direction. For example, "Watered Down Love" evokes "the gentle, almost Zen precepts of Chapter 13 of I Corinthians,"[21] which speaks of the power of love prevailing over faith by protecting, trusting, hoping, and preserving.

Both "Shot of Love" and "The Groom's Still Waiting at the Altar" bring Dylan's songwriting back to the "world of contradiction, polity, violence and catastrophe, seething with nebulous omens and hopeless ambiguity."[22] According to the latter song's analysis of society, "Cities on fire, phones out of order,/ They're killing nuns and soldiers, there's fighting on the border." Despite the gospel implications of these lyrics, which emphasize the need for *agape* as well as the multiple ways people fall short and alienate the "Groom" (aka Jesus), the lyrics are filled with doubt and trepidation rather than a forced sense of security.

The non-gospel songs take this trend one step further by their immersion in the realm in which the death of St. Augustine, according to Dylan's late 1960s song, means that there are no traditional martyrs in the contemporary world. On the other hand, Dylan finds that there are secular heroes, as depicted in "Lenny Bruce" (and also in "Blind Willie McTell," another outtake from *Infidels* a couple of years later), who serve as models of fortitude and integrity that provides inspiration and moral support just as substantial as theological belief. "Sick comedian" Lenny Bruce, who was "More of an outlaw than you ever were," as Dylan tells himself while playing piano chords that borrow heavily from gospel rhythms, is celebrated for being a maverick or rebel who flaunted conventions: "Lenny Bruce is dead but he didn't commit any crime/ He just had the insight to rip off the lid before its time." In reaping unfortunate consequences for his scathing social criticism, he became a secular saint as a suffering servant in the everyday world.

One way of reading "Lenny Bruce" is that Dylan views the martyred comedian as more Jesus-like in the sacrifices made for the sake of principle than the singer himself, and also as someone whose all-too-human stage presence vitiates the need for devotion to a higher power. "They said that he was sick 'cause he didn't play by the rules," Dylan laments. "He just showed the wise men of his day to be nothing more than fools . . . . He fought a war on a battlefield where every victory hurts./ Lenny Bruce was bad, he was the brother that you never had." Similarly, Dylan celebrates Willie McTell, also known as Georgia Sam, as the ultimate bluesman who never made it big and always remained humble and true to his craft. McTell is also evoked in "Highway 61 Revisited" and "Gonna Change My Way of Thinking," plus several songs he made famous, especially "Delia," that have been performed by Dylan.

In his contemporary hymn "Every Grain of Sand" about the "time of my confession, in the hour of my deepest need," Dylan begins a cycle of deeply spiritual songs produced in the 1980s in which biblical teachings and citations are prevalent, but are no longer viewed as the revelation of a single truth as in the gospel stage. Instead, they are internalized in terms of an ongoing process of self-discovery launched against a cultural landscape filled with multiple, fragmented relative truths.

In the song's first verse, Dylan uses the symbolism of flowers and weeds to comment inspirationally on the inner struggle to come to terms with the impact of karma on spiritual life: "The flowers of indulgence and the weeds of yesteryear,/ Like criminals they have choked the breath of conscience and good cheer." Dylan suggests that the indulgent flowers and karmic weeds are not obstacles so much as challenges to be overcome—akin to what Zen discourse refers to as the "Gateless Gate" (*mumonkan* 無門間) to nirvana—even as he hears "ancient footsteps like the motion of the sea" and is "hanging in the balance of the reality of man."[23]

A fascinating comparison can be made with "Genjokoan," perhaps Zen master Dogen's most famous philosophical essay originally written as a letter to a lay disciple. The opening passage describes the need to reconcile the polarity of form or phenomena, that is, daily existence, with emptiness or the manifestation of enlightenment. After delineating the overcoming of oppositions such as delusion and realization, life and death, or sentient beings and buddhas, Dogen remarks, "Weeds still spring up to our dismay, and flowers still fall to our chagrin." For Dogen, these flowers fade while weeds proliferate as the Buddha Way "leaps clear of abundance and scarcity," and of all polarity. He thereby acknowledges the continuing presence of *samsara* or the frailty of impermanence, and the causal effects of desire and aversion that exist within the efforts to realize the transcendental state of nirvana. To put it in Western terms, heaven and hell are never so far apart.

In the even-numbered verses (second, fourth, sixth) of "Every Grain of Sand," Dylan proclaims that "every leaf that trembles," "every hair [that] is numbered," and "every sparrow falling" are like "every grain of sand." This emphasis on the value of each and every particular element no matter how seemingly miniscule or irrelevant is no doubt influenced by biblical teaching such as Psalm 139.17-18 as well as Matthew 10.28-31 and Luke 12.6-7. The image of sand recalls the naturalism found in "Tomorrow is a Long Time," "Lay Down Your Weary Tune," and "Chimes of Freedom." It is also similar to the opening stanza of William Blake's *Songs of Innocence* published in the early 1800s: "To see a World in a Grain of Sand/ And a Heaven in a Wild Flower/ Hold Infinity in the palm of your hand/ And Eternity in an hour."[24]

Despite the dualistic background in Dylan's reference to seeing "the Master's hand . . . In the fury of the moment," his message is comparable to a pantheistic poem Dogen composed on his return from the remote mountains to the capital city of Kyoto to seek medical care shortly before his death, which in turn reminds us of the opening lines of Walt Whitman's *Song of Myself*: "Like a blade of grass,/ My frail body/ Treading the path to Kyoto,/ Seeming to wander/ Amid the cloudy mist on Kinobe Pass."[25] The comparison with Christian mysticism, American Transcendentalism, and Zen Buddhist thought strongly suggests that Dylan's post-gospel religiosity is striving for a balance of the forces of dualism and non-dualism.

SECOND STAGE: CONVERSION DISILLUSIONMENT (NON-DUALITY III)

In the early 1980s, Dylan leaves behind but never fully departs from gospel belief, but by the time of *Infidels* he is again recording and touring folk-rock music minus distaff backup singers.[26] As with *Shot of Love*, the *Infidels* sessions produce a remarkable number of original songs, including several important numbers that are released either on subsequent albums or on *The Bootleg Series: Volume 3*. The official version of *Infidels* includes eight songs that show Dylan making a new dramatic foray into the world of chaos and uncertainty, and doubt and despair, without any hesitation or reservation about taking this on through an authentic commitment and resolve to maintain autonomy.

Several songs demonstrate Dylan's most sustained interest in topical issues since the early 1960s, including "Union Sundown," which is a kind of update of "North Country Blues" in focusing on how the effects of globalization undermine American workers. Other numbers place overt political implications in a theological context that reveals the continuing influence of Duality III, including the antiwar anthems "License to Kill" and "Man of Peace," as well as the ironically titled, pro-Israeli message of "Neighborhood Bully." Two other songs express the mixed-up confusion of romance that encompasses the apocalyptic nuances of "I and I," which says "The world could come to an end tonight," and the profound degree of disillusionment in "Don't Fall Apart on Me Tonight," which notes that "the streets are filled with vipers/ Who've lost all ray of hope,/ You know, it ain't even safe no more/ In the palace of the Pope."

The nightingale's tune

A song that takes *Infidels* in another important direction is "Sweetheart Like You," which appears on the surface to be a romantic putdown by saying, "You can be known as the most beautiful woman/ Who ever crawled across cut glass to make a deal." But at its core, this is a highly confessional, post-evangelical lyric. Dylan makes a subtle use of biblical allusions so that the meaning of the song's message is as ambiguous as Nietzsche's proclamation that "God is dead," which could be seen as either a blessing or a curse. The song opens with the boss having "gone North . . . after sundown," which may refer to the resurrection of Jesus or to the desertion of humanity by divine forces. It continues with, "They say in your father's house, there's many mansions," a reference to John 14.2 that also alludes to medieval mystic Teresa of Avila, but comments sardonically, "Each one of them got a fireproof floor."

In the remaining verses, Dylan is either critiquing himself in the second person or turning his attack on society symbolized by the so-called sweetheart. He challenges all those who resort to patriotism as "the last refuge/ To which a scoundrel clings," or to extortion since big thievery is rewarded when "they make you king" while a petty criminal is put in jail. In "Sweetheart Like You," Dylan sees the situation of humanity as having "only one step down from here, baby, It's called the land of permanent bliss," and he asks rhetorically either of himself or his audience, "What's a sweetheart like you doin' in a dump like this?" Nearly a decade after, "Up to Me" claims proudly, "And the harmonica around my neck, I blew it for you, free,/ No one else could play that tune,/ You know it was up to me," "Sweetheart Like You" declares that you "Got to play your harp until your lips bleed," thus transforming the pathos of dualistic self-sacrifice to the mockery of non-dualistic self-criticism.

The signature song of *Infidels* is the intensely introspective "Jokerman," one of the most important lyrics in Dylan's entire career for understanding the delicate interaction between Duality and Non-Duality in the post-gospel phase. Since it is the opening number of the album that follows "Every Grain of Sand," which is the finale song of *Shot of Love*, the two songs can be seen in tandem. Together, they reveal post-gospel Dylan seeking the middle path of spirituality that integrates seemingly opposite perspectives. Whereas "Every Grain of Sand" uses non-dual, especially naturalist imagery in support of a dualistic message that God has a master plan for each and every person, "Jokerman" uses dualistic notions in referencing "casting your bread" from Ecclesiastes and "the Book of Leviticus and Deuteronomy" for the sake of bearing an essentially non-dualistic message about one who also learns from the "law of the jungle and the sea," but is "Resting in the fields, far from the turbulent space."

The meaning of the title is delightfully vague and thus open to several possible interpretations. It could represent an extension of the Outsider persona of the joker, drifter, Alias, or Jack of Hearts who is "born with a snake in both of your fists while a hurricane was blowing," and who challenges but stays free from the confines of ordinary society. Or Jokerman, who is "Friend to the martyr, a friend to the woman of shame,/ You look into the fiery furnace, see the rich man without any name," could be the great liberator who exposes the flaws and therefore functions as a kind of modern-day savior. Another implication is that "Jokerman" suggests an Antichrist who "is going to Sodom and Gomorrah/ But what do you care? Ain't nobody there who would want to marry your sister." Perhaps this is Dylan's devastating self-criticism for his own foibles and weaknesses in trying to live up to the gospel's unwavering moral standard.

In the post-born-again phase Dylan explores and embraces anew the vagaries and inconsistencies implicit in a non-dual worldview, so that "Jokerman," which sounds like "Zimmerman," could be seen at once as a messiah and as a deficient version of Jesus. Or the message could be the irrelevancy of Jesus compared to the "Jokerman dance to the nightingale tune." According to Michael Gray, "The invocation of the dance is after all an assertion of the *idea* of renewal, of the *concept* of submission to the muse. And it insists, as the verses do, on the impossibility of unconditional surrender to any fixed position."[27] Gray cites Aidan Day who writes: "It's a dance invested with paradox in that it is both a dance of death and a dance of life: a dance simultaneously of matter and spirit." Day also describes it as "at once a dance of death and a flight of the soul by a light that governs both creativity and waste."[28]

Evoking a passage in T. S. Eliot's poem *Burnt Norton*, which says of dance, "And do not call it fixity," as cited by Gray, Day shows that Dylan's dance is in "the unfixed terrain between the flesh and the spirit, between death and rebirth, between the Trickster and the transcendent self, and in the unfixed terrain that is unfixed because nothing, not even the figure of

Christ, can be singularly anything." According to Day the song cannot settle for:

> Containment within a dualistic frame of reference ... even the unstableness of the opposition between time and non-time, life and death, is called into question ... Generating questions which it does not resolve, the lyric itself is presented to its audience in the form of a question or riddle. In its refusal to close lies its strength, its commitment to confront and challenge. And in that refusal it epitomizes the most distinctive perspective of Dylan's lyrical career: a continually renewed skepticism regarding the possibility of attaining absolutely final positions and a protest at the paralyzing intolerance of such as settling for closed and fixed points of view. The work neither simply despairs nor simply celebrates. Recognising a "hateful siege/ Of contraries" it simultaneously exults in that siege.[29]

The realm of riddles that Dylan occupies recalls the Zen notions of the "True Man with No Rank" or the "Wanderer with No Fixed Abode," who embraces all polarities from the standpoint of understanding that their non-dualistic basis is ultimately grounded in that which is beyond yet remains interconnected with the dichotomy of dualism and non-dualism.

Something only dead men know

The next release during the phase of Non-Duality III, *Empire Burlesque*, has been criticized for a lack of consistency in both lyrical and musical dimensions. Many of the songs seem to be rediscovering, for better or worse, categories stemming from the stage of Non-Duality I twenty years earlier. The putdown lyrics, including "Seeing the Real You at Last," "When the Night Comes Falling from the Sky," and "Something's Burning, Baby," recall songs like "Can You Please Crawl Out Your Window?" A poignant expression of hurt in "Never Gonna Be the Same Again," along with the enthusiastic celebrations of love in "I'll Remember You" and "Emotionally Yours" are also similar to the atmosphere of mid-1960s songs.

In the powerful finale, "Dark Eyes," an acoustic folk song written in the studio during the final recording sessions (reminiscent of "Restless Farewell" on *The Times They are A-Changin'*), the main image is again ambiguous. While "a drunken man is at the wheel ... [amid] the falling gods of speed and steel," Dylan "live[s] in another world where life and death are memorized,/ Where the earth is strung with lovers' pearls." We can only wonder whether dark eyes, which are "all I see," according to the narrator, are something to be prized or vilified. It is likely that they refer to the ignorance that Dylan sees around him in people who fail to understand his spiritual message.

"Brownsville Girl" (cowritten with playwright Sam Shepard, and originally an outtake from *Empire Burlesque* then titled "New Danville Girl") on *Knocked Out Loaded* is perhaps the most extraordinary narrative Dylan has ever sung. It plays off the story of Gregory Peck in the 1950s film *The Gunslinger* and features pithy, obtuse lyrics and wordplays that convey the intricacies as well as inconsistencies of a non-dual worldview.

In the original film, Peck, who presented Dylan with Kennedy Center honors in 1997, plays the fastest gun in the west who, when finally gunned down, wishes to save his killer so that he too can suffer the fate of constant anxiety in being on the run from the law and the outlaw alike. In this song, Dylan plays the role of a desperado about to be framed who feels "too over the edge . . . [ready to] go out of control." He confesses his feelings of angst:

> Now I've always been the kind of person that doesn't like to trespass but sometimes you just find yourself over the line.
> Oh if there's an original thought out there, I could use it right now.
> You know, I feel pretty good, but that ain't sayin' much. I could feel a whole lot better.

On the run, the narrator visits a friend named Ruby, who reinforces all the feelings of loss and vulnerability, as she "changed the subject every time money came up . . . You could tell she was so broken-hearted./ She said, 'Even the swap meets around here are getting pretty corrupt.'"

The message of "Brownsville Girl" is that in the midst of relativism and falsity, one can take a step back and with detachment comment that it is:

> Strange how people who suffer together have stronger connections than people who are most content.
> I don't have any regrets, they can talk about me plenty when I'm gone.
> You always said people don't do what they believe in, they just do what's most convenient, then they repent.

But is this repentant attitude authentic, or merely a ploy to disguise ongoing deception? The song expresses the need to accept the world of illusion: "You know, it's funny how things never turn out the way you had 'em planned./ The only thing we knew for sure about Henry Porter is that his name wasn't Henry Porter." Perhaps it does not matter that it can never be known who the real person is, or perhaps there is no real identity.

While "Brownsville Girl" may be seen to be wallowing in non-dualism, "Silvio" (cowritten with Robert Hunter of the Grateful Dead) on *Down in the Groove* is the song near the end of Non-Duality III that comes closest to developing a non-theological approach that seeks a balance between the confirmation and the refutation of truth. The opening verse accepts without complaint that expectations generally fall short in the crush of time moving from past to future, so that the present often gets overlooked and taken for granted: "Stake my future on a hell of a past/ Looks like tomorrow is coming on fast/ Ain't complaining 'bout what I got/ Seen better times, but who has not?" Of course, Dylan is aware that his own role is special because of his seemingly magical powers of persuasion: "I can snap my fingers and require the rain/ From a clear blue sky and turn it off again/ I can stroke your body and relieve your pain/ And charm the whistle off an evening train." Yet, he remains content with his loner status: "I'm an old boll weevil looking for a home/ If you don't like it you can leave me alone."

Although the stage of Non-Duality III is consistent with preceding phases in conveying disillusionment with personal relations and social structures as well as in accepting relativism, a new element of non-dualism is introduced in "Silvio." By understanding the limits inherent in the conversion syndrome that expects any given radical ideological transition, whether embracing family values or born-again religiosity, to provide a firm and conclusive solution to human trials and tribulations, Dylan gains a greater awareness of the shortcomings of all truth claims. In the final analysis acceptance and resignation to what reality is without blinders, while encompassing both sides of the paradox, provides the only release: "I can tell you fancy, I can tell you plain/ You give something up for everything you gain/ Since every pleasure's got an edge of pain/ Pay for your ticket and don't complain."

Yet Dylan continues to affirm an intense longing for truth and still uses the Bible along with the Blues as vehicles for "finding out something only dead men know," and expressing this in a compelling yet cryptic fashion. In what proves to be the final phase before he is able to achieve a middle road perspective during the Modern Era, Dylan finds a way of articulating a dialectical compromise and integration of the previously distanced and mutually exclusive standpoints of dualism and non-dualism. The ultimate arbiter of truth-claims is neither of the human nor the divine realm. Rather, true experience, as also suggested in the final verse of "A Hard Rain's A-Gonna Fall," is based on turning to nature as mentor (or mirror and

model for behavior), but at the end of the line it is self-understanding alone
that discovers what is authentic and what is not:

> One of these days and it won't be long
> Going down in the valley and sing my song
> I will sing it loud and sing it strong
> Let the echo decide if I was right or wrong.

Chapter 9

The Modern Era (1989–Present)

Never-Ending Middle Way Lost or Found?

OVERVIEW: STUCK IN THE MIDDLE WITH YOU

The Modern Era begins in the late 1980s with a thoroughly rejuvenated approach to music-making that Dylan describes vividly in the chapter of his autobiography *Chronicles* titled "Oh Mercy."[1] According to this account, several years of decline in his overall level of interest in performing and songwriting culminates in a disabled hand mangled in a freakish accident in 1987 that incapacitates him for a spell. By turning once again to the Delta Blues for inspiration, however, Dylan finds that he is able to draw on inner resources to create a dramatic reversal from his downward spiral. This is based on using an innovative style of guitar playing and singing derived on the old bluesmen Dylan emulated from the earliest days of recording. Although Dylan enjoys a remarkable revival of his performing and composing skills, the full recovery of his songwriting is slow moving. It takes almost a decade for this to gather sufficient momentum and result in the outpouring of creativity that begins in 1997 with *Time Out of Mind* and continues with *"Love and Theft"* in 2001 and *Modern Times* in 2006.

From the time the reversal starts at the end of the 1980s through the present day, Dylan averages over a hundred performances a year while playing nearly 500 different songs at various venues large and small

Figure 9.1   Dylan and the Pope

throughout the world. In 1989, he releases *Oh Mercy*, produced in New Orleans by Daniel Lanois, which is one of his great comeback efforts, and this is followed a year later by *Under the Red Sky*, which gets a decidedly mixed reception. Then, after not writing new material for seven years, starting in the late 1990s, he releases three consecutive bestselling and critically acclaimed albums in addition to several singles produced for films and other creative ventures. This includes an acclaimed autobiography, a series of innovative radio shows, an exhibition along with a book of paintings, and a new feature film. With *Modern Times* released at age 65, Dylan becomes the oldest person in history to have a chart-topping #1 record, and he also garners numerous prestigious honors and awards, as well as performing for the Pope and the President.[2]

These accomplishments demonstrate convincingly that Dylan stands at the top of his game and remains perhaps the most respected and revered figure in American popular culture. How does he bounce back from the nadir of the mid-1980s to reach and sustain this peak of creativity during the later stages of his career twenty years later? The key to his success lies in achieving a Zen-like middle way position with regard to the spiritual quest. The approach initially explored in songs like "Every Grain of Sand,"

"Jokerman," and "Silvio" during the phase of Non-Duality III integrates diverse paths into a unified and comprehensive or holistic standpoint that Dylan previously pursued in random zigzag fashion. The veering and swerving between seemingly incompatible extremes is transmuted into a coherent yet open-ended approach.

Each of the first three career periods reveal Dylan starting out by finding a safety net in a particular ideological viewpoint and musical style rooted in dualism, and then redefining himself through adopting a specific approach that makes him feel secure for the moment. Eventually, this outlook comes to feel like a ball and chain or a cage cramping his style from which he needs to break free and escape in order to continue to seek authenticity and autonomy through non-dualism. What was once the cause of freedom becomes a dungeon, but at the same time what was imprisoning can turn into a liberating force and serve as the source of a new commitment.

Once disengaged from a particular approach, Dylan pursues and attains the opposite path, which he espouses fervently until its failure to offer a satisfactory resolution for personal or social problems becomes all too concise and too clear, thus causing considerable frustration and anguish. At this point, he starts looking again for yet another answer. The impact of the inconclusive changes he underwent in the first three main career periods leaves Dylan ripe and ready for . . . either retirement or renewal, that is, standing still as a living icon or taking up the ongoing challenge of continual enhancement.

The music of the Modern Era encompasses all of the main themes and outlooks that were treated by Dylan in previous phases, and innovatively fits them together in a dynamic pattern. In pursuing the middle path, Dylan stays true to his commitment to keep on bargainin' for salvation while knowing it cannot be easily gained. World-weary from a lifetime of suffering, he sticks to the Outsider's commitment to pursue integrity and resists being turned into a pop idol or mere cultural symbol by pressing on with musical innovation.

In the three consistently brilliant records of the Modern Era, Dylan attains an integrative perspective in which the polarities of Duality and Non-Duality as well as that of light and darkness, and freedom and constraint, are allowed to play off and support one another but without collapsing into a simplistic identity. Near the end of a career in which he has always chosen one side or the other in ways that aggravated and alienated a sector of his fans, this tension subsides as he accepts that oppositions coexist and constructs a holistic viewpoint. Dylan no longer feels compelled to lurch from one extreme to the other, and back. He conveys regret and desolation yet shows that these states are uplifting and comforting in that self-understanding, while complex and limited, is simply the only vehicle to spiritual fulfillment.

For the new Dylan, to paraphrase Ecclesiastes, "There is a time for dualism, and a time for non-dualism," which recalls the Zen affirmation of everyday life, "I eat when I am hungry, and sleep when I am tired." This is echoed in "Standing in the Doorway" from *Time Out of Mind*: "I'll eat when I'm hungry, drink when I'm dry/ And live my life on the square." The non-dualistic implications of this lyric are complemented by the dualism suggested in the lines that complete the verse, "And even if the flesh falls off of my face/ I know someone will be there to care," which imply a recourse to divine grace.

Throughout the Modern Era, Dylan keeps a focus on commentary about society and remains true to his career-long passion of exposing "the incestuous relationship among authoritarianism, social evils, militarism and materialism" by arguing that "the solutions to corruption are spiritual ... [and involve] judgment, or a 'hard rain,' on people who perpetrate evil."[3] Modernization is certainly no blessing for Dylan, who refers to "these modern times [as] (the New Dark Ages)" in the liner notes to *World Gone Wrong*.[4] He regards modernity in an unconventional sense of representing anything but a linear path moving inevitably toward progress. Rather, it is an obstacle to spiritual fulfillment that must be overcome in order to attain a constructive compromise of dualism and non-dualism.

As with Charlie Chaplin's great silent film *Modern Times*, which expressed a mute protest against the soulless mechanized world during the era when talkies were already popular, Dylan rails against the robot-like materialism and lack of genuine spirituality that pervades the contemporary world. He remarks wistfully in "Highlands," the sixteen-minute finale of *Time Out of Mind* based on a Charley Patton blues shuffle, "I wish someone would come/ And push back the clock for me," and many other songs of the Modern Era are filled with pre-technology images of riding in buggies and looking at fountains. However, in seeking to resolve the conflict between spirituality and modernity Dylan does not look for escape in a false, un-modern utopia.

Instead, Dylan realizes that to achieve resilience and renewal he must come to terms with and juggle more or less harmoniously, but without eradicating the tension between, several sets of polarities. These include the stimulation of awakening and the restfulness of passivity, as well as the need for exercising compassion and forgiveness with the instinct to gain revenge for betrayal. Furthermore, the self-image of Dylan as heretic/outlaw/nonconformist and as repentant/sheriff/enforcer must be brought into balance, along with Dylan the preacher who seeks to convert others and the Dada-iconoclast whose aim is to subvert all ideologies and institutions.

The middle path is evident in all of Dylan's recent works, particularly in songs such as "Tryin' to Get to Heaven" and "Not Dark Yet" on *Time Out of Mind*, "High Water" and "Sugar Baby" on *"Love and Theft"*, and "Thunder on the Mountain" and "Ain't Talkin'" on *Modern Times*. As Thom Jurek has pointed out of the integrative spirit and content of the music of the Modern Era, "bawdy joy, restless heartache, a wild sense of humor, and bottomless sadness all coexist and inform one another as a warning and celebration of this precious human life while wondering openly about what comes after."[5] Furthermore,

> *Modern Times* is the work of a professional mythmaker, a back-alley magician, and a prophetic creator of mischief. He knows his characters because he's been them all and can turn them all inside out in song: the road-worn holy man who's also a thief; the tender-hearted lover who loves to brawl; the poetic sage who's also a pickpocket; and the Everyman who embodies them all and just wants to get on with it.[6]

Thus, the middle way for Dylan, as in Zen discourse, is not a simple compromise or half–half approach but a dynamic way of exploring options that are played off one another and significantly modified yet never fully abandoned. In Dylan's middle path, we find both Duality and Non-Duality in ample evidence in ways that juxtapose, interconnect, or mutually exchange these options. A prominent example of this outlook is "Highlands" on *Time Out of Mind*, in which feelings of desolation and despair are given full vent, yet are offset by the idealistic hope for spiritual attainment achieved from a standpoint that unifies harsh judgment with stoic resignation, as well as self-mockery with feelings of joy and elation.

In reaching this goal, Dylan seems to heed what Zen masters know about the value of discourse, which is that "Rhetoric can no longer reasonably be reduced to relativism, nor separated from argument, but must be seen as a vehicle for understanding and interrogating 'the problematic and the questionable.'"[7] The following turn of phrase epitomizes the Zen approach to the middle way. The saying begins, "With realization, all things are unified/ Without realization, all things are disparate," and then it reverses the pattern by asserting, "Without realization, all things are unified,/ With realization all things are disparate."[8] In this way, Zen advises that from the middle way standpoint it is possible to think and speak appropriately from each and every angle, even if the causes and/or effects appear to be nearly opposite on the surface. This outlook is succinctly expressed in another saying, "When it is time for life the master uses the sword to give life, and when it is time for death he uses the sword to give death."

Dylan in the Modern Era similarly uses poetic language not as a tool for advocating a succession of exclusive standpoints in perpetual conflict. Rather, it informs and inspires a sense of the inclusive quality and compatibility of approaches to convey eternal verities of dignity and honor maintained despite countless obstacles and shackles. As in Zen, Dylan shows that one can find beauty in the midst of illusion by being aware of a deep sense of transgression and fragmentation and accepting the absurdity while never quite trusting it or allowing oneself to be constrained in trying to choose between a stark set of contrasts. Relinquishing the need for insistence which may become strident or for resignation which may reflect world-weariness is a crucial element for attaining the middle path.

GATEWAY: A NEW WAY OF PICKIN'

How low had Dylan sunk by the time he was ready and primed for his Modern Era revival? On the one hand, in the mid- to late 1980s he was still a productive and highly visible if perhaps not altogether viable artist, still releasing an album nearly every year. Yet in "Don't Fall Apart on Me Tonight" on *Infidels* in 1989 he expressed regret, albeit somewhat disingenuously, for a lack of productivity during that phase: "I wish I'd have been a doctor,/ Maybe I'd have saved some life that had been lost,/ Maybe I'd have done some good in the world/ 'Stead of burning every bridge I crossed." Keeping in mind that Nietzsche considered himself a "physician for the soul," perhaps Dylan doubted the value of his contribution to mending the ways of human suffering—or else he ironically praised it.

A major participant in the benefit concerts for Live Aid in 1985 and Farm Aid in 1986 (which originated based on a suggestion Dylan made during the previous performance), he also toured with Tom Petty and the Grateful Dead. The latter group, which enjoys a fanatical following, has regularly performed Dylan songs and referred to him as "The Oracle."[9] However, Dylan was uneasy about the quality of his own participation in these outings, and he felt that by his (incredibly high) standards this phase of music-making was increasingly problematic. He released his three least successful albums from a commercial and critical standpoint back to back (*Knocked Out Loaded* in 1986, and *Down in the Groove* and *Dylan and the Dead* both in 1988), and he played in the film, *Hearts of Fire*, produced in Britain but never even released stateside.

More significantly, Dylan has in retrospect complained of feeling totally distant from his songs and his sense of identity, and at age 48 he was literally on the verge of giving up on his career altogether. He was trapped in a cage of his own making. To cite images from several songs,[10] he felt that he was blown out from exhaustion or, while resembling a painting hanging in the Louvre his throat would start to tickle and his nose itch but he knew that he could not move. Like Mona Lisa, he must have had a bad case of the highway blues that no doctor or priest could possibly cure.

During one particular performance, Dylan reports feeling so lost and dismayed that he could not pronounce the lyrics, and "For an instant I fell into a black hole." However, all this despair is about to change for the better in a dramatic and radical fashion. After spontaneously turning to a tried and true performance method, he is able to recover his standing:

> Instantly, it was like a thoroughbred had charged through the gates. Everything came back, and it came back in multidimension. Even I was surprised. It left me kind of shaky. Immediately, I was flying high .... Now the energy was coming from a hundred different angles, completely unpredictable ones. I had a new faculty and it seemed to surpass all the other requirements.... I saw that instead of being stranded somewhere at the end of the story, I was actually in the prelude to the beginning of another one.[11]

This passage recalls countless records of Zen masters who, with their back against the wall due to a psychological torment or challenge generated in the training process, metaphorically box their way out of the corner in a fashion that unleashes the floodgates of creative inspiration.

The approach to performing that overcomes his demons and restores his vitality is based on what Dylan had learned as a novice in the early 1960s when he received instruction from an old bluesman, Lonnie Johnson. Once a mentor for Robert Johnson, Lonnie Johnson's career continued and he had a hit in the late 1940s with "Tomorrow Night," a song Dylan covers on *World Gone Wrong*. The method is based on using an odd- instead of an even-number chords system, which may sound like a simple enough adjustment, but for Dylan the Johnson approach, although overlooked by most contemporary performers, opens up an infinite variety of inspirational expressions. In the midst of his depression, Dylan writes, "now all of a sudden it came back to me, and I realized that this way of playing would revitalize my world."[12] His explanation of multidimensionality resembles the meaning of the traditional East Asian nine-turn or zigzag bridge, which enables the observer to view the world from an immense multiplicity of complementary perspectives.

Following this epiphany, Dylan embarks on a series of comeback efforts that mark the beginning of the Modern Era when he strives to integrate dualistic and non-dualistic tendencies. This includes the release of *Oh Mercy* in 1989 and two Traveling Wilburys albums recorded with other rock superstars, in addition to initiating the Never-Ending Tour. In tapping into "that wellspring of creativity," he fulfills what he says in the liner notes to a tribute album he produced about Jimmie Rodgers, known as the "Father of Country Music." According to Dylan, Rodgers "seamlessly combined Anglo-Saxon folk ballads and African–American country blues."[13] For Dylan, the "Man Who Started It All" was "a thousand-and-one tongues yet singularly his own," and "was a performer of force without precedent with a sound as lonesome and mystical as it was dynamic. He gives hope to the vanquished and humility to the mighty . . ."

Oh my goodness

The *Oh Mercy* sessions in 1989, like those six years earlier for *Infidels*, his other creative peak of the 1980s, yield an exceptional number of important songs, including several that are left off the official album but released subsequently.[14] In *Chronicles*, Dylan gives a rare insight into his songwriting techniques as he describes how he spontaneously composes the lyrics at odd times of the day and in various settings, and also mentions some verses excised from the final versions. However, he does admit that he does not feel these numbers quite match his classic efforts like the romance of "Girl From the North Country" or the protest of "With God on Our Side."

The songs on *Oh Mercy* include broad-based social criticism in "Everything is Broken" and "Political World," released with a subtly crafted video. Both songs cryptically depict the failures of institutions to accomplish their goals because they are reduced to struggles for power based on deceit. "Disease of Conceit" along with the outtake "Dignity" also fit into this category by showing how people either commit sin, which is distastefully prevalent, or are unable to live up to virtue that is all too elusive when reduced to being sought as a mere material object or commodity. As "Dignity" points out, "Someone showed me a picture and I just laughed;/ Dignity's never been photographed." Also, "Series of Dreams" explores the nature of illusion and the difficulties of escaping this state: "Thinking of a series of dreams/ Where the time and the tempo fly/ And there's no exit in any direction/ 'Cept the one that you can't see with your eyes."

Another important category includes deeply confessional songs in which Dylan seems to be singing sincerely, and for once without donning a mask or disguise as he fully bares his soul directly to the audience in "Most of the Time," "What Was It You Wanted?," and the second of two queries, "What Good Am I?" The lyrics of the last song forcefully asks of his inability to live up to what may be inflated expectations, "What good am I if I know and don't do/ If I see and don't say if I look right through you/ If I turn a deaf ear to the thunderin' sky/ What good am I?" All of these songs express a restrained moodiness and sustained sense of resignation that show a strong tendency toward non-dualism.

In fact, on first listening, *Oh Mercy* may seem like the logical extension of the stage Non-Duality III in the mid-1980s, a phase that was never completely fulfilled after the promise of *Infidels*. However, another set of songs indicates that the greatness of the album lies not in non-dualism but in the delicate yet complex interrelation between the two worldviews of Duality and Non-Duality, which is expressed in four distinct ways.

The first way is in "Ring Them Bells," which initially appears to have an overt Christian flavor by talking of various saints and rites. But the song also speaks of the "sun going down upon the sacred cow" and "breaking down the distance between right and wrong" in a way that corresponds with a Zen style of non-dualism regarding moral dichotomies.[15] Yet this is articulated with enough ambiguity that it is difficult to determine whether the post-modern condition, like Nietzsche's "God is dead" proclamation, is to be considered a relief or a tragedy.

A second way of attaining a constructive compromise on *Oh Mercy* is the overlapping of dualism and non-dualism found in another confessional song, a solo acoustic number that concludes the album, "Shooting Star." According to producer Daniel Lanois' recollection, this song was written in the studio and recorded in one take, like its album-finale predecessors "Restless Farewell" on *Another Side of Bob Dylan* and "Dark Eyes" on *Empire Burlesque*. The three main verses offer feelings of regret, yet also express an acceptance of the fact that the narrator has apparently let down a partner in an intimate relationship because of a fundamental disagreement about expectations and levels of commitment. While watching the proverbial star as it "slips away" in the middle of the night, he beseechingly wonders "If I ever became what you wanted me to be/ Did I miss the mark or/ Overstep the line/ That only you could see."

However, the song's bridge contains millenarian imagery which implies that one can never escape God's power and divine judgment:

> Listen to the engine, listen to the bell
> As the last fire truck from hell
> Goes rolling by, all good people are praying,
> It's the last temptation
> The last account
> The last time you might hear the sermon on the mount.

It is noteworthy that this is recorded four years after the release of the apparent repudiation of Christianity in "Tight Connection to My Heart" and fifteen years since "Up to Me" referred to Christ's sermon as nothing more than what a broken glass reflects.

The third approach is evident in "Born in Time," if this is treated as an *Oh Mercy* outtake since it seems out of place stylistically on *Under the Red Sky*, where it was first released. The song's title implies that there is a time-less or eternal realm, which although not mentioned or defined in the lyr-ics suggests a dualistic contrast with the here-and-now realm, which is illusory in that "we were made of dreams." Life's purpose, it appears, is to live and accept the non-dualistic world of relativism as experienced "In the hills of mystery,/ In the foggy web of destiny," since "the ways of nature will test every nerve,/ You won't get anything you don't deserve/ Where we were born in time."

Who was that man in the long black coat?

Perhaps the most important way of interweaving opposing views that is crucial for understanding how *Oh Mercy* fits into Dylan's overall career trajectory in light of a Zen-based dialectical theory is the juxtaposition of dualism and non-dualism in back-to-back verses of "Man In The Long Black Coat." It tells an enigmatic love story in which a woman is mysteri-ously whisked away in the dead of night by an inscrutable outsider dressed in black, and the audience remains unclear about his intentions and the impact on the woman. The Man In The Long Black Coat is like earlier quixotic Dylan personae or characters in narratives, such as the Joker and Drifter on *John Wesley Harding*, the Gypsy on *New Morning*, Alias in *Pat Garret and Billy the Kid*, the Jack of Hearts on *Blood on the Tracks*, and Jokerman on *Infidels*. All we know is that he hangs out at dance halls on the outside of town with dust on his coat while wearing a mask and quoting the Bible.

Does the mysterious figure represent liberation from bondage or a new kind of imprisonment for which the woman has leapt out of the fire, so to speak, and into the frying pan? It is very difficult to discern the answer as the lyrics leave it deliberately ambiguous since she did not take time to leave a note: "She never said nothing, there was nothing she wrote." In inter-preting the event of her departure, two radically different interpretations are given in the heart of the song, one in the context of a preacher's sermon which expresses Duality and the other through the vehicle of the narrator's commentary which conveys Non-Duality. The first, dualistic interpreta-tion is as follows:

> Preacher was a talkin' there's a sermon he gave,
> He said every man's conscience is vile and depraved,

> You cannot depend on it to be your guide
> When it's you who must keep it satisfied.
> It ain't easy to swallow, it sticks in the throat,
> She gave her heart to the man in the long black coat.

According to this passage, people tend to rely on their conscience but this is not a sufficient tool because it is potentially corruptible at every turn and therefore cannot serve as a reliable guiding light. The implication is that one's own judgment and will must give way to a higher authority which provides answers based on truth versus falsity. This is the only path to deliverance from being lost in a relativistic world where there is no standard or regularity for determining correct behavior. The dualistic view probably condemns the man as well as the woman for falling prey to deception.

The second interpretation of the primary event in the song's story line is evoked in the narrator's comments regarding the floating quality of the world of human behavior and its repercussions:

> There are no mistakes in life some people say,
> It is true sometimes you can see it that way.
> But people don't live or die, people just float.
> She went with the man in the long black coat.

This resembles the Eastern worldview of the balancing of opposites symbolized by Yin/Yang forces. In this approach, the question of what is true, right, or good versus contradictory elements of falsity, illusion, and evil is transformed into an affirmation that relativity or horizontal paradoxicality is the highest truth. To look for anything beyond this is an illusion that creates its own level of ignorance and bondage. The non-dualistic view may well accept the woman's actions as a matter of her working out fateful encounters.

The final verse leaves us with a sense of chaos and confusion about whether to reject or accept what has taken place in the aftermath of a violent storm that reflects the Man's impact on the town. We know something disturbing has transpired for better or worse, and can only scratch our heads and wonder what to think, as members of the community toil in vain or try in their own way to make the best of things: "There's smoke on the water, it's been there since June,/ Tree trunks uprooted, 'neath the high crescent moon/ Feel the pulse and vibration and the rumbling force/ Somebody is out there beating the dead horse."

It seems likely that at an earlier stage of his career, Dylan would have endorsed a single interpretation of the main action, but at this important transitional juncture he is not moving from one extreme to the other but allows for a juxtaposition of opposing views that does not exclusively support a particular perspective. Even though Dylan does not come out and endorse the Non-Duality approach over Duality, there seems to be a Zen-like emphasis in seeing the inseparability of absolute and relative. Therefore, the paradoxical view that dualism is intertwined with non-dualism brings Dylan's experience into another, more deeply rooted level of Non-Duality.

To another rendezvous

Just as *Empire Burlesque* was considered disappointing by many fans after the success of *Infidels* even though it consisted of entirely new material, *Under the Red Sky* coming on the heels of *Oh Mercy* is given short shrift by many critics. Facing writer's block once again, Dylan then takes a long reprieve from songwriting before recording another new album of original material. As with other records that got disappointing receptions including *Street-Legal*, a major contributor to the problem with *Under the Red Sky* is production quality, which does not compare favorably with Lanois' meticulous handiwork on *Oh Mercy*. This is due in part to the fact that Dylan's time and attention is no doubt divided with his efforts in recording for the Traveling Wilburys.

The main factor for the way *Under the Red Sky* is received, however, has more to do with an apparent disconnect between its style and its content, which sends to jaded fans a very mixed message. For nearly every song, Dylan chooses to use the nursery rhyme as a musical conceit to house—or perhaps hide in a sly and subtle fashion—an apocalyptic tale of the degradation and decline of the world as we know it accompanied by hope for the second coming of the messiah. The album title evokes Matthew 16.2-3, which refers to an ominous and foreboding landscape also well known to sailors, shepherds, and other wayfarers.

The opening number "Wiggle Wiggle," which probably antagonizes some followers on first listening for seeming inane, is intended to suggest that the world is infested with the devil who will "Wiggle, wiggle, wiggle, rattle and shake,/ Wiggle like a big fat snake." In the title cut, "the little boy and the little girl were both baked in a pie," conjuring a sense of Jonah contained in the belly of the beast, but the man in the moon who commits this act promises, perhaps falsely, to give the girl "the key to the kingdom and this is the town/ This is the blind horse that leads you around." The song "10,000 Men," which is composed in the AAB twelve-bar Blues structure, sets up a moral showdown between the thousands of men who are "dressed in oxford blue," symbolizing their advantageous position, and thousands of women who are "all dressed in white," symbolizing the purity of their sacrifice.

Then, "2 x 2" implies divine judgment causing a flood as "Two by two, they stepped into the ark,/ Two by two, they step in the dark." Next, "Handy Dandy," another ambivalent image in the tradition of "Jokerman," could be taken to represent the savior, who "got a basket of flowers and a bag full or sorrow/ He finishes his drink, he gets up from the table he says,/ 'Okay, boys, I'll see you tomorrow.'" The arrival of the messiah is presaged in the final song, which also follows an AAB structure, when "The cat's in the well and the servant is at the door./ The drinks are ready and the dogs are going to war."

While for many listeners the childlike quality of the lyrics may seem like an overdoing of the cleverness featured in the gospel song "Man Gave Names to All the Animals" on *Slow Train Coming* a decade earlier, several prominent critics have seen the signs of genius in this album. Andrew Muir finds *Under the Red Sky* an altogether disarmingly humorous and challenging way for Dylan to deal with his longtime concern of warning of the inevitability and catastrophic impact of Armageddon. He particularly notes that Dylan's approach is a reworking of his ability to conjure "nonsense" composition, which has been such a crucial element of modern literary and intellectual history from the "great art movements of surrealism, impressionism *et al*, following on from the philosophical and psychological works of such thinkers as Freud and Jung."[16]

Similarly appreciative of the performer's innovative creativity on this unusual album, Michael Gray highlights that Dylan, who has shown that blues lyrics can capture the cadences of the King James Bible, demonstrates here how material that comes from the playground, such as ring-games, chants, and rhymes that children learn from each other easily enters into grown-up songs (and is also a tool for proselytizing and modes of religious conversion both east and west).[17] Alan Lomax had long noted a variety of examples revealing affinities between children's and adult's lyricism in Delta Blues songs and Gray recommends that Dylan's significant achievements on *Under the Red Sky* should be seen in this light.

From the standpoint of the dialectical theory of Dylan's trajectory, the strengths and shortcomings of the *Under the Red Sky* have to do with the ways he seeks to create a balance between dualism and non-dualism. In this case, his message is clearly dualistic but the medium for delivering it is non-dualistic. It is natural to raise the question, what is his real intention? Perhaps Dylan himself is uncertain at this point, and feels he must make another major foray into the realm of Classic, Country, or Deep Delta Blues for inspiration that will bring his songwriting closer to the middle path.

AHEAD TO THE PAST

During the lengthiest drought in the career of this most prolific and productive of songwriters, Dylan releases three consecutive acoustic albums without an original composition, including two records of solo covers of old folk/blues material, *Good As I Been to You* in 1992 and *World Gone Wrong* in 1993, along with *MTV Unplugged* two years later. While sales are modest by Dylan standards and many followers assume that he might never write again, in retrospect, it is clear that this is all a necessary part of a retooling phase. As with the stage that produced *The Basement Tapes* and *Self Portrait* two and a half decades before, Dylan is in the process of touching base with his Blues roots in order to recharge, so to speak, his songwriting batteries.

Although my discussion of previous stages generally has not considered live albums, I include *MTV Unplugged* in the list of new records from this phase because it fits in with the pattern of acoustic performances and reinforces the image of a back-to-basics approach to music-making. In addition to standards from his 1960s and early 1970s catalogue, *MTV Unplugged* features refurbished versions of more obscure older numbers such as "John Brown," a devastating antiwar song that was previously unreleased, and "Tombstone Blues," one of the most ironic of social commentaries from the stage of Non-Duality I. The album also includes two numbers from the *Oh Mercy* sessions with profound underlying spiritual implications: "Shooting Star" and the unveiling of a live version of "Dignity," which was first released on a greatest hits collection the year before.

In evaluating the contributions of *Good As I Been to You* and *World Gone Wrong*, it is necessary to return to his initial album to see that Dylan has come full circle back to being a Blues interpreter who seeks to transmit the tradition by transgressing its rules and putting his own stamp onto old songs such as "Frankie and Albert," "Hard Times," "Broke Down Engine," and "Delia." Perhaps as an extension of *Under the Red Sky*, Dylan's version of the nursery rhyme "Froggie Went A-Courtin'" is transformed into a subtle yet probing social commentary about how people lose out in the system when they are crushed by the pecking order that tries to enforce the status quo of immobility. The song also makes a distinctive statement in its last verse by telling an audience that seems to have turned its back, "A little piece of cornbread layin' on a shelf./ If you want anymore, you can sing it yourself, Uh-huh."

The main lesson Dylan learns by plugging into Blues sources as a sense of inspiration for future songwriting has a twofold dimension that expands upon Basic Bob categories: the public or communal side that features a critique of society; and the private or personal side that deals with the inner turmoil of romantic conflict. On the public side, according to Michael Gray, Dylan uses the songs to evoke and celebrate what critic Greil Marcus has called the "weird, old America" or the "invisible republic," which is "the past of down-home pre-corporate, pre-Pentagon America and of the sometimes obscure inspired recording artists, black and white, who sang of and belonged to those faded-photo worlds." For Gray, "There is immense multiplicity here, and re-opening these gates is, for someone in Bob Dylan's position, a far greater action against the grain than could possibly be achieved with a rock album."[18] It is clear that Dylan is able to reflect on widespread implications of social and historical conditions of a world gone wrong in ways that will contribute prominently to songs on subsequent albums like "High Water" and "Thunder on the Mountain," which highlight the specter of divine retribution for injustice and inequities.

On the personal side, Dylan finds a way to express cryptically but eloquently his private feelings of distress or outrage by depersonalizing through projecting them into the kind of storytelling that sees truth in small, intimate details of how one reacts to tragedy and strife. As Chris Gregory notes:

> The secret language of the blues has always enthralled Bob Dylan. From his earliest days as a performer he has been irresistibly attracted to its sly, lascivious poetic sensibility, its subtle use of imagery and nuance, the codes and sub-codes and complex patterns of reference within its corpus. His ambition has always been to *inhabit* the mental condition of the great blues singers, to . . . *carry myself like Big Joe Williams* . . . as he once put it, to locate the body of his own work within the emotional world that the greatest blues singers of the form's classic mid twentieth century period (particularly between the 1920s and the 1950s) had constructed . . . [to] speak from a mysterious, dangerous, yet often hilarious, place where life was being experienced to the full, in all its horror and ecstasy.[19]

In the Blues context, criticism of others is exaggerated and expressed with a sense of irony in order to shed light on one's own weaknesses and on the limitations of the self which is innately restricted yet ever striving for freedom. Concrete instances of betrayal or regret explode into metaphysical metaphors for understanding sin and redemption on an individual as well as on a collective level. This is perhaps most compellingly conveyed by Dylan's remarkably moving performance of the Blind Willie McTell version of "Delia" on *World Gone Wrong*. In this rendition, the narrator only very reluctantly and with great trepidation is able to disclose that he is the killer of the girl who is doomed to keep suffering from feelings of mortality and decay while imprisoned. The chorus in Dylan's version's laments that "All the friends I ever had are gone," which includes not only Delia but also the narrator himself who has to live in prison with the results of his crime.

Another aspect of the personal side is that Dylan's approach on these records shows that in singing the blues, any and every situational context can serve as a backdrop for the sadness and regret of an emotional response to the ongoing, underlying quest for paradise. The songs also eloquently reveal how suffering and sacrifice can mark a turning point that makes one ready to manifest genuine concern for and commitment to others as a stepping stone to salvation. This hope is expressed in "Diamond Joe": "And when I'm called up yonder/ And it's my time to go,/ Give my blankets to my buddies/Give the fleas to Diamond Joe." Furthermore, songs like "Lone Pilgrim" convey the tale of a narrator imagining that "My soul flew to mansions on high." Paradise may be reached, yet only with a price that is paid by one who "ain't got no drivin' wheel," according to "Broke Down Engine."

BACK TO THE FUTURE

In each of the first three decades of his career during the 1960s, 1970s, and 1980s, Dylan alternated between conviction based on dualism and resignation to non-dualism, or moved from conversion to de-conversion and back. But by the 1990s he feels that he has run the course and is out of options, and faces two possibilities for continuing as a performer: singing oldies, either his own or those of the folk/blues tradition; or developing a synthetic outlook that would engender a new wave of insight and originality. The Blues interlude of the early 1990s as an extension of the Lonnie Johnson-inspired performance, paves the way for a music-making renewal. For the first time in Dylan's career, this is based not on a conversion but rather on a standpoint of non-conversion since the old pattern of reversal and reversion has fallen by the wayside.

In reaching for the middle path, Dylan's songwriting during the recordings of the Modern Era gains inspiration by returning to and recapturing themes, rhythms, and lyrics borrowed from prominent Delta Blues musicians including his perennial heroes Charley Patton and Robert Johnson, along with the whole motif of minstrelsy that pervaded the musicology of an older, turn-of-the century era. While the Delta Blues musically and lyrically infuses almost the entirety of the three albums *Time Out of Mind*, "*Love and Theft*", and *Modern Times*,[20] just as in the 1960s when Dylan absorbed the impact of the Beats and Modernists, there are numerous other musical influences. These range from obscure slave ballads and the Civil War era poetry of Henry Timrod to Merle Haggard songs and *Confessions of a*

Yakuza, and from the literary works of Robert Burns and Lewis Carroll to the classical verse of Virgil and Ovid.

Although these additional influences play an important role, Dylan draws heavily on the Blues for structure, phrasing, atmosphere, and content. Beginning in 1997, five songs feature the twelve-bar AAB style, including "Dirt Road Blues" on *Time Out of Mind*, "Summer Days" and "Lonesome Day Blues" on *"Love and Theft"*, and "Rollin' and Tumblin'" and "The Levee's Gonna Break" on *Modern Times*, with "Someday Baby" functioning as a variant of this pattern that uses a constant ending to three-line verses. Although "Nettie Moore" on *Modern Times* does not adhere to the AAB structure, in evoking a romantic poem from the time of slavery it is one of the best examples of a song that uses a specific story of love and betrayal in Blues fashion to feature concrete imagery which is clearly identifiable in order to evoke lofty abstractions. It weaves an intricate tale of the woe begotten and deprived who only reluctantly but with a need to confess disclose the true source of their angst.

A trilogy?

Dylan has disclaimed what his record company once promoted, which is that the three albums of the Modern Era form a unified trilogy, yet it is clear that they have much in common. Each includes an integrated collection of songs that as a whole tells a story of spiritual attainment, somewhat like predecessor productions during earlier stages of his career. Whereas *John Wesley Harding* and *Slow Train Coming* were narratives about the transition from non-dualism to dualism, and *Blood on the Tracks* depicted a spiritual movement in the reverse direction, the Modern Era albums represent a mixture of dualism and non-dualism. They overcome the tendency to relinquish oneself to the taint of nihilism based on too much adherence to Non-Duality or to remain attached to a dependence on otherness derived from an over-adherence to Duality. Instead, they focus on possibilities for self-attainment through love or appreciation of nature in light of the inevitability of being judged for missteps and misdemeanors.

All three records lay out their main themes based on a model of problem–solution in the opening tracks. The all-encompassing torment of unrequited love is expressed in "Love Sick" on *Time Out of Mind*; chaos, confusion, and loss more generally is the main theme in "Tweedle Dee and Tweedle Dum" on *"Love and Theft"*; and ominous signs of destruction are evoked in "Thunder on the Mountain" on *Modern Times*. Each album also features an inventive final song, including "Highlands," which deals with aspirations for transcendence, "Sugar Baby" that highlights the need to face judgment day, and "Ain't Talkin'" which leads the narrator to travel "In the last outback, at the world's end."

Time Out of Mind is the story of personal vulnerability as well as the ascent of the heart and mind to attain spiritual heights. Apparently at an early stage of recording, *Time Out of Mind* had a working title of "A Stormy Season" and it was referred to as "spooky" by Dylan during interviews because it reflects that he is "not in tune with myself." The album applies the Blues to an intimate and intensely personal view of what is happening to the narrator at the stage of his life when, instead of dreaming of possibilities to come, he laments lost opportunities yet continues to pursue his goals despite despair and disappointment. It reveals the raw power of angst with waves of insanity challenging the soul, plus the gentle sweetness of love and faith since "God is my shield," yet in the end offers a brutally realistic and fair confessional. This record further expresses an upward movement or spiritual ascension from "walking through streets that are dead" while being "tired" and "wired" in "Love Sick" to saying "my heart's in the Highlands gentle and fair" and "I'm gonna go there when I feel good enough to go."

"Love and Theft" puts emphasis on a critique of horizontal relations or interpersonal connections between self and others, which includes feelings of vengeance as well as the need to change the ways of rivals and allies. Whereas the previous record was somewhat monolithic in its Grammy Award-winning musical production, the self-produced *"Love and Theft"* provides a panoramic survey of the old, weird state of Americana with the narrator rambling about and gambling away his feelings. As Andrew Muir notes, "You will find blues, pop, rock, crooning, bebop, Texan swing, country boogie, balladeering, rockabilly and more."[21] Despite the apparently disconcerting disarray and changes of style, *"Love and Theft"* achieves overall coherence because "the tracks all interlock to create a vibrant community all of this album's own . . . depicting the struggle of authentic Americans trying to survive in the machine age."[22] Therefore, stylistic diversity functions as a perfect reflection of the prevalence of relativism in the modern world.

Modern Times returns to Dylan's apocalyptic view of the contemporary world with what a commentator has called "heart-wrenching warmth and sagacious wit." The direction indicated by the narrative pathway of the songs complements the other two albums by evoking a sense of descent from the mountaintop evoked in the opening lines of the first track. This comments on communal or collective plight and shows that it is likely too late for many people to save themselves through repentance or devotion. After receiving a revelation and feeling "like my soul is beginning to expand," Dylan metaphorically blows his trombone in order to help to disclose the "hot stuff" and to show us the "writing on the wall." He then proceeds to highlight the causes and consequences of controversy and conflict, and finishes the album by depicting the end of the world. There are no conclusive answers as he embraces the relative non-dualistic universe while ever longing for dualistic responses to the problems.

STAIRWAY TO THE STARS

On these albums, light and darkness, and commitment and indifference as reflections of how dualism and non-dualism are vying for dominance, with battles being won, lost, held to a draw, and altogether abandoned. Given the convergence and intertwining of spiritual themes operating on so many levels simultaneously, I think that the best way to appreciate the achievement of the Modern Era is not to look at each record as a discrete entity but, rather, holistically. This enables us to see that in the later stages of his career Dylan has created a distinctive system of thought that analyzes the problems of life and points to the possibilities for a resolution. His approach is comparable to the Zen view of "disentangling tangled vines" (kattō 葛藤) by using the vines themselves as tools for the path of self-extrication. Therefore, I will examine the songs of the Modern Era by reconstructing the middle-way worldview and organizing the message into five steps of a spiritual developmental process. The steps, for which I provide labels based on phrasing taken from album or song titles or lines, are as follow:[23]

1) **World Gone Wrong**, or the deep blues and sense of angst felt in its fundamental existential meaning on physical and mental levels, which stimulates the spiritual path;
2) **Love Sick**, or an awareness of how unrequited love or heartbreak becomes a crossroads that opens one up to experiencing either degradation or higher states of consciousness;
3) **Judge Is Comin' In**, reflecting the moral need to confront and overcome one's own limitations and wrongdoings at their root either through facing judgment day or the apocalypse;
4) **Ain't No Altars**, or the urgency of the spiritual quest that is undermined by profound uncertainty about the rectitude of the various paths to salvation that may be attempted;
5) **Tryin' to Get to Heaven**, by attaining a constructive compromise that is able to admire and appreciate frail beauty amid the transient world where there is simply no firm knowledge regarding the basic questions of why and wherefore.

World gone wrong

The deep blues represents a desolate internal landscape matched by outer signs, or a shadowy world that is also evoked in "Jokerman" on *Infidels* where lies, deceit, and betrayal go unchecked and a person who tries to maintain integrity feels that he is in the middle of nowhere, with no place to hide, and nothing left to lose. He is wandering in the wilderness with blues wrapped around his head or falling down like hail and leaving a greasy trail. To create another sentence that links various examples of Dylanesque imagery, "World Gone Wrong" is a case where I'm just going down that long and lonesome valley's highway of regret while feeling bad. Or, according to "Ain't Talkin'," "The sufferin' is unending/ Every nook and cranny has its tears/ I'm not playing, I'm not pretending/ I'm not nursin' any superfluous fears."

Much of the suffering is quite physical and palpable, as in "'Til I Fell in Love With You," "Well my nerves are exploding/ And my body is tense/ I feel like the whole world/ got me pinned up against the fence," or in "Mississippi" on *"Love and Theft"*, "Got nothing for you, I had nothing before/ Don't even have anything for myself anymore/ Sky full of fire, pain pourin' down."

Suffering is often reflected in the natural environment when we are forced to walk through "high and muddy water" while "clouds are weeping." According to "Standing in the Doorway" on *Time Out of Mind*, "The light in this place is so bad/ Makin' me sick in the head/ All the laughter is just makin' me sad./ The stars have turned cherry red." Furthermore, "I can see for myself that the sun is sinking" in "Workingman's Blues #2" on *Modern Times*, "the temperature dropped" in "Nettie Moore," and in "Cold Irons Bound" on *Time Out of Mind* and elsewhere severe weather is a harbinger of hardships. In these cases, nature becomes a mirror for a devastated internal landscape.

The anguish of the deep blues is also experienced as a mental phenomenon in that time and space become warped, as Jack Fate remarks in *Masked and Anonymous*, "We try to kill time but time ends up killing us." In a similar vein according to "Tryin' to Get to Heaven" on *Time Out of Mind*, "Yesterday everything was going too fast/ Today, it's moving too slow/ I got no place left to turn/ I got nothing left to burn." Other examples of lyrics emphasizing the role of mental anguish include "Can't Wait" on *Time Out of Mind* in which everything is disintegrating in the "graveyard of my mind"; "Not Dark Yet" on *Time Out of Mind* which shows that "Behind every beautiful thing there's some kind of pain"; and "Nettie Moore" on *Modern Times* which complains that "Everything I've ever known to be right has been proven wrong/ I'll be drifting along." As a preacher pro-claims in the opening scene of *Masked and Anonymous*, "Man has the mind of God, but the body of dust."

There is also a communal side to the deep blues. On the one hand, peo-ple are a distraction and only voice a "mind polluting word," or they "will tear your mind away from contemplation/ They will jump on your misfor-tune when you're down." Although "Workingman's Blues #2" is not a topical protest song, it speaks to the issue of oppression that trickles down from the leanings of a rulership that is aloof and entrenched: "Now the place is ringed with countless foes/ . . . No man, no woman knows/ The hour that sorrow will come/ . . . Well, they burned my barn, and they stole my horse/ I can't save a dime/ I got to be careful, I don't want to be forced/ Into a life of continual crime."

The impact of the physical, mental, natural, and social suffering is to heighten an awareness of metaphysical angst according to "Tryin' to Get to Heaven": "Gonna sleep down in the parlor, and relive my dreams./ I'll close my eyes and I wonder,/ if everything is as hollow as it seems." In "Not Dark Yet," Dylan says his "soul has turned into steel," and based on a Talmudic passage laments that he lives and dies without knowing why but in any case he is forced to act against his will in not being able to prolong life. This enhanced level of consciousness based on angst dialectically causes one to seek salvation through a process of either dualistic redemption based on a single, higher truth or non-dualistic resignation to relative truths. However, it is necessary first to look more closely at the causes and consequences of the deep blues.

Love sick

The basis of the most profound suffering according to the songs of the Modern Era—and this was also true for the stages of Non-Duality I, II, and III—is the heartbreak of unrequited love as in "'Til I Fell in Love With You" on *Time Out of Mind*: "I've been hit too hard/ I've seen too much/ Nothing can heal me now/ But your touch/ I just don't know what I'm gonna do/ I was all right 'til I fell in love with you." The pain affecting this raw nerve gets aggravated the more one feels aggrieved by romantic conflict. Accord-ing to "Standing in the Doorway": "Don't know if I saw you if I would kiss you or kill you/ It probably wouldn't matter to you anyhow/ You left me standing in the doorway cryin'/ I got nothin' to go back to now."

One option is to try to seduce a potential partner by putting her on a pedestal as in "Make You Feel My Love," "I'd go hungry, I'd go black and blue/ I'd go crawling down the avenue. Oh there's nothing that I wouldn't do/ to make you feel my love," or "Spirit on the water,/ Darkness on the face of the deep . . . Now your sweet voice/ Calls out from some old familiar shrine." When a lover treats you right all day but then turns around and is able to "do wrong all night," another option is to be aggressive and to put down the partner. According to "Someday Baby," in which the narrator wants to "ring your neck . . . as a matter of self-respect": "Well you take my money and you turn it out/ You fill me up with nothin' but self doubt/ Someday baby, you ain't gonna worry po' me any more," because "You can take your clothes put 'em in a sack/ You goin' down the road, baby and you can't come back."

While love may be the primary trigger it is by no means the only area in which a need for vengeance is in all too abundant supply. According to "Floater (Too Much to Ask)" on *Love and Theft*, "If you ever try to interfere with me or cross my path again/ You do so at the peril of your own life/ I'm not quite as cool or forgiving as I sound/ I've seen enough heartaches and strife." Similarly, "Thunder on the Mountain" proclaims, "Gonna raise me an army, some tough sons of bitches/ I'll recruit my army from the orphanages," and in "Ain't Talkin'," "If I catch my opponents ever sleeping/ I'll just slaughter 'em where they lie," or "I'll burn that bridge before you can cross." Also, "Ain't Talkin'" further explains how difficult it is to suppress the instinct for revenge: "They say prayer has the power to help/ So pray from the mother/ In the human heart an evil spirit can dwell/ I'm trying to love my neighbor and do good unto others/ But oh, mother, things ain't going well."

In romantic conflict, the passive and aggressive approaches are only successful if not taken to the extreme and the partner responds accordingly. Unfortunately, they can both lead to dire consequences according to two songs which, like the tale in "Delia" of the murder of a lover, speak of a homicide that has taken place out of a jealous rage as subtly revealed by an unreliable narrator who is in a state of denial. In "Spirit on the Water" on *Modern Times* the narrator confesses, "I only mean it for the best/ I want to be with you any way I can/ I been in a brawl/ Now I'm feeling the wall." He then laments the impact of the crime, "I wanna be with you in paradise/ And it seems so unfair/ I can't go to paradise no more/ I killed a man back there."

In the case of "Nettie Moore," in a moment of rage the narrator blurts out, "I'm gonna make you come to grips with fate/ When I'm through with you, you'll learn to keep your business straight," but admits, "The woman I'm loving she rules my heart/ No knife could ever cut our love apart." Tragically, however, the knife has done just that as the narrator seeks to escape by going where the Southern crosses the yellow dog to "Get away from all these demagogues." Yet, knowing deep down that there is no easy path to salvation without passing through judgment he concludes by saying, "I'm standing in the light/ I wish to God that it were night."

Judge is comin' in

When the impulse for vengeance leads to murder by an enraged lover who either kills a rival for his partner's affections or the partner herself, or if a social injustice or an act of hostility in response to this is severe enough, then judgment and retribution for transgressions committed must automatically take place. As Dylan said in "Up to Me," a *Blood on the Tracks* outtake from 1974, "When you bite off more than you can chew, you got to pay the penalty." This moral process occurs whether it is interpreted from the perspective of being enforced by a dualistic divine force or a non-dualistic mechanism of karmic causality. In "Nettie Moore," the narrator regrets, "I'm beginning to believe what the scriptures tell." We all know the home truth that it is the perpetrator rather than the victim of wrongdoing who will invariably "come to grips with fate," and punishment befalls anyone who tries vainly to avoid this result or fails to transmute it into an opportunity to gain salvation.

The experience of a moral crisis becomes a formidable crossroad or intersection that determines spiritual possibilities leading either to damnation or salvation. Seen from an individual perspective this crossroad is known as judgment day, and from a communal perspective it is known as the apocalypse. Both of these experiences are explored in great depth in the songs of the Modern Era. According to the Oscar-winning single in the film *Wonder Boys* from 1999, "Things Have Changed," the feeling of desperate anticipation in the face of a potentially catastrophic crisis is felt in the same way in moments of both judgment and apocalypse: "Standing on the gallows with my head in a noose/ Any minute now I'm expecting all hell to break loose/ If the bible is right then the world will explode/ The next sixty seconds could be like an eternity."

A grim sense of the ominous expectation of an apocalyptic catastrophe is expressed in "The Levee's Gonna Break," a rewrite of a classic blues number "When the Levee Breaks," also recorded by Led Zeppelin. Like "High Water," the song is literally about the 1927 flood of the Mississippi River that devastated the Delta farmlands but Dylan transforms it into a timeless expression of how and why we must await retribution. Looking at the song's opening and closing verses, the impact of the natural disaster is to learn a vivid lesson about the significance of divine judgment and how this puts an emphasis on the need for individual responsibility-taking:

"If it keep on rainin', the levee gonna break/ Everybody saying this is a day only the Lord could make . . . If it keep on rainin', the levee gonna break/ Some people still sleepin', some people are wide awake." The song ironically promises millennial hopes even to those who wear their "cat clothes" so that "Few more years of hard work, then there'll be a 1,000 years of happiness."

"Thunder on the Mountain" updates the commentary on the significance of catastrophic events by focusing on current world affairs to reflect on America's experience of 9/11 as a possible sign of retribution:

> Thunder on the mountain, fires on the moon
> There's a ruckus in the alley and the sun will be here soon . . . .
> Mean old twister bearing down on me
> All the ladies of Washington scrambling to get out of town
> Looks like something bad gonna happen, better roll your airplane down.

This song also evokes a harsh judgment of injustice and inequity: "Shame on your greed, shame on your wicked schemes/ I'll say this, I don't give a damn about your dreams. . . . For the love of God, you ought to take pity on yourself,"

Like the final verse of "Sugar Baby" on the inevitable confrontation with the Maker as an opportunity for stocktaking at the final moment of truth signaled by the angel of death, "Nettie Moore" recognizes how fragile the time factor is in accounting for transgressions: "Got a pile of sins to pay for and I ain't got time to hide." The agonizing sense of anticipation is further highlighted by "Tryin' to Get Heaven": "People on the platforms, waitin' for the trains./ I can hear their hearts a-beatin', like pendulums swingin' on chains./ When you think that you've lost everything . . . Tryin' to get to heaven before they close the door." However, coming face to face with an encounter with judgment does not in itself guarantee that destructive tendencies will be weeded out and overcome, according to "Nettie Moore": "The Judge is coming in, everybody rise/ Lift up your eyes/ You can do what you please, you don't need my advice/ 'Fore you call me any dirty names you better think twice."

Ain't no altars

In a summer 2007 interview with *Rolling Stone*, Dylan indicates that he is not tied to any particular ideology but underneath it all continues his commitment to the ongoing search for salvation as suggested in "Ain't

Talkin'," which refers to an unnamed code of faith: "All my loyal and much loved companions/ They approve of me and share my code/ I practice a faith that's been long abandoned/ Ain't no altars on this long and lonesome road."

For Dylan, the spiritual quest is urgent and immediate, but at the same time the role of religion per se is limited and tentative.[24] According to "Standing in the Doorway," faith is effective in that someone stands by caringly despite the anguish and hardship so that "I know the mercy of God must be near." In "Ain't Talkin'": "It's bright in the heavens and the wheels are flying/ Fame and honor never seem to fade/ The fire's gone out but the light is never dyin'/ Who says I can't get heavenly aid?"

Yet it is far from certain whether conventional religious alternatives are able to work, so that Dylan greatly prefers a life of faith to the role of "religion" in the sense of some institution or ideology that in the end delimits more that it liberates. There is simply no guarantee for salvation because according to "Not Dark Yet," regardless of whether we accept or reject any given religious ideology, "I've still got the scars that the Son/sun didn't heal." In "Til I Fell In Love With You," religion offers little or no comfort: "But I know God is my shield/ And he won't lead me astray/ Still I don't know what I'm gonna do/ I was allright 'til I fell in love with you." What may go wrong with misguided or half-hearted religious belief is also alluded to in the last verse of the movie single "Huck's Tune" from 2007, "All the merry little elves can go hang themselves/ My faith is as cold as can be." Faith must be steady and firm in its conviction, and not succumb to one of the perennial theological pitfalls.

One kind of weak faith which results from too much emphasis on stoicism, leading to nihilism, occurs when you feel your back is against the wall, and sincere concern and commitment to others is abandoned out of fear or paralysis. The refrain "don't care" reverberates through songs of the Modern Era. In "High Water" Dylan sings, "I'm preachin' the word of God, I'm puttin' out your eyes/ . . . I told her I didn't really care/ High water everywhere," and in "Things Have Changed," "People are crazy and times are strange/ I'm locked in tight, I'm out of range/ I used to care, but things have changed." This echoes "Not Dark Yet, "I just don't see why I should even care/ It's not dark yet, but it's getting there."

Trying to withdraw to a state of meditation is problematic because so many others seek to distract and take advantage of your misfortune so that one is left in "Million Miles" on *Time Out of Mind*, "drifting in and out of dreamless sleep . . . Maybe in the next life I'll be able to hear myself think." Another kind of weak faith continues to pay the price for acts of hedonism, as in "Tryin' to Get to Heaven": "Some trains don't pull no gamblers,/ No midnight ramblers like they did before./ I've been to Sugartown, I shook the sugar down,/ Now I'm tryin' to get to heaven before they close the door." But at least awareness of this can bring one to a moment of regret, which can be a crucial turning point leading to spiritual realization.

Whereas nihilism represents an extreme form of non-dualism, an excessive state stemming from the side of non-dualism is a slavish attachment to devotion that rings hollow as in "Thunder on the Mountain," "I been to St. Herman's church, said my religious vows/ I've sucked the milk out of a thousand cows." What is needed is to achieve righteous indignation and devout commitment through genuine repentance. "Bye and Bye" recommends, "I'm gonna baptize you in fire so you can sin no more," and in "Nettie Moore," "I'd walk through a blazing fire, baby, if I knew you was on the other side." In "The Levee's Gonna Break," the baptism comes not by fire but by water, "Well, I worked on the levee, mama, both night and day/ I worked on the levee, mama, both night and day/ I got to the river and I threw my clothes away." When this rite is successful, according to "Thunder on the Mountain," caring and compassion is the result: "Gonna forget about myself for a while, gonna go out and see what others need ... Remember this, I'm your servant both night and day." However, this is not necessarily sufficient to guarantee the attainment of salvation.

Tryin' to get to heaven

Attaining transcendence according to Dylan's middle-path approach combines dualistic forgiveness and compassion with non-dualistic resignation to harsh reality, and this mix generates authentic care and concern for each and every grain of sand primarily achieved through either a profoundly sincere relationship with a woman or by intense communion with nature. Unlike earlier career stages, however, when Dylan's idealization of romantic patterns or an inspiring environmental context was sometimes taken to an extreme, in the songs of the Modern Era any kind of celebration is tempered by sensitivity to frailty and fragility, which has a resonance with the Buddhist view of impermanence and instability affecting all people and things. Dylan is no longer the wild-eyed idealist or the world-weary nihilist but a seasoned, savvy traveler on the highways and byways of the path to salvation who sees all the flux and change yet accepts it all with good nature and aplomb.

This outlook is eloquently expressed in "When the Deal Goes Down" on *Modern Times*, which derives in part from "Last Fair Deal Gone Down" by Robert Johnson (also referenced in "Changing of the Guards") and uses the melody from Bing Crosby's signature song "When the Blue of the Night Meets the Gold of the Day." The Crosby tune is transformed from a gentle love song into a song that uses romance as a vehicle to articulate a vision of the joys of an awareness of the strengths and limitations of personal relationships. The lyric admits, "We live and we die, we know not why," which touches base with "Not Dark Yet," "I was born here and I'll die here against my will." It also includes the following expression of finite transcendence sung in a sustained tone of lamentation:

> I heard the deafening noise, I felt transient joys
> I know they're not what they seem
> In this earthly domain, full of disappointment and pain
> You'll never see me frown
> I owe my heart to you, and that's sayin' it true
> And I'll be with you when the deal goes down.

According to a reviewer who explains the depth of the lyrics of "When the Deal Goes Down":

> What makes the song so moving is the way it depicts a struggle for, and perhaps a final attainment of, a kind of grace, or spiritual enlightenment, achieved not through any conventionally "religious" path but through making a personal "deal" with the spirit of creativity. Dylan has stated that he now places his faith not in any deity but in the old songs he constantly revisits and refers to in his art.[25]

The vision is reinforced in several other numbers from the Modern Era, including "Beyond the Horizon," which evokes a deceptively simple awareness that conjoins dualistic elements involving a divine force making moral judgments with non-dualistic realization of the need for overcoming divisions. According to the song:

> Beyond the horizon, across the divide
> 'Round about midnight, we'll be on the same side
> Beyond the horizon, 'neath crimson skies
> In the soft light of morning I'll follow you with my eyes
> Somebody there always cared
> There's always a reason
> Why someone's life has been spared.

While these songs focus on human relations as the source of transcendence, another set of songs highlights the role of nature, especially in "Highlands" and "Bye and Bye" on *Love and Theft* which proclaims: "I'm rollin' slow—I'm doing all I know/ I'm tellin' myself I found true happiness/ That I've still got a dream that hasn't been repossessed/ I'm rollin' slow, goin' where the wild roses grow." The realm of the Highlands provides a perfect platform for gazing at the humdrum world with a sense of aloofness and quietude, although it is located more in the imagination than as a physical reality.

The song opens by examining the depths of suffering:

> Insanity is smashing up against my soul
> You can say I was on anything but a roll
> If I had a conscience, well I just might blow my top
> What would I do with it anyway
> Maybe take it to the pawn shop.

It also celebrates the heights of redemption that can be gained when "my heart's in the Highlands gentle and fair/ Honeysuckle blooming in the wildwood air/ Bluebelles blazing, where the Aberdeen waters flow." The image of the Highlands has dualistic implications as the place "when I get called home . . . [with] Big white clouds, like chariots that swing down low," but the intense emphasis on naturalism in symbolizing an internal experiential domain modifies and complements the gospel tone by suggesting an Asian-style mystical view.

"Highlands" continues with a vivid and haunting evocation of what is involved in reaching (or not) the long sought realm. The narrator says, "I got new eyes, everything looks far away," which indicates a radical shift in perception and perspective:

> Well my heart's in the Highlands at the break of day
> Over the hills and far away
> There's a way to get there, and I'll figure it out somehow
> Well I'm already there in my mind and that's good enough for now.

The Highlands is not an utopia in the sense of being an unattainable realm because it represents a description of something real, but at the same time it is so idealized that the narrator realizes that he will never actually get there. But the beauty of this realm is that it restores and inspires his mind while his heart is enraptured by longing and aspiration, whether or not he is actually there.

The song makes an important distinction between the heart which aspires to reach the heights and the mind which in its own way, despite its deep blues, can already glimpse and experience it regardless of the obstacles. There is thus a basic disconnect between reality and hope, the physical and the spiritual as in the Robert Burns poem which serves as one of Dylan's sources, "My heart's in the Highlands, my heart is not here,/ . . . My heart's in the Highlands, wherever I go." But the disparity or dualism is exactly what drives rather than impedes Dylan's approach to non-dualism through attaining finite transcendence. It is this creative tension that is the key to fulfillment.

The state of mind expressed by this song consists of an intriguing mixture of spiritual elements. On the one hand, it is eerily reminiscent of "Desolation Row" from 1965 in evoking the non-dualism of loss and powerlessness, hollowness and isolation, with little relief in sight other than to withdraw from and rise above the madding crowd. At the same time, it creates a dualistic uplifting note of energy and excitement in evoking a sparkling natural landscape that is a vehicle to or a reflection of heavenly reward, even though the descriptions are no doubt deliberately skewed since bluebells do not "blaze" and Aberdeen is the name of a town rather than a waterway. This delicate combination of Duality and Non-Duality brings consolation and reprieve in a world of transiency and pain.

In a comparable expression of a creative seeker who longs for the authenticity of the inexpressible haven of solitude amid a world of rank uncertainty and ambiguity, fifth century Chinese Daoist poet Tao Qian, an important precursor of Zen verse, wrote "Drinking Wine:"[26]

> I made my home amidst this human bustle,
> Yet I hear no clamor from the carts and horses.
> My friend, you ask me how this can be so?
> A distant heart will tend towards like places.
> From the eastern hedge, I pluck chrysanthemum flowers,
> And idly look towards the southern hills.
> The mountain air is beautiful day and night,
> The birds fly back to roost with one another.
> I know that this must have some deeper meaning,
> I try to explain, but cannot find the words.

This verse has a contemporary resonance in highlighting the non-dual dualism of the level of finite transcendence Dylan has reached . . . at least in his mind, which is good enough for now, he says. I believe that Tao Qian would heartily agree with Dylan's notion of experiencing transient joys as a constructive compromise or middle path between seeking a single truth and finding no truth whatsoever.

A ZEN MASTER?

Some critics have argued that Christianity is the central factor in understanding Dylan's approach to religiosity, primarily because biblical apocalypticism especially influenced by the *Book of Revelations* affects all periods of his career, both the phases of answers and those of disillusion. However, a Christian-based view can easily be challenged in that, by looking over the trajectory of Dylan's career, it might well be said that the first half (1960s and 1970s) had more of a Zen flavor until his gospel conversion, whereas the second half (1980s and 1990s) reflected a commitment to Christian faith.

Having documented that this simplistic division is rather misleading, yet another argument could be made that turns the Christian standpoint on its head. Just a couple of years of born-again compositions have been used to justify the notion of a lifelong embracing of Christian faith that outranks other religious themes. It is therefore reasonable to assert that while direct links to Zen or the East more generally are relatively limited and primarily confined to the mid-1970s, Dylan has long held a Zen-like attitude that is crucial for considering his entire career trajectory.

While Dylan's Zen outlook remains for the most part under the surface, it comes to the fore at times of disillusionment with conventional forms of authority, be it social, political, religious, or familial and the kinds of answers to life's problems they typically represent. This rejection of authority was especially pronounced in three main phases of the mid-1960s, mid-1970s, and mid-1980s, when Dylan found himself at a crucial turning point and was struggling with the question of how to make sense of the relativity of truth by gaining consolation through the detachment of solitude and compassion.

However, my aim is not simply to claim that Dylan is a master of Zen Buddhism, and so I stop short of such a highly problematic suggestion, which surely contradicts all of the evidence to the contrary based on his considerable Western influences and orientation. Rather, the spirit of this book, in accord with Dylan's unwillingness to be put in any one camp, is reflected in the subtitle, which concludes with a question mark.[27] The merits, along with the questionability, of linking Dylan with Zen Buddhist thought, as one way among many of exploring his enigmatic worldview, have been explored.

Opposing views based on a single vision of truth derived from a higher power and the acceptance of relative truths devoid of unity—or the dichotomies of retribution and resignation, or justice and detachment—coexist more or less harmoniously in the Modern Era. Transitions are evident from verse to verse in some cases and this creative use of dialectic, I argue, is what makes for Dylan's creative resurgence that is abundantly in evidence in each of the three most recent albums.

In Zen fashion, the middle way for Bob Dylan is not a simplistic compromise, as oppositions do not merely vanish into an abstract oneness.

Visions of heavenly wheels and chariots are inseparable from the enduring tensions of the concrete world that is filled with the intermingling of conflict and hope, tragedy and sublimity, and betrayal and trust. Having said that the Modern Era reflects balance, it can also be argued that by emphasizing the point that Duality does not exist apart from Non-Duality, this juxtaposition tends to surpass the veracity of the dualistic view and suggests that the weight of the balance falls on the non-dualistic side.

Is Dylan a Zen master? The question itself provides the answer to the question. Meanwhile, may the non-dual dual dialectical trajectory of finite transcendence achieved while wandering in and out of the wilderness, even as it is doom alone that counts, continue to go unbroken! No one else can sing that tune. Or show us the scars for having made a few bad turns.

Appendix A

Citations of Dylan Lyrics*

"2 x 2"   Copyright ©1990 Special Rider Music

"4th Time Around" (2)   Copyright ©1966; renewed 1994 Dwarf Music

"10,000 Men"   Copyright ©1990 Special Rider Music

"Absolutely Sweet Marie"   Copyright ©1966; renewed 1994 Dwarf Music

"A Hard Rain's A-Gonna Fall" (2)   Copyright ©1963; renewed 1991 Special Rider Music

"Ain't Talkin'" (6)   Copyright © 2006 Special Rider Music

"All Along The Watchtower" (2)   Copyright ©1968; renewed 1996 Dwarf Music

"All I Really Want To Do"   Copyright ©1964; renewed 1992 Special Rider Music

"All The Tired Horses"   Copyright ©1970 Big Sky Music

"Angelina"   Copyright ©1981 Special Rider Music

"Ballad In Plain D"   Copyright ©1964; renewed 1992 Special Rider Music

"Beyond The Horizon"   Copyright © 2006 Special Rider Music

"Billy 1"   Copyright © 1972 Ram's Horn Music

"Black Crow Blues"   Copyright ©1964; renewed 1992 Special Rider Music

"Black Diamond Bay" (Bob Dylan and   Copyright ©1975 Ram's Horn Music
   Jacques Levy)

"Blowin' In The Wind"   Copyright ©1962; renewed 1990 Special Rider Music

"Born In Time"   Copyright ©1990 Special Rider Music

Bringing It All Back Home liner   Copyright ©1965 Special Rider Music
   notes (4)

"Brownsville Girl" (6)   Copyright ©1986 Special Rider Music

"Buckets of Rain" (3)   Copyright ©1974 Ram's Horn Music

"Bye And Bye" (2)	Copyright ©2001 Special Rider Music
"Can You Please Crawl Out Your Window?"	Copyright ©1965; renewed 1993 Special Rider Music
"Cat's In The Well"	Copyright ©1990 Special Rider Music
"Changing Of The Guards" (2)	Copyright ©1978 Special Rider Music
"Chimes Of Freedom"	Copyright ©1964; renewed 1992 Special Rider Music
Chronicles (2)	New York: Simon & Shuster, 2004
"Clean-Cut Kid"	Copyright ©1985 Special Rider Music
"Cold Irons Bound"	Copyright ©1997 Special Rider Music
"Copper Kettle"	Copyright ©1970 Big Sky Music
"Country Pie" (2)	Copyright ©1969; renewed 1997 Big Sky Music
"Covenant Woman"	Copyright ©1980 Special Rider Music
"Dark Eyes"	Copyright ©1985 Special Rider Music
"Day Of The Locusts"	Copyright ©1970 Big Sky Music
"Death Is Not The End"	Copyright ©1988 Special Rider Music
Desire liner notes	Copyright ©1975 Ram's Horn Music
"Desolation Row" (6)	Copyright ©1965; renewed 1993 Special Rider Music
"Diamond Joe"	Copyright ©1992 Special Rider Music
"Dignity" (3)	Copyright ©1989 Special Rider Music
"Dirge" (3)	Copyright ©1973 Ram's Horn Music
"Dirt Road Blues"	Copyright ©1997 Special Rider Music
"Don't Fall Apart On Me Tonight" (2)	Copyright ©1983 Special Rider Music
"Down In The Flood (Crash On The Levee)"	Copyright © 1967; renewed 1995 Dwarf Music
"Drifter's Escape"	Copyright ©1968; renewed 1996 Dwarf Music
"Every Grain Of Sand" (2)	Copyright ©1981 Special Rider Music
"Father Of Night"	Copyright ©1970 Big Sky Music
"Floater (Too Much To Ask)"	Copyright ©2001 Special Rider Music
"Forever Young"	Copyright ©1973 Ram's Horn Music
"Froggie Went A-Courtin'"	Copyright ©1992 Special Rider Music
"Gates of Eden"	Copyright ©1965; renewed 1993 Special Rider Music

"George Jackson"	Copyright ©1971 Ram's Horn Music
"Going, Going, Gone"	Copyright ©1973 Ram's Horn Music
"Gonna Change My Way Of Thinking" (2)	Copyright ©1979 Special Rider Music
"Gotta Serve Somebody" (2)	Copyright ©1979 Special Rider Music
"Handy Dandy"	Copyright ©1990 Special Rider Music
"Highlands" (4)	Copyright ©1997 Special Rider Music
"High Water (for Charlie Patton)" (4)	Copyright © 2001 Special Rider Music
"Highway 61 Revisited" (2)	Copyright ©1965; renewed 1993 Special Rider Music
Highway 61 Revisited liner notes (3)	Copyright ©1965 Special Rider Music
"Huck's Tune"	Copyright © 2007 Sony BMG Music Entertainment
"Hurricane" (Bob Dylan and Jacques Levy) (3)	Copyright ©1975 Ram's Horn Music
"I Am A Lonesome Hobo"	Copyright ©1968; renewed 1996 Dwarf Music
"I And I" (3)	Copyright ©1983 Special Rider Music
"I Believe In You"	Copyright ©1979 Special Rider Music
"Idiot Wind"(6)	Copyright ©1974 Ram's Horn Music
"If Not For You"	Copyright ©1970 Big Sky Music
"I Pity The Poor Immigrant"	Copyright ©1968; renewed 1996 Dwarf Music
"I Shall Be Free No. 10"	Copyright © 1971 Special Rider Music
"I Threw It All Away" (2)	Copyright ©1969; renewed 1997 Big Sky Music
"It's Alright, Ma (I'm Only Bleeding)" (6)	Copyright ©1965; renewed 1993 Special Rider Music
"It Takes A Lot To Laugh, It Takes A Train To Cry" (2)	Copyright ©1965; renewed 1993 Special Rider Music
"I Want You" (2)	Copyright ©1966; renewed 1994 Dwarf Music
"John Wesley Harding" (2)	Copyright ©1968; renewed 1996 Dwarf Music
John Wesley Harding liner notes	Copyright ©1968 Dwarf Music
"Jokerman" (5)	Copyright ©1983 Special Rider Music
"Just Like A Woman" (2)	Copyright ©1966; renewed 1994 Dwarf Music
"Just Like Tom Thumb's Blues" (5)	Copyright ©1965; renewed 1993 Special Rider Music
"Knockin' On Heaven's Door"	Copyright ©1973 Ram's Horn Music

"Lay Down Your Weary Tune"	Copyright ©1964; renewed 1992 Special Rider Music
"Lenny Bruce"	Copyright ©1981 Special Rider Music
"License to Kill"	Copyright ©1983 Special Rider Music
"Like A Rolling Stone" (2)	Copyright ©1965; renewed 1993 Special Rider Music
"Lily, Rosemary and the Jack of Hearts"	Copyright ©1975 Ram's Horn Music
Live At Budokan liner notes	Produced by Don DeVito, 1979
"Lo And Behold!"	Copyright ©1967; renewed 1995 Dwarf Music
"Long Distance Operator"	Copyright © 1971 Dwarf Music
"Love Minus Zero/No Limit" (3)	Copyright ©1965; renewed 1993 Special Rider Music
"Love Sick"	Copyright ©1997 Special Rider Music
"Maggie's Farm"	Copyright ©1965; renewed 1993 Special Rider Music
"Make You Feel My Love"	Copyright ©1997 Special Rider Music
"Man In The Long Black Coat" (2)	Copyright ©1989 Special Rider Music
"Man Of Peace"	Copyright ©1983 Special Rider Music
Masked And Anonymous (2)	Sony Pictures Classic © 2003
"Masters Of War" (2)	Copyright ©1963; renewed 1991 Special Rider Music
"Million Dollar Bash"	Copyright ©1967; renewed 1995 Dwarf Music
"Million Miles"	Copyright ©1997 Special Rider Music
"Mississippi"	Copyright ©1997 Special Rider Music
"Mozambique" (Bob Dylan and Jacques Levy)	Copyright ©1975 Ram's Horn Music
"Mr. Tambourine Man"	Copyright ©1964; renewed 1992 Special Rider Music
"My Back Pages" (2)	Copyright ©1964; renewed 1992 Special Rider Music
"Nettie Moore" (6)	Copyright © 2006 Special Rider Music
"Nobody 'Cept You"	Copyright ©1973 Ram's Horn Music
"Not Dark Yet" (5)	Copyright ©1997 Special Rider Music
"Nothing Was Delivered"	Copyright ©1968; renewed 1996 Dwarf Music
"No Time To Think" (2)	Copyright ©1978 Special Rider Music
"Oh, Sister" (Bob Dylan and Jacques Levy)	Copyright ©1975 Ram's Horn Music
"One Too Many Mornings"	Copyright ©1964; renewed 1992 Special Rider Music

"Open The Door, Homer"	Copyright ©1968; renewed 1996 Dwarf Music
Pat Garrett And Billy The Kid	Copyright ©1973 Ram's Horn Music
"Peggy Day"	Copyright ©1969; renewed 1997 Dwarf Music
Planet Waves liner notes (3)	Copyright ©1974 Ram's Horn Music
"Please Mrs. Henry"	Copyright © 1967; renewed 1995 Dwarf Music
"Political World"	Copyright ©1989 Special Rider Music
"Positively 4th Street" (2)	Copyright ©1965; renewed 1993 Special Rider Music
"Precious Angel" (3)	Copyright ©1979 Special Rider Music
"Property Of Jesus"	Copyright ©1981 Special Rider Music
"Quinn The Eskimo (The Mighty Quinn)"	Copyright © 1970 Dwarf Music
"Restless Farewell"	Copyright ©1964; renewed 1992 Special Rider Music
"Ring Them Bells"	Copyright ©1989 Special Rider Music
"Sad-Eyed Lady Of The Lowlands"	Copyright ©1966; renewed 1994 Dwarf Music
"Señor (Tales of Yankee Power)"	Copyright ©1978 Special Rider Music
"Series Of Dreams"	Copyright ©1991 Special Rider Music
"Shelter From The Storm" (5)	Copyright ©1974 Ram's Horn Music
"Shooting Star" (2)	Copyright ©1989 Special Rider Music
"Sign On The Window"	Copyright ©1970 Big Sky Music
"Silvio" (4)	Copyright ©1988 Special Rider Music
"Simple Twist of Fate" (5)	Copyright ©1974 Ram's Horn Music
"Slow Train" (5)	Copyright ©1979 Special Rider Music
"Solid Rock"	Copyright ©1980 Special Rider Music
"Someday Baby"	Copyright © 2006 Special Rider Music
"Song To Woody"	Copyright ©1962; renewed 1990 MCA
"Spirit On The Water" (4)	Copyright © 2006 Special Rider Music
"Standing In The Doorway" (3)	Copyright ©1997 Special Rider Music
"Stuck Inside Of Mobile With The Memphis Blues Again" (4)	Copyright ©1966; renewed 1994 Dwarf Music
"Subterranean Homesick Blues"	Copyright ©1965; renewed 1993 Special Rider Music
"Sugar Baby" (5)	Copyright ©2001 Special Rider Music

"Sweetheart Like You" (3)	Copyright ©1983 Special Rider Music
"Talkin' World War III Blues"	Copyright ©1963; renewed 1991 Special Rider Music
"Tangled Up In Blue" (5)	Copyright ©1974 Ram's Horn Music
Tarantula	New York: The Macmillan Company, 1971
"Tears Of Rage" (2)	Copyright ©1968; renewed 1996 Dwarf Music
"Temporary Like Achilles"	Copyright ©1966; renewed 1994 Dwarf Music
"The Ballad Of Frankie Lee And Judas Priest" (3)	Copyright ©1968; renewed 1996 Dwarf Music
"The Groom's Still Waiting At The Altar"	Copyright ©1981 Special Rider Music
"The Levee's Gonna Break" (3)	Copyright © 2006 Special Rider Music
"The Man In Me" (2)	Copyright ©1970 Big Sky Music
"The Times They Are A-Changin'" (2)	Copyright ©1963; renewed 1991 Special Rider Music
The Times They Are A-Changin' liner notes	Copyright ©1964 Special Rider Music
"Things Have Changed" (7)	Copyright ©1999 Special Rider Music
"This Wheel's On Fire"	Copyright ©1967; renewed 1995 Dwarf Music
"Three Angels"	Copyright ©1970 Big Sky Music
"Thunder On The Mountain" (2)	Copyright © 2006 Special Rider Music
"Tight Connection To My Heart (Has Anybody Seen My Love)"	Copyright ©1985 Special Rider Music
"Til I Fell In Love With You" (2)	Copyright © 1997 Special Rider Music
"Time Passes Slowly"	Copyright ©1970 Big Sky Music
"Tombstone Blues" (4)	Copyright ©1965; renewed 1993 Special Rider Music
"Too Much Of Nothing" (2)	Copyright ©1967; renewed 1995 Dwarf Music
"Tough Mama"	Copyright ©1973 Ram's Horn Music
"True Love Tends To Forget" (2)	Copyright ©1978 Special Rider Music
"Trust Yourself"	Copyright ©1985 Special Rider Music
"Tryin' To Get To Heaven" (8)	Copyright ©1997 Special Rider Music
"T.V. Talkin' Song"	Copyright ©1990 Special Rider Music
"Under The Red Sky"	Copyright ©1990 Special Rider Music
"Union Sundown"	Copyright ©1983 Special Rider Music

"Up To Me" (4)	Copyright ©1974 Ram's Horn Music
"Visions of Johanna" (6)	Copyright ©1966; renewed 1994 Dwarf Music
"Watching The River Flow"	Copyright ©1971 Big Sky Music
"We Better Talk This Over" (2)	Copyright ©1978 Special Rider Music
"Wedding Song"	Copyright ©1973 Ram's Horn Music
"What Can I Do For You?"	Copyright ©1980 Special Rider Music
"What Good Am I?"	Copyright ©1989 Special Rider Music
"When He Returns" (5)	Copyright ©1979 Special Rider Music
"When I Paint My Masterpiece"	Copyright ©1971 Big Sky Music
"When The Deal Goes Down" (4)	Copyright © 2006 Special Rider Music
"When The Ship Comes In" (2)	Copyright ©1965; renewed 1991 Special Rider Music
"When You Gonna Wake Up?" (4)	Copyright © 1979 Special Rider Music
"Where Are You Tonight? (Journey Through Dark Heat)" (2)	Copyright © 1978 Special Rider Music
"Wiggle Wiggle"	Copyright ©1990 Special Rider Music
'Workingman's Blues #2" (3)	Copyright © 2006 Special Rider Music
World Gone Wrong liner notes	Copyright ©1993 Special Rider Music
"You Ain't Goin' Nowhere"	Copyright ©1967; renewed 1995 Dwarf Music
"You're A Big Girl Now"	Copyright ©1974 Ram's Horn Music
"You're Gonna Make Me Lonesome When You Go" (2)	Copyright ©1974 Ram's Horn Music

* Permission granted by Jeff Rosen, courtesy of the Web site bobdylan.com

Appendix B

Dylan Discography in Relation to Career Periods

PERIOD 1: FROM "PROTESTING" TO "DETESTING"

Duality I: Topical Protest

Gateway: Basic Bob Typology (Bootleg Series Vol.1)	1961–1963
Bob Dylan (also part of Basic Bob)	1962
The Freewheelin' Bob Dylan (also part of Basic Bob)	1963
The Times They Are A-Changin'	1964
Crossroad: Another Side of Bob Dylan	1964

Non-Duality I: Social Disillusionment

Bringing It All Back Home	1965
Highway 61 Revisited	1965
Blonde on Blonde	1966

PERIOD 2: FROM "I'LL BE YOUR BABY" TO "YOU'RE AN IDIOT, BABE"

Gateway: The Basement Tapes, John Wesley Harding	1967

Duality II: Country/Family

Nashville Skyline	1969
Crossroad: Self Portrait, New Morning	1970

Non-Duality II: Personal Disillusionment

Planet Waves	1974
Blood on the Tracks	1975
Desire	1976

PERIOD 3: FROM "SERVING SOMEBODY" TO "LETTING THE ECHO DECIDE"

Gateway: Street-Legal	1978

Duality III: Gospel

Slow Train Coming	1979
Saved	1980
Crossroad: Shot of Love	1981

Non-Duality III: Conversion Disillusionment

Infidels	1983
Empire Burlesque	1985
Knocked Out Loaded	1986
Down in the Groove	1988

MODERN ERA: MIDDLE WAY FOUND

Gateway: Oh Mercy and Under the Red Sky	1989–1990

Ahead to the Past

Good as I Been to You	1992
World Gone Wrong	1993
MTV Unplugged	1994

Back to the Future

Time Out of Mind	1997
"Love and Theft"	2001
Modern Times	2006

Appendix C

Dylan Pendulum Diagram

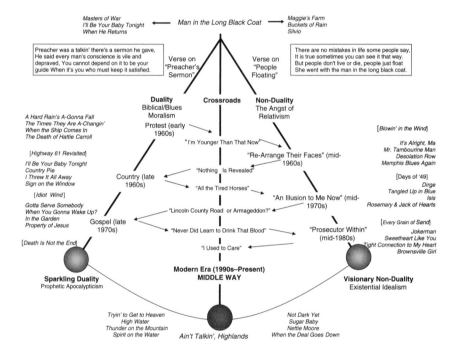

Notes

PREFACE

1 Mikal Gilmore. "Hard-boiled, Raw Bootlegs Document Dylan's Late-period Revival," *Rolling Stone* 1063 (10/16/2008), p. 75.

CHAPTER 1

1 M. Cooper Harriss. "Sightings," *Religion in Modern Times*, http://marty-center. uchicago.edu/sightings/archive_2006/0810.shtml (8/10/2006).

2 Catherine Mason and Richard Thomas. "Introduction [to special issue on Bob Dylan]," *Oral Tradition* 22/1 (2007): 3.

3 See Bert Cartwright. *The Bible in the Lyrics of Bob Dylan.* Lancashire, UK: Wanted Man, 1985; Michael J. Gilmour. *Tangled Up In the Bible: Bob Dylan and Scripture.* New York: Continuum, 2004; and Stephen H. Webb. *Dylan Redeemed: from Highway 61 to Saved.* New York, NY: Continuum, 2006.

4 Andy Gill and Kevin Odegard. *A Simple Twist of Fate: Bob Dylan and the Making of Blood on the Tracks.* Cambridge, MA: Da Capo Press, 2005, p. 4.

5 Gill and Odegard. *A Simple Twist of Fate*, pp. 4 and 6.

6 Greeted with the newspaper headline "Bob Dylan has arrived!" ("Bobu Diran ga yatte-kita"), Dylan was also asked if he should be considered a "god of folk songs," to which he responded, "no," and when queried how he should be thought of, he replied, "I'm just a person." Skeptics have seen the motive for the tour tied to a need for money to pay alimony after a difficult, contested divorce. See Naoki Urasawa and Koji Wakui. *Talkin' About Bob Dylan: Diran wo katarou.* Tokyo: Shogakukan, 2007; and also see Mihashi Kazuo. *60 nendai no Bobu Diran.* Tokyo: Shinko Music Pub. Co., 1991.

7 The live album was originally planned along with the greatest hits collection *Masterpieces* for a Japan-only release.

8 The liner notes also refer to Dylan's remembering a geisha, showing his movement between the physical and spiritual.

9 The officially released version is, "I ran into the fortune-teller, who said beware of lightning that might strike/ I haven't known peace and quiet for so long I can't remember what it's like." One wonders why Dylan removed the Asian reference.

10 The officially released version is, "She was born in spring, but I was born too late/ Blame it on a simple twist of fate."

11 This is the opening passage that introduces the thirteenth-century Chinese collection of koans known as the *Wumenguan* (Jap. *Mumonkan*), which means "Gateless Gate."

12 See Clinton Heylin. *Bob Dylan: Behind the Shades Revisited*. New York: HarperCollins Publishers Inc., 2000, pp. 368–369.

13 In *Chronicles: Volume One*. New York: Simon & Shuster, 2004, p. 288, Dylan associates this theme with Robert Johnson.

14 Dylan's Christian albums sold far less than his non-religious albums, and in a 1980 interview in Dayton, Ohio he replied to a question about whether becoming a Christian was an easy choice by saying: "It would have been easier if I had become a Buddhist, or a Scientologist, or if I had gone to Sing Sing."

15 See Richard F. Thomas. "The Streets of Rome: The Classical Dylan," *Oral Tradition* 22/1 (2007): 30–56. For a complete listing of the *Confessions of a Yakuza* passages, see Jonathan Eig and Sebastian Moffett. "Did Bob Dylan Lift Lines From Dr. Saga? Don't Think Twice, It's All Right Is the View of This Japanese Writer," *Wall Street Journal*, http://www.csudh.edu/dearhabermas/plagiarbk010.htm (7/08/2003).

16 Dylan's case is somewhat similar to that of Leonard Cohen, another 1960s Jewish singer-songwriter who explored many diverse forms of religiosity such as the Hebraic Kabbalist mystical tradition along with Christianity and other esoteric and mythical disciplines, including Yoga and Zen Buddhism. Although it is clear that for both Dylan and Cohen spiritual experimentation was often undertaken as a matter of self-discovery to enhance music-making, unlike the former, Cohen did become a practicing Zen Buddhist beginning in the early 1970s under Sasaki Roshi, and for long stretches gave up songwriting and performing altogether in order to dedicate himself to meditative training and a life of humility in practice. See David Boucher. *Dylan & Cohen: Poets of Rock and Roll*. New York: Continuum International Publishing, 2004. Also there is no doubt that other Dylan companions over the years have had more than a passing interest in Asian mysticism, such as Robbie Robertson, lead guitarist of The Band who was known to read writings on Zen by D. T. Suzuki and Alan

Watts, and Willie Nelson who penned the national bestseller, *The Tao of Willie: A Guide to the Happiness in Your Heart*. New York: Gotham Books, 2006 with Turk Pipkin.

17 Michael Gray. *Song and Dance Man III: The Art of Bob Dylan*. New York: Continuum, 2000, p. 399.

18 For more on the comparison of Dylan and Dogen, see Steven Heine and Taigen Dan Leighton. "Dylan and Dogen: Masters of Spirit and Words," *Kyoto Journal* 39 (1999): 4–11. An audiofile of Leighton's lecture on "Visions of Johanna" and Zen meditation called "Bob Dylan's Song about Sesshin and Zen Mind" is available at http://www.ancientdragon.org/dharma/dharma_talks_audio.

19 Another sign of rebellion was that Dylan rather slyly performed offbeat, almost unrecognizable versions of the anti-war anthem "Masters of War" at the unlikely venues of West Point and the Grammy Awards ceremony on the eve of the first Gulf War in the early 1990s, yet he has kept to himself whether he rejects or supports American conflicts from Vietnam to Iraq. He has suggested the song is not against war per se, but the "military-industrial complex," as Eisenhower once termed the forces of greed for power that dominate society with hostilities and inhibit individualism. It is interesting that during the worldwide Live Aid show of 1985 to help the famine-stricken in Africa, Dylan sang "Ballad of Hollis Brown," an early, obscure protest song about poverty leading to a man murdering himself and his family. He also used this to open Tour '74, when he said "Gotcha" to perplexed reporters expecting to hear one of the big hits who did not at first recognize this song. At Live Aid, Dylan commented that more should be done to reduce poverty among the farmers of America, and this led his friends and associates like Willie Nelson to originate the annual Farm Aid fundraisers. On the other hand, Dylan has been criticized for using himself and/or his music for ads for Victoria's Secret and Cadillac Escalade.

20 Personal interview in Hibbing, Minnesota (3/25/2007).

21 Galatians 6.7: Be not deceived; God is not mocked: for whatsoever a man soweth, that shall he also reap.

CHAPTER 2

1 Arlo Guthrie performing in the same city at that time said to his audience, "You will hear more Dylan songs here than in his concert."

2 Albertina Lloyd. "Bob Dylan on screen," http://www.femalefirst.co.uk/ entertainment/ Bob+Dylan-43210.html (11/03/2007).

3 Mike Devlin. "Top 10 musical geniuses," *Canwest News Service*, http://www. canada.com/globaltv/globalshows/et_story.html?id=c80f66b2-ead1 -49dd-80cb-c9c124451644 (11/05/2007).

4 Jim Sullivan. "Dylan Changin' with the Times," *Christian Science Monitor*, http://www.csmonitor.com/2006/0901/p11s03-almp.html (9/01/2006).

5 Lawrence Toppman. "Everybody's 'There' Except Bob D. But the Search for the 'Real' Dylan Makes for a Fascinating Experiment in Haynes' Biopic," *Charlotte Times* (11/23/2007).

6 See Eric Lott. *Love and Theft: Blackface Minstrelsy and the American Working Class*. New York: Oxford University Press, 1993. The book's title was no doubt the source of Dylan's own love and thievery for his 2001 album. Spike Lee's 1999 film *Bamboozled* is an excellent resource for understanding the historical roots of minstrelsy, especially in the final scene which is a montage of clips from pre-war films, and its continuing impact on contemporary culture wars.

7 Other songs that refer to lies include: "I Pity the Poor Immigrant" ("lies with ev'ry breath"), "Tell Me" ("tell me no lies"), "License to Kill" ("And his eyes, they just tell him lies"), and "Million Miles" ("You told yourself a lie; that's all right mama, I told myself one too").

8 Jody Rosen. "Bob Dylan's Make-Out Album: The Romantic—and Spectacular— *Modern Times*," *Slate*, http://www.slate.com/id/2148563 (8/30/2006).

9 Apparently the original working title of *Time Out of Mind* was "A Stormy Season."

10 According to Michael Gilmour, "hilltop village" refers to Jerusalem and "gambling for my clothes" alludes to five passages including Psalms 22.18 and all four Gospels, and "I offered up my innocence" alludes to two Old Testament and three New Testament passages; see *Tangled Up in the Bible: Bob Dylan and Scripture*. New York: Continuum, 2004, p. 116. But the song can also be seen to have an Eastern flavor according to Andy Gill and Kevin Odegard by symbolizing "the classic Taoist principles of yin and yang that help sustain the balance of the world," in *A Simple Twist of Fate: Bob Dylan and the Making of Blood on the Tracks*. Cambridge, MA: Da Capo Press, 2005, p. 162.

11 In a scene in *I'm Not There*, director Todd Haynes has President Lyndon Baines Johnson (LBJ) mouthing these words while giving a television address at the time of the escalation of the Vietnam War. LBJ was known to say that he wanted to bomb the Viet Cong back to the Stone Age. But I think the Dylan line in the context refers to religious institutions.

12 In "Foot of Pride," a 1983 *Infidels* outtake: "Yeah, from the stage they'll be tryin' to get water outta rocks/ A whore will pass the hat, collect a hundred grand and say thanks/ They like to take all this money from sin, build big universities to study in/ Sing 'Amazing Grace' all the way to the Swiss banks."

13 Stephen H. Webb. *Dylan Redeemed: From Highway 61 to Saved*. New York: Continuum, 2006, p. 37.

14 Dave Van Ronk tells the story of how Dylan in the early days in Greenwich Village would tell everyone tall tales of his hanging out with bluesmen in remote or exotic locations when he was just a teenager, such as riding a train

with Big Joe Williams all the way down to Mexico. Nobody believed him, until one day Williams walked by and without prompting blurted out, "Hey Bobby! I haven't seen you since that boxcar down in Mexico!" See Van Ronk with Elijah Wald. *The Mayor of MacDougal Street: A Memoir*. New York: Da Capo Press, 2005, p. 163.

15 Robert Palmer. *Deep Blues: A Musical and Cultural History from the Mississippi Delta to Chicago's South Side to the World*. New York: Penguin Books, 1981, p. 81.

CHAPTER 3

1 Linda Hocking, co-owner of Zimmy's restaurant in Hibbing that hosts many events celebrating Dylan told me she thought his music was a kind of living Rorschach test for all kinds of interpretations to be read into.

2 Andrew Muir. *Troubadour: Early and Late Songs of Bob Dylan*. Cambridgeshire, UK: Woodstock Publications, 2003, p. 264.

3 Mikal Gilmore. "The Rolling Stone Interview: Bob Dylan (2001)," *Rolling Stone*, 882 (11/22/2001).

4 Igor Stravinsky and Pablo Picasso were other major twentieth-century musicians or artists who used folk elements to enrich their "high" art.

5 Robert Palmer. *Deep Blues: A Musical and Cultural History from the Mississippi Delta to Chicago's South Side to the World*. New York: Penguin, 1981, p. 75.

6 Dylan also says, "He seems to know almost everything, he even throws in Confucius-like sayings whenever it suits him," in *Chronicles: Volume One*. New York, Simon & Shuster, 2004, p. 286.

7 Dylan has also said:

> The blues is more than something to sit home and arrange. What made the real blues singers so great is that they were able to state all the problems they had; but at the same time, they were standing outside them and could look at them. And in that way, they had them beat. What's depressing today is that many young singers are trying to get inside the blues, forgetting that those older singers used them to get outside their troubles.

8 Also,

> The influence of the Mississippi Delta . . . has had more impact on American music than any other geographical area: A place that exists in that razor-thin dividing line between shadow and hellfire, a place that percolates artistry from an ancient wellspring that is protective of its offspring—a place ever ready to express its passion in music or words.

See also James L. Dickerson. *Mojo Triangle: Birthplace of Country, Blues, Jazz and Rock 'n' Roll.* New York: Schirmer Trade Books, 2005.

9 Nigel Williamson. *The Rough Guide to the Blues.* London: Rough Guides, 2007, pp. 2–15.

10 Palmer. *Deep Blues*, p. 69.

11 See W. C. Handy. *Father of the Blues: An Autobiography.* New York: Da Capo Press, rpt. 1969; original 1941.

12 This may have been influenced by Johnny Maddox's 2002 recording of blues favorites by the title *Where The Southern Crosses The Yellow Dog.*

13 Dylan. *Chronicles*, pp. 240–241.

14 Victoria Spivey has said,

> I know Bob Dylan loved Big Joe Williams and Big Joe Williams loved Bob Dylan, and they used to get on the stage at Gerde's and play together. Big Joe and Little Joe or Joe Junior we used to call them. Joe and Bobby told us Bobby used to follow Joe up and down the streets of Chicago, that Big Joe was an inspiration.

15 See Matthew Zuckerman. "If There's An Original Thought Out there, I Could Use It Right Now: The Folk Roots of Bob Dylan," *Dylan Influences*, www.expectingrain.com/kok/div/influences.html (3/21/08).

16 Palmer notes of Muddy Waters when he first traveled to Chicago from the Delta that he "was a vigorous twenty-six-year-old with high cheekbones and cool, hooded eyes, features that lend him a certain Oriental inscrutability," in *Deep Blues*, p. 3.

17 Palmer. *Deep Blues*, p. 19, quoting literary critic Paul Garon paraphrasing Andre Breton.

18 Palmer. *Deep Blues*, p. 18.

19 Palmer. *Deep Blues*, p. 69.

20 Dylan. *Chronicles*, p. 282.

21 Dylan. *Chronicles*, p. 285.

22 Bono. "Foreword," *Dylan: Visions, Portraits, & Back Pages.* London: DK ADULT, 2005, p. 8.

23 McCartney implicitly disputes those who tend to view the 1960s material as the only true high point of Dylan's career and to see nearly everything else, save one or two exceptional albums like *Blood on the Tracks*, as a comedown. According to McCartney,

> I'm in awe of Bob. Y'know, people say, "Who's your hero?" And he's always been ... In The Beatles, he was our hero. I think he's great. He hit a period where people went, "Oh, I don't like him now." And I said, "No. It's *Bob Dylan*." To me, it's like Picasso, where people discuss his various periods, "*This* was better than *this*, *that* was better than *this*." But I go, "No. It's *Picasso*. It's *all* good." Whether it's bad or good, it's all Picasso.

A.V. Club, Interview with Robert Siegel, http://www.avclub.com/content/interview/paul_mccartney/2 (6/27/2007).

24 Michael Gray. "Dylan and the Blues," *Uncut Legends #1*, 1/1 (2003), p. 24.

25 Since he apparently never attended college, Dylan went instead to the "University of Dinkytown," in Nigel Williamson. *The Rough Guide to Bob Dylan*. London: Rough Guides, 2006, p. 14.

26 Dylan. *Chronicles*, p. 247.

27 See Deborah Baker. *A Blue Hand: The Beats in India*. New York: Penguin Press, 2008.

CHAPTER 4

1 Naoki Urasawa and Koji Wakui. *Talkin' About Bob Dylan: Diran wo katarou*. Tokyo: Shogakukan, 2007, p. 17.

2 In the liner notes to *John Wesley Harding* Dylan says, "A lightbulb fell from one of [Frank's] pockets and he stamped it out with his foot."

3 "Tangled Up in Blue" was rewritten from a gospel and a post-gospel perspective during performances in 1978 and 1984, respectively.

4 When asked in 1966 whether the trapeze image was meant to allude to the "carnival sound" that had been introduced into songs such as "I Want You," which speaks of circus instruments mocking the narrator, he replied, "That isn't a carnival sound, that's religious. That's very real, you can see that." Dylan thereby called attention to the role of risk-taking and verbal acrobatics needed to carry out the spiritual quest.

5 Curtis Schieber. "Dylan, Costello diverge as echoes of anti-war movement," *The Columbus Dispatch* (10/14/2007).

6 In *Modern Times*, Dylan borrows passages from Civil War poet Henry Timrod.

7 Richard Brown. "Highway 61 and Other American States of Mind," in Neil Corcoran. *"Do You, Mr. Jones?": Bob Dylan with the Poets and Professors*. London, England: Pimlico, 2003, p. 183.

8 People in town recall that Dylan busted the foot pedal of a very old and expensive piano by pumping it so hard.

9 Al Alexander. "I'm Not There (A-)," *GateHouse News Service*, http://www.wickedlocal.com/middleton/archive/x1908579544 (11/28/2007).

10 Dylan also refers to Dr. Filth in "Desolation Row," "doctors got no cure" in "Tombstone Blues," and to the futility of cures in "Just Like Tom Thumb's Blues" and "Shot of Love."

11 The conflict between Garrett and Billy is also played out in the Riddle, Missouri sequence that concludes *I'm Not There*. This theme is echoed when a guard about to release the imprisoned Jack Fate played by Dylan in *Masked and*

Anonymous tells him that "Keeping people from being free is big business," and Fate responds, "I'll keep it in mind," with the phrase uttered sardonically, as if to say that he was not going to let a little thing like that get in his way.

12 John Hammond, the famed producer who discovered other legendary musicians, has remarked that what impressed him most from the outset was not so much Dylan's skill with voice, guitar, or harmonica, but rather his attitude of dissatisfaction with society. Hammond knew that the key to Dylan's success would lie in distilling and bottling the sense of hostility and outrage as creative, dynamic energy. For Dylan, those who are outcast become attractive because their ambiguous status reflects a purposeful transcendence of conventional values that are petty or easily corruptible. However, one of Dylan's most famous lines celebrating the proverbial renegade, "To live outside the law you must be honest," has become ironic in relation to persistent abuses of power in the highest places.

13 Clinton Heylin. *Bob Dylan: Behind the Shades Revisited.* New York: HarperCollins Publishers Inc., 2000, p. 70.

14 Heylin. *Behind the Shades Revisited*, pp. 69–70. James Dunlap argues that Dylan is more influenced by the tradition of Emersonian self-reliant idealism, which seeks to stimulate individual consciences to stand up and be counted, than the Lomax-oriented folk revival movement, in "Through the Eyes of Tom Joad: Patterns of American Idealism, Bob Dylan, and the Folk Protest Movement," *Popular Music and Society* 29/5 (December 2006): 549–573.

15 This phrase was frequently evoked in Jimmy Carter's first, winning 1976 presidential campaign, which emphasized renewal in the aftermath of both the Watergate scandal and the war in Vietnam.

16 In *Masked and Anonymous*, the reporter Tom Friend played by Jeff Bridges tells Jack Fate, "You've got all the answers."

CHAPTER 5

1 Nigel Williamson. *The Rough Guide to Bob Dylan.* London: Rough Guides, 2006, p. 13.

2 Kierkegaard's identit(ies) were profoundly confusing. It was not until posthumous research was conducted on all available writings including journals and diaries that the real motives for his techniques were for the first time convincingly interpreted, although perhaps still never clearly understood. It turned out that Kierkegaard all along was a lifelong committed Christian. While he endorsed the priority of making individual choices as a matter of what he called existential subjectivity, it became clear that for him the ultimate decision in becoming an authentic Christian believer was to take a leap of faith into the realm of a complete affirmation of the Incarnation despite its reason-defying

basis for doubt, as opposed to the sheep-like acquiescence to institutional doctrine and ritual which he referred to as "Christendom." Yet he favored a Socratic dialectical method of reasoning, as do Dylan and Zen in their respective ways.

3 Stephen Webb. *Dylan Redeemed: From Highway 61 to Saved.* New York: Continuum, 2006, pp. 31 and 32.

4 Webb. *Dylan Redeemed*, p. 94.

5 Webb. *Dylan Redeemed*, p. 95.

6 Apparently, Haynes decided to leave out a seventh actor playing a character called Charley, since Dylan's very early performances resembled Chaplin's tramp-like quality. The film does not cover at least two other important stages: the smiling country gentleman who is content with married life of *Nashville Skyline*, and the Vegas-style touring superstar with full band and distaff singers of the *Street-Legal* phase in the late 1970s that occurred just before the gospel conversion (inspired in large part by Dylan's backup singers).

7 Jonathan Romney says, "Todd Haynes took on the challenge of a lifetime by making a film about the legendarily enigmatic troubadour. The resulting biopic is almost as hard to pigeon-hole as the man himself," "How *I'm Not There* reveals another side of Bob Dylan," *The Independent on Sunday*, http://arts.independent.co.uk/film/features/article3276686.ece (12/30/2007).

8 Cosmo Landesman. "I'm Not There—the Sunday Times review," *The Sunday Times* (12/22/2007).

9 According to a dialogue in *I'm Not There* on this dilemma, "You strive for freedom to live a certain way, but the more you live that way, the less it feels like freedom."

10 Professor Donald Mitchell shared this story as part of memorial panel for Masao Abe during the annual meeting of the American Academy of Religion in San Diego, CA (November 2007).

11 Andy Hertzfield. "Dylan's Song Sequencing in Albums and Concerts" http://www.differnet.com/Dylan/ (3/11/1997). According to the author, the first song and the last song on many Dylan albums are particularly important for understanding his transitions to new themes and styles. Thus, "Opening songs as announcements or declarations of change" and "Closing songs as song of farewell or transition," as well as "Final songs [that are] set apart from the rest of the album" are particularly noteworthy.

CHAPTER 6

1 The first side only was electric on the original vinyl release.

2 A reviewer once said of *Blonde on Blonde* that Dylan shot at one target and hit fourteen (songs).

3 Benjamin Filene. *Romancing the Folk: Public Memory & American Roots Music.* Chapel Hill, NC: University of North Carolina Press, 2000, p. 222:

> He is both drawing on and altering the down home blues to create a personalized form that can communicate the messages he wants to convey. His blues have ceased being tributes to his idols and have become vibrant and expressive contemporary outlets.

4 Nigel Williamson. *The Rough Guide to Bob Dylan.* London: Rough Guides, 2006, p. 168.

5 Ronnie Gilbert of The Weavers introduced Dylan at the Newport Folk Festival by telling the audience, "He's yours," to which Dylan strenuously objects in his *Chronicles: Volume One.* New York: Simon & Shuster, 2004, p. 115.

6 A strong retort was published in the magazine at the time by Johnny Cash, who later wrote on the liner notes to *Nashville Skyline,* "This man can rhyme the tick of time/ The edge of pain, the what of sane/ And comprehend the good in men, the bad in men/ Can feel the hate of fight, the love of right/ And the creep of blight at the speed of light/ The pain of dawn, the gone of gone/ The end of friend, the end of end/ By math of trend . . . And Know/ The yield of rend; the break of bend/ The scar of mend/ I'm proud to say that I know it,/ Here-in is a hell of a poet./ And lots of other things/ And lots of other things."

7 Watching the Newport concert recorded in *The Other Side of the Mirror,* it seems that the audience may not have been upset with Dylan, who was called back to stage for an acoustic rendition of "Mr. Tambourine Man," as much as with the back-up band, especially Mike Bloomfield's fierce electric guitar which has received so much praise for its contribution to several songs on *Highway 61 Revisited,* especially "Tombstone Blues." The concert's first song, "Maggie's Farm," was based on Blues songs, and it was just a matter of time before Dylan did what the Delta bluesmen had accomplished—go electric by connecting with Chicago, in this case some of the Paul Butterfield's Blues Band, which included both black and white players.

8 Mark Polizzotti. *Highway 61 Revisited.* New York: Continuum, 2006, p. 11.

9 Cited in Andy Gill. *Don't Think Twice, It's All Right: Bob Dylan, The Early Years.* New York: Thunder's Mouth Press, 1998, p. 66.

10 I am including the songs from Dylan's first and second albums as part of Basic Bob, mainly because the protest label did not really take hold until the following album, *The Times They Are A-Changin',* in addition to other early material that was eventually released on *The Bootleg Series, Volume I.*

11 Of the approximately two dozen unreleased songs from this phase, at least nine can be classified as protest "The Ballad of Donald White," "The Death of Emmett Till," "Talking Bear Mountain Picnic Massacre Blues," "Walls of Red Wing," "Talkin' John Birch Paranoid Blues," "I'd Hate to Be You on That Dreadful Day," "John Brown," "Man on the Street," and "Who Killed Davey Moore?"

The remaining lyrics occupy one of the other four categories, such as "Hard Times in New York Town" as social commentary; "Let Me Die in My Footsteps," "Tomorrow is a Long Time," "Eternal Circle," and "Paths of Victory" expressing spiritual longing; "Only a Hobo," "Ramblin' Gamblin' Willie," "Standing on the Highway," "Poor Boy Blues," "Ballad for a Friend," "Man on the Street," "Walkin' Down the Line," "Mixed Up Confusion," and "Hero Blues" as loner blues; and "Quit Your Low Down Ways" as an example of romantic conflict.

Furthermore, the thirteen traditional folk/blues songs covered on *Bob Dylan*, which are an important indicator of Dylan's interests and future directions also tend to fit into this pattern. Interestingly enough, the categories of topical protest and social commentary are not evident, but the other three are. For example, "Gospel Plow," "Fixin' to Die," "In My Time of Dyin'," and "See That My Grave is Kept Clean" express spiritual longing, with a special emphasis on a Hellhound Blues-based anticipation of death, which could strike at any time; "Man of Constant Sorrow" and "Freight Train Blues" represent existential loner blues; and "You're No Good," "Pretty Peggy-O," "Highway 51 Blues," "Baby, Let Me Follow You Down," and "House of the Rising Sun" are in the category of romantic conflict.

12 Because transportation was needed to enable the miners to get to work, the Greyhound Bus Company was founded in Hibbing and quickly spread down Highway 61 and fanned out in every direction to become a giant national chain. According to a Robert Johnson line, "So my old evil spirit can catch a Greyhound bus and ride"; see Robert Palmer. *Deep Blues: A Musical and Cultural History from the Mississippi Delta to Chicago's South Side to the World*. New York: Penguin, 1981, p. 116. Today, a museum stands near the old Hibbing, although ironically bus service has been recently cut off to the area for lack of demand. The 1930s art deco station in Clarksdale is now a tourist information center, although Greyhound remains active in nearby Memphis, a major metropolitan area on the main highway (55, which links to St. Louis and points further north).

13 The other two sites built by the mining companies were the Androy Hotel and City Hall, which emulated Philadelphia's Independence Hall.

14 See Dan Bergan. *The Hibbing High School*. Hibbing, MN: Manney's Shopper, 2001.

15 When I spoke with Miller and his wife on August 25, 2008, it was clear that he and Rolfzen, who has been celebrated by many Dylan followers including Natalie Goldberg who filmed him in *Tangled Up in Bob*, had remained close friends a couple of decades after retirement and often shared meals where they talked about Dylan. Rolfzen is still revered by his other students in town, who said that every day he would come to his office at 5:30 a.m. to prepare and got so worked up while teaching that he broke a sweat and perspired through his shirt. Miller said he was particularly pleased with "Blowin' in the Wind," which

he referred to as a "good song," while beaming with a sense of pride, since his wife commented that when the song came out many people attributed its social message to Miller's influence. Also, Miller was adamant about the role of free speech and said that he frequently told critics who accused him of being a rabble-rouser that "Communist is what you call anyone that you disagree with." Miller's comment on Dylan, who was said to sit attentively in the front row of Rolfzen's classroom: "a good student period . . . not a wise ass, he listened and learned."

Seeking an escape from Hibbing which was after all a small and isolated Midwestern town lacking in culture, Dylan during his teenage years was particularly fascinated by itinerant carnivals that passed through town. These were a holdover from the days of minstrelsy when black and white communities were sharing forms of musical creativity, but interacting unevenly socially and with a tragic festering bias and hatred. Dylan also managed to listen to Blues Highway rockabilly sounds picked up dimly late at night on airwaves that accessed radio stations playing Delta sounds from nearby Little Rock. In addition, he caught the latest films starring teen idols James Dean and Marlon Brando at the downtown movie theater. The Lybba Theater where Dylan first saw *Rebel Without a Cause* happened to be owned by his family and named for one of his relatives. Also, by the time of Dylan's youth, this part of the state extending upwards from Minneapolis through the area around Duluth was the home of longtime American Communist Party leader Gus Hall and the place where the progressive Minnesota Democratic-Farmer-Labor Party thrived. This nexus helped to produce several noted liberal senators who gained national prominence, including vice president and three-time presidential candidate Hubert Humphrey, a former mayor of Minneapolis, his protégé Walter Mondale, who also served as vice president, in addition to Eugene McCarthy, a senator who ran for the presidency, and Paul Wellstone, another senator who may have become a candidate but died prematurely. A memorial at the site of the plane crash that killed Wellstone in 2002 stands in a rural area near Hibbing. At a Duluth concert shortly after the time of the accident, Dylan dedicated a song to "my friend Paul."

16 This is just weeks before his appearance, along with a host of celebrities, in front of a throng of several hundred thousand white and black protestors who participate in the March on Washington for Jobs and Freedom led by Martin Luther King on August 28.

17 Mike Marqusee. *Wicked Messenger: Bob Dylan and the 1960s*. New York: Seven Stories Press, 2005, p. 81. It is clear that Emmet Till was mercilessly kidnapped and savagely murdered by white supremacists. Commemorated in plays by James Baldwin and Toni Morrison in addition to numerous other cultural productions, a sign on Highway 49 near where the incident took place was defaced and stolen in 2006–2007, with a replica replacement later installed. However,

the details of the account of the circumstances of Bessie Smith's untimely demise are contested. John Hammond, Dylan's first producer who also discovered Smith several years earlier, said that racism denied her access to a white hospital in Clarksdale, Mississippi after a car accident, and she died by the time she reached a black hospital (the building was eventually turned into a hotel that once housed John F. Kennedy, Jr.). This narrative was long taken at face value, and was the inspiration for a one-act play by Edward Albee. But, recent research has shown that apparently the black and white facilities were not that far apart at the time, and the problems in her getting proper treatment were more complicated, involving some questionable personal decisions by participants in the tragedy rather than blatant racism.

18 Marqusee. *Wicked Messenger*, p. 82.

19 Dylan also sang during his 1981 post-gospel tour Jim Krueger's "We just disagree": "So let's leave it alone / 'cause we can't see eye to eye/ There ain't no good guy./ There ain't no bad guy./ There's only you and me, and we just disagree."

20 *The Times They Are A-Changin'* was recorded at the end of October 1963, several weeks before the Kennedy assassination, although by the time of the release a few months later in January 1964 Dylan was upset about keeping too high a political profile, worried that "if they can kill the president, they can kill a folksinger."

21 Dylan also sang in 1981 concerts Barry McGuire's famous late '60s protest song, "Abraham, Martin, and John."

22 The importance of this song is demonstrated by performances as an emotional encore during the first Rolling Thunder Revue tour in 1975, as well as at the thirtieth Anniversary Concert at Madison Square Garden in 1993 with Eric Clapton, Neil Young, Tom Petty, George Harrison, and Roger McGuinn.

23 Note that while humor certainly remains, perhaps in a heightened, more sophisticated form, blatantly funny songs do not continue.

24 During this stage, Dylan delves into his Blues roots for inspiration from Charley Patton and Kokomo Arnold for "It Takes a Lot to Laugh, It Takes a Train to Cry," Sleepy John Estes for "From a Buick 6," Lightnin' Hopkins for "Leopard Skin Pill-Box Hat," and Robert Johnson for "Pledgin' My Time." He also draws from Beat poetic and other literary sources ranging from Allen Ginsberg and Jack Kerouac to T. S. Eliot and William Blake.

25 Mark Lawrence McPhail. *Zen in the Art of Rhetoric: An Inquiry into Coherence*. Albany, NY: State University of New York Press, 1996, p. 37, citing Eugen Herrigel. *The Method of Zen*. New York: Random House, 1974, p. 80. A concrete example of this is to say that the best offense is a good defense, which implies the inverse, that is, that the best defensive plan is to take the offensive.

26 *Bringing It All Back Home* features five songs on social commentary, three on romance including one that is a putdown, plus two on existential blues and one spiritual lyric ("Mr. Tambourine Man"). Also, *Highway 61 Revisited* has four

songs dealing with social criticism, two on loner blues, and three on romance, but several of these lyrics are so complex that they cross over two or more categories.

27 From the standpoint of Jewish mystical Kabbalistic/Hasidic symbolism, the act of "reciting the alphabet" can have a very positive, salvific meaning in that the Hebrew language is considered sacred and the foundation of world-creation. This was something that the founder of Hasidism, Baal Shem Tov, was known to do when he was fighting with demons, and it is very similar to a Zen saying that counting "1, 2, 3, 4, 5," is the key to universal truth. Other angles on naming as the primordial linguistic creative act are in the final verse of "Desolation Row," in which Dylan rearranges the faces of his former friends and gives "them all another name," and in the gospel song "Man Gave Names to All the Animals."

28 McPhail. *Zen in the Art of Rhetoric*, p. 37, citing Herrigel. *Zen in the Art of Archery*, p. 93.

29 Aidan Day. *Jokerman: Reading the Lyrics of Bob Dylan*. Oxford: Basil Blackwell, 1985, as cited in Andrew Muir. *Troubadour: Early and Late Songs of Bob Dylan*. Cambridgeshire, UK: Woodstock Publications, 2003, p. 109.

30 Ibid.

31 According to Charley Patton's "Pea Vine Blues," which is about an old railway that served the Delta, "But the good book tells us you got to reap just what you sow."

32 A typical Japanese ritual, no doubt borrowed from mainland Asia, is to hang divination strips or votive banners out on trees, poles, or wires in order to allow the karmic energy to circulate, thus enabling the benefits to be enhanced.

33 The latter song plays off the title of what was perhaps the most famous early Blues tune first recorded by "father of the blues" W. C. Handy in 1911. Handy played a pivotal role as a former minstrel singer and bandleader, who recognized the importance of Blues rhythms, but his own musical compositions have much more in common with Dixieland and Ragtime genres than the kind of Delta Blues that generally influenced Dylan. In the early twentieth century these styles along with Jazz were mixed up in the public consciousness, as in Bing Crosby's 1940s film *Birth of the Blues*, which is really about Jazz.

CHAPTER 7

1 Three of the songs appeared on The Band's *Music from Big Pink* in 1969, "Tears of Rage," "This Wheel's on Fire," and "I Shall Be Released"; one was on *Self Portrait* in 1970, "Quinn the Eskimo (The Mighty Quinn)"; three were on *Greatest Hits, Vol. 2* in 1971, "You Ain't Going Nowhere," "Down in the Flood," and "I Shall Be Released." Also, "Santa Fe" appeared on *Bootleg Series, Vol. I* in 1991. In addition, two singles from period two, "Watching the River Flow" and "When I Paint My Masterpiece," were on *Greatest Hits, Vol. 2.*

2 Sid Griffin. *Million Dollar Bash: Bob Dylan, The Band, and The Basement Tapes*. London, England: Jawbone Press, 2007.

3 The musical approach Dylan takes at this time greatly influences the emerging country-rock genre successfully employed by The Band on *Music from Big Pink* (for which Dylan wrote or co-wrote three songs), the Byrds on *Sweetheart of the Rodeo*, and the Grateful Dead on *Workingman's Dead*, among many other productions. Dylan's stylistic innovations also had a tremendous impact on the post-psychedelic music on the Beatles' *White Album* and on the Rolling Stones' *Beggars Banquet*.

4 Greil Marcus. *The Old, Weird America: The World of Bob Dylan's Basement Tapes*. New York: Picador, 2001.

5 In a passage in the album's liner notes that alludes to a Zen epiphany, Frank, who is trying to accommodate the three kings' request to learn just enough about "Mr. Dylan's new record," "so's we can say that we've been there," "took a deep breath, moaned and punched his fist through the plate-glass window." After this incident, Frank's wife criticizes him, but Frank insists that his hand is okay as the workmen replace the window.

6 Some of this blockage may have been due to the apparently dead-end nature of the times, when it was common to feel frustration and fatigue with promoting social causes or resolving personal crises. In France, for instance, New Wave filmmaker Jean-Luc Godard, who had been one of the bright lights of a mid-1960s cultural revolution by combining innovative artistry with political commitment, suddenly felt stymied and lost his productivity for a few years following the failures of the student protest movement of May 1968.

7 Unlike the previous three records, *Self Portrait* was not actually recorded in Nashville but tapes were sent for studio musicians he had worked with before like Charlie McCoy and Kenny Buttrey to fill in the gaps. In many ways, the album was way ahead of its time, and today would be considered a great retrospective reflection on the roots of Dylan's music-making.

8 Nigel Williamson. *The Rough Guide to Bob Dylan*. London: Rough Guides, 2006, pp. 180–181: "if the albums was released now, many of the songs would be regarded as modern Americana classics and that the record's simple verities and absence of ego seem far more in tune with the spirit of our times today .... can finally be seen for what it is—a personal scrapbook of the music that provided the backdrop to the evolution of Dylan's genius." Williamson refers to the album as "Self Parody."

9 Eugen Herrigel. *Zen in the Art of Archery*. New York: Vintage Books, 1971.

10 Clinton Heylin. *Bob Dylan: Behind the Shades Revisited*. New York: HarperCollins Publishers Inc., 2000, p. 369; and Andy Gill and Kevin Odegard. *A Simple Twist of Fate: Bob Dylan and the Making of Blood on the Tracks*. Cambridge, MA: Da Capo Press, 2005, pp. 37–39.

11 Herrigel. *Zen in the Art of Archery*, p. 44.

12 Gill and Odegard. *A Simple Twist of Fate*, p. 39.

13 "George Jackson" asserted, "Some of us are prisoners, some of us are guards."

14 Just before its release in January 1976, Dylan completed the Rolling Thunder Revue tour, including a finale "Night of the Hurricane" benefit concert held at Madison Square Garden and also attended by Muhammed Ali, which was the basis for the filming of *Renaldo and Clara* released in January 1978. During the second leg of the Rolling Thunder Revue Dylan consistently included Woody Guthrie's "Deportees" on the set list, and this led observers to sense that Dylan was on the verge of a renewed social awareness.

15 For a Zen Buddhist approach see Bernard Faure. *Double Exposure: Cutting Across Buddhist and Western Discourses.* Stanford, CA: Stanford University Press, 2003.

CHAPTER 8

1 This recording features sidemen like keyboard player Barry Beckett and the Muscle Shoals Horns, who are also accompanied by the Albert King-like guitar work of the Dire Straits' Mark Knopfler.

2 Benjamin Filene. *Romancing the Folk: Public Memory and American Roots Music.* Chapel Hill, NC: University of North Carolina Press, 2000, p. 227, also notes:

> As a folk stylist, then, Dylan strove both to absorb the essence of individual roots traditions and to stretch the boundaries of each genre. The ultimate expression of this goal came when Dylan tried to break down generic boundaries altogether.

3 An interesting point is that *Blonde on Blonde* was recorded in Nashville with Opry sidemen, but the group also included Robbie Robertson from The Band and Al Kooper from the Highway 61 Revisited sessions.

4 Sales of *Street-Legal* coming on the heels of the commercial flop of *Renaldo and Clara* were not strong. After the initial success of the well-produced and highly promoted *Slow Train Coming*, which ranked #3 on the charts for over a month and yielded Dylan's first Grammy with "Gotta Serve Somebody," the born-again stage seemed to lead to a decline. Beginning with *Saved*, which no doubt alienated much of Dylan's audience base because of its extreme emphasis on evangelism, album sales did again reach bestselling proportions for seventeen years as the critics savaged many of the releases of period III until *Time Out of Mind* released in 1997 commenced a new series of hits (including *"Love and Theft"* in 2001 and *Modern Times* in 2006, despite commercial flops like the 2003 film *Masked and Anonymous*).

5 Dylan also participated in a Chabad fundraiser in the 1980s. His Japan connection is reestablished with the video for "Tight Connection to My Heart," produced in 1983.

6 For example, it was generally considered that the release of *Dylan*, which included throwaways from *Self Portrait*, in fall 1973 was the fault of the record company which was taking revenge on Dylan for signing with another producer for a couple of albums.

7 Furthermore, the cover art of *Saved* and *Shot of Love* is ridiculed. The retrospective *Biograph* released in 1985 is deemed of limited significance because it does not contain new material. The two live albums from this stage, *Real Live* released in 1984 and *Dylan and the Dead* in 1988, plus the video of a tour with Tom Petty, *Hard to Handle* in 1986, are generally savaged. Also criticized is Dylan's participation in mid-1980s benefit activities, including the recording of the single "We Are the World" as well as the Live Aid and Farm Aid concerts. As suggested in note 19 in Chapter 1, Dylan, who sang "North Country Blues" and "Ballad of Hollis Brown" during his Live Aid performance, took the opportunity, which rankled some in the audience, to suggest the concept which eventually was turned into Farm Aid by Willie Nelson and others.

8 Clinton Heylin. *Bob Dylan: The Recording Sessions 1960-1994*. New York: St. Martin's Griffin, 1995, p. 157. In contrast to Heylin, my view is that *Empire Burlesque* which contains all original songs, albeit over-produced, is of significantly different value than *Knocked Out Loaded* and that it is misguided to conflate the two.

9 This includes the *Gotta Serve Somebody* collection of covers of Dylan's gospel songs that contains Dylan redoing "Gonna Change My Way of Thinking" with Mavis Staples, complete with a put-on Southern accent dialogue about frying chickens, and film documentaries *Gotta Serve Somebody—the Gospel Songs of Bob Dylan* and *Rolling Thunder Revue and the Gospel Years 1975–1981*. Paul Williams, interviewed in the films, was Dylan's main champion at the time with publications praising the gospel tour.

10 Nigel Williamson. *The Rough Guide to Bob Dylan*. London: Rough Guides, 2006, p. 191.

11 Maybe written the previous summer (1977)—but as early as late November he started referring to the Bible in a changed verse of "Tangled Up in Blue" and in early December was singing "Slow Train" and "Do Right to Me Baby (Do Right to Others)" at preconcert soundchecks for the end of the fall tour's performances.

12 Michael Gray. *Song and Dance Man III: The Art of Bob Dylan*. New York: Continuum, 2000, p. 215.

13 "I beheld till the thrones were cast down, and the Ancient of days did sit, whose garment was white as snow, and the hair of his head like the pure wool: his throne was like the fiery flame, and his wheels as burning fire."

14 Dylan also began to hint at his new faith halfway through the North American (last) leg of his 1978 world tour, when "Street Legal" was his current album, and he began to perform what became a series of rewrites of a passage in "Tangled Up in Blue." Instead of "She opened up a book of poems and handed

it to me / Written by an Italian poet from the thirteenth century," Dylan sang, "She opened up the Bible and started quotin' it to me/ Gospel According to Matthew, verse 3, Chapter 33," or "She opened up the Bible and started quotin' it to me / Jeremiah Chapter 31, verses 9–33."

15 Gray. *Song and Dance Man III*, p. 230.

16 The affinity with the East is at first indirect in the mid-1960s in evoking themes of naturalism, nothingness, and relativism, and then more direct in 1970s passages such as the *Planet Waves* liner notes, an outtake line of "Idiot Wind," an image in "Hurricane," and the liner notes to *Live at Budokan*. Note that even though the US release date of this album was subsequent to *Street-Legal*, its original Japan distribution was earlier.

17 Gray. *Song and Dance Man III*, p. 218. Gray also notes that it is "a typically audacious leap for Dylan that he can use Mexico as the symbol of earthly pleasures in this song while using it as an opposite symbol in 'Señor (Tales of Yankee Power).'"

18 Robert Palmer. *Deep Blues: A Musical and Cultural History from the Mississippi Delta to Chicago's South Side to the World*. New York: Penguin, 1981, pp. 83–84.

19 Gray. *Song and Dance Man III*, p. 247.

20 Varda Branfman. "Knockin' on Heaven's Door; My travels with Bob Dylan," www.writingforhealing.blogspot.com (6/29/2008).

21 Gray. *Song and Dance Man III*, p. 432. I Corinthians 13.2-7, "if I have a faith that can move mountains, but have not love, I am nothing. If I give all I possess to the poor and surrender my body to the flames, but have not love, I gain nothing. Love is patient, love is kind. It does not envy, it does not boast, it is not proud. It is not rude, it is not self-seeking, it is not easily angered, it keeps no record of wrongs. Love does not delight in evil but rejoices with the truth. It always protects, always trusts, always hopes, always perseveres."

22 Gray. *Song and Dance Man III*, p. 427.

23 The alternative wording is "hanging in the balance of a perfect finished plan."

24 Gray. *Song and Dance Man III*, p. 415.

25 Steven Heine, trans. *The Zen Poetry of Dogen: Verses from the Mountain of Eternal Peace*. Mt. Tremper, NY: Dharma Communications, 2005, p. 106.

26 Except for Clydie King's performance on "Union Sundown," but this more closely resembles Emmylou Harris' contribution to *Desire* than albums beginning with *Street-Legal*. Dylan recaptures a classic folk–rock sound with high-profile British rockers Mark Knopfler and Mick Taylor on guitar and Alan Clark on keyboards, along with the reggae rhythm section of Robbie Shakespeare on bass and Sly Dunbar on drums/percussion. On *Empire Burlesque* backup vocals are provided for over half of the songs.

27 Gray. *Song and Dance Man III*, p. 510. Several modern philosophers including Martin Heidegger and Eugen Herrigel have pointed to the Greek notion of play or dance as an alternative to the Judeo-Christian moralistic worldview.

28 Ibid. Note that the first quotation is from Aidan Day. "*Bob Dylan: Escaping on the Run*. London: Wanted Man Series 3, 1984; and the second is from his

book *Jokerman: Reading the Lyrics of Bob Dylan*. Oxford, UK: Basil Blackwell, 1985.

29 Ibid., cited from Day. *Jokerman*.

CHAPTER 9

1 Bob Dylan. *Chronicles: Volume One*. New York: Simon & Shuster, 2004, especially pp. 153–174.

2 *Tell Tale Signs* is a compilation of Dylan's Modern Era outtakes and live tracks released in fall 2008. Some examples of Dylan and Dylan-related productions during this phase which are helpful in understanding retrospectively his overall career production include additional volumes of *The Bootleg Series*, compilations like *Essential Bob Dylan* and *Dylan, The Other Side of the Mirror*, *The Gaslight Tapes*, special collections produced by Barnes & Noble and Starbucks of Dylan recordings or featuring songs he has selected; the first volume of *Chronicles*, Theme Time Radio Hour, the *Drawn Blank Series*; and Martin Scorsese's *No Direction Home* as well as a compilation of songs that no doubt influenced him called *Bob Dylan's Jukebox*. There have also been numerous academic conferences and music festivals in recent years, and Dylan has been covered in whole albums by leading artists such as Maria Muldauer, Judy Collins, and Brian Ferry. The only non-hit during the Modern Era is *Masked and Anonymous* distributed in 2003 that is, I believe, a compelling art-film drama that focuses on minstrelsy and politics.

3 John W. Whitehead. "No Shelter from the Storm: Bob Dylan's Apocalypse," http://www.rutherford.org/articles_db/commentary.asp?record_id=535 (5/27/08).

4 In discussing "Blood in My Eyes," Dylan says the song is "faultlessly made" by the Mississippi Sheiks because it goes against the grain of modernity.

5 Thom Jurek. "Review of *Modern Times*," *The Allmusic Blog*, http://www.allmusic.com/cg/amg.dll?p=amg&sql=10:4ojteay84xs7~T1. See also M. Cooper Harriss. "Sightings," "*Religion in* Modern Times," http://marty-center.uchicago.edu/sightings/ archive_2006/0810.shtml (8/10/2006).

6 Jurek. "Review of *Modern Times*."

7 This is the role that Michel Meyer gives to rhetoric, a role that suggests its potentially coherent properties: "When seen as based on the use of questioning, rhetoric ceases to be rhetoric of figures (or literary rhetoric) and the rhetoric of conflict (or argumentation, legal or not)." See Meyer. *Rhetoric, language, and reason*. University Park, PA: Pennsylvania State University Press, 1994, pp. 155–156.

8 This is from verse commentary on koan case 16 known as "Yunmen's Sound of the Bell." in the twelfth century Chinese collection of 48 koan records, the *Wumenguan* (Jap. *Mumonkan*).

9 Dylan has talked about how much he learned from hearing the Grateful Dead covers of his songs and he even asked to join the group around 1991, and after the death of Jerry Garcia a few years later Dylan was frequently playing distinctive renditions of Dead songs in his concerts.

10 These images come from "Shelter from the Storm," "Don't Fall Apart on Me Tonight," "Visions of Johanna," and a live version of "I Shall Be Released."

11 Dylan. *Chronicles*, pp. 152–153.

12 Dylan. *Chronicles*, p. 157.

13 Larry Katz. "Putting on the Brakeman: Bob Dylan's Egyptian Label Debuts with Tribute to Forgotten 'Father of Country Music'," *Boston Herald* (8/15/97).

14 "Born in Time" and "God Knows" appear on *Under the Red Sky*, "Series of Dreams" is on *The Bootleg Series, Volume 3* released in 1991, and "Dignity" is on *Greatest Hits, Volume 3* in 1994.

15 In *Chronicles*, Dylan remarks that this is an odd turn of the phrase, which should probably refer to "right *from* wrong."

16 Andrew Muir. *Troubadour: Early and Late Songs of Bob Dylan*. Cambridge-shire, UK: Woodstock Publications, 2003, p. 150.

17 Michael Gray. *Song & Dance Man III/: The Art of Bob Dylan*. New York: Continuum, 2000, pp. 645–646.

18 Gray. *Song & Dance Man III*, p. 705. Gray also suggests, "The two main features... have been black balladry and the history of its infusion into American popular music, and the private dramas of a particular clutch of pre-war blues: the grand dustclouds of oral history and the small intensities of a particular milieu, both equally revitalized into a Bob Dylan vision of then and now and the world gone wrong.... There is the evocation of another great sweep of history, that of the American Civil War, with all its psychic divides, its North-South, then-now, slave-abolitionist flames never extinguished, the South's defeat," p. 758.

19 Chris Gregory. "*Modern Times* track-by-track part 9: The Levee's Gonna Break," http://www.chrisgregory.org/blog/PermaLink,guid,f482a5e0-1392-4287-a887-c71c51db555c.aspx (9/13/2007).

20 For example, "Thunder on the Mountain" is an update on Chuck Berry's "Johnny B. Goode"; "Rolling and Tumbling" is a blues standard recorded by Muddy Waters, Cream, Canned Heat, Robert Johnson, and Eric Clapton, with over sixty recorded versions of this song; "When the Deal Goes Down" borrows the melody from Bing Crosby's "When the Blue of the Night Meets the Gold of the Day" while some of the lyrical force is drawn from Robert Johnson's "Last Fair Deal Gone Down"; "Someday Baby" is based off a song by Sleepy John Estes as well as a Muddy Waters song called "Trouble No More"; "Beyond the Horizon" lifts the entire structure and melody of "Red Sails in the Sunset," written by Jimmy Kennedy and Hugh Williams in 1935; "Nettie Moore" lifts the title and some of its chorus from an obscure Civil War era composition although

Dylan's melody and lyrics are significantly different; "The Levee's Gonna Break" is based on the blues standard "When the Levee Breaks" by Kansas Joe McCoy and Memphis Minnie, also recorded by Led Zeppelin who similarly reworked the song into their own composition that is much different from Dylan's; "Ain't Talkin'" derives its chorus from the more up-tempo "Highway of Regret" by the Stanley Brothers; and "Workingman's Blues #2" is a take-off on Merle Haggard's country classic.

21 Muir. *Troubadour*, p. 264.

22 Muir. *Troubadour*, pp. 264–265.

23 In addition to citing three song titles, the phrase "Judge is comin' in" is from "Nettie Moore," and "Ain't no altars" is from "Ain't Talkin'," both on *Modern Times*.

24 In 1949 as her only hit in the spiritual market, Wynona Carr sang a unique gospel song called "The Ball Game," which related the Christian salvific experience in baseball terms that became one of the top selling gospel records of the day. The flip side was called "I Know By Faith." According to Dylan's Theme Time Radio Hour account during the now famous "Baseball" broadcast after Sister Wynona Carr's "The Ball Game" is played:

> Sister Wynona Carr talking about life being a ballgame, where everyday life is a ballgame and everybody can play: Jesus is at the home plate and at the first base is Temptation, second base is Sin and at third is Tribulation. King Solomon is the umpire, Satan's doing all he can to psych you out and Daniel's up at bat, Satan pitches a fastball and Job hits a home run, you've got to just swing at the ball, give it your all, Moses is on the sidelines, he's waiting to be called . . . Sister Wynona Carr, "The Ball Game."

25 Chris Gregory. "*Modern Times* track-by-track part 4: When the Deal Goes Down," http://www.chrisgregory.org/blog/PermaLink,guid,0819fdf8-46c1-49f2-863f-2f2e3da4b29d.aspx (10/19/2006).

26 Tao Qian is also the author of the famous poetic essay "Peach Blossom Spring," which depicts a fisherman wandering and stumbling upon an idyllic village where time has stopped and there are no conflicts, but when the traveler leaves and tries to return later he is unable to find this utopia again. "Peach Blossom Spring" has influenced countless examples of literature and art in East Asian history including, as a recent example, the final episode in famed Japanese director Akira Kurosawa's eight-sequence film *Dreams* (*Yume*).

27 This was used as the subtitle for my presentation at the symposium on Dylan held at the University of Minnesota in March 2007, and the first version of conference program deleted the question mark, unwittingly transforming the phrase into an assertion rather than leaving it as an inquiry.

Bibliography

WORKS ON DYLAN AND POPULAR MUSIC

Alexander, Al. "I'm Not There (A-)," *GateHouse News Service*, http://www.wickedlocal.com/middleton/archive/x1908579544 (11/28/2007).

Baker, Deborah. *A Blue Hand: The Beats in India*. New York: Penguin Press, 2008.

Ball, Gordon. "Dylan and the Nobel," *Oral Tradition* 22/1 (2007): 14–29.

Bauldie, John. *Wanted Man: In Search of Bob Dylan*. New York: Citadel Underground, 1991.

Bergan, Dan. *The Hibbing High School*. Hibbing, MN: Manney's Shopper, 2001.

Bieri, Guido. *Life on the Tracks: Bob Dylan's Songs*. Switzerland: Guido Bieri, 2007.

Bono. "Foreward," *Dylan: Visions, Portraits, and Back Pages*. London: DK ADULT, 2005.

Boucher, David. *Dylan & Cohen: Poets of Rock and Roll*. New York: Continuum International Publishing, 2004.

Bouquerel, Laure. "Bob Dylan, the Ordinary Star," *Oral Tradition* 22/1 (2007): 151–161.

Bowden, Betsy. *Performed Literature: Words and Music by Bob Dylan Second Edition*. Lanham, MD: University Press of America, 2001.

Branfman, Varda. "Knockin' on Heaven's Door; My Travels with Bob Dylan," www.writingforhealing.blogspot.com (6/29/2008).

Cartwright, Bert. *The Bible in the Lyrics of Bob Dylan*. Lancashire, UK: Wanted Man, 1985.

Charters, Samuel B. *The Country Blues*. New York: Da Capo Press, 1959.

Cheseborough, Steve. *Blues Traveling: The Holy Sites of Delta Blues*. Jackson, MS: University Press of Mississippi, 2004.

Corcoran, Neil. *"Do You Mr. Jones?" Bob Dylan with the Poets and Professors.* London, England: Pimlico, 2003.

Daley, Michael. "Vocal Performance and Speech Intonation: Bob Dylan's 'Like a Rolling Stone'," *Oral Tradition* 22/1 (2007): 84–98.

Davis, Francis. *The History of the Blues.* Cambridge, MA: Da Capo Press, 2003.

Day, Aidan. *Jokerman: Reading the Lyrics of Bob Dylan.* Oxford, UK: Basil Blackwell, 1985.

—. *Bob Dylan: Escaping on the Run.* London: Wanted Man Study Series 3, 1984.

Désveaux, Emmanuel. "Amerindian Roots of Bob Dylan's Poetry," *Oral Tradition* 22/1 (2007): 134–150.

Devlin, Mike. "Top 10 Musical Geniuses," *Canwest News Service*, http://www.canada.com/globaltv/globalshows/et_story.html?id=c80f66b2-ead1-49dd-80cb-c9c124451644 (11/05/2007).

Dickerson, James L. *Mojo Triangle: Birthplace of Country, Blues, Jazz and Rock'n'Roll.* New York: Schirmer Trade Books, 2005.

Dunlap, James. "Through the Eyes of Tom Joad: Patterns of American Idealism, Bob Dylan, and the Folk Protest Movement," *Popular Music and Society* 29/5 (December 2006): 549–573.

Dylan, Bob. *Chronicles: Volume One.* New York: Simon & Shuster, 2004.

—. *Inspirations.* Kansas City, MO: Andrews McMeel Publishing, 2005.

—. *Lyrics 1962–2001.* New York: Simon & Shuster, 2004.

—. *Tarantula.* New York: The Macmillan Company, 1971.

—. Dir. *Renaldo and Clara*, 1977.

—. Dir. *Masked and Anonymous*, 2003.

Eig, Jonathan and Moffett, Sebastian. "Did Bob Dylan Lift Lines From Dr. Saga? Don't Think Twice, It's All Right Is the View of This Japanese Writer," *Wall Street Journal*, http://www.csudh.edu/dearhabermas/plagiarbk010.htm (7/08/2003).

Filene, Benjamin. *Romancing the Folk: Public Memory & American Roots Music.* Chapel Hill, NC: University of North Carolina Press, 2000.

Froeliger, Nicolas. "Nothing's Been Changed, Except the Words: Some Faithful Attempts at Covering Bob Dylan Songs in French," *Oral Tradition* 22/1 (2007): 175–196.

Gill, Andy. *Don't Think Twice, It's All Right: Bob Dylan, The Early Years.* New York: Thunder's Mouth Press, 1998.

—. and Odegard, Kevin. *A Simple Twist of Fate: Bob Dylan and the Making of Blood on the Tracks.* Cambridge, MA: Da Capo Press, 2005.

Gilmore, Mikal. "The Rolling Stone Interview: Bob Dylan (2001)," *Rolling Stone* 882 (11/22/2001).

—. "Hard-boiled, Raw Bootlegs Document Dylan's Late Period Revival," *Rolling Stone* 1063 (10/16/2008).

Gilmour, Michael J. *Tangled Up In the Bible: Bob Dylan and Scripture.* New York: Continuum, 2004.

Gray, Michael. "Dylan and the Blues," *Uncut Legends #1* 1/1 (2003): 93–99.

—. *The Bob Dylan Encyclopedia*. New York: Continuum, 2006.

—. *Song and Dance Man III: The Art of Bob Dylan*. New York: Continuum, 2000.

Gregory, Chris. "*Modern Times* track-by-track part 9: The Levee's Gonna Break," http://www.chrisgregory.org/blog/PermaLink,guid,f482a5e0-1392-4287 -a887-c71c51db555c.aspx (9/13/2007).

—. "*Modern Times* track-by-track part 4: When The Deal Goes Down," http://www. chrisgregory.org/blog/PermaLink,guid,0819fdf8-46c1-49f2-863f- 2f2e3da4b29d.aspx (10/19/2006).

Griffin, Sid. *Million Dollar Bash: Bob Dylan, The Band, and The Basement Tapes*. London, England: Jawbone Press, 2007.

Hajdu, David. *Positively 4ᵗʰ Street: The Lives and Times of Joan Baez, Bob Dylan, Mimi Baez Fariña and Richard Fariña*. New York: Farrar, Straus and Giroux, 2001.

Hamilton, Marybeth. *In Search of the Blues*. New York: Perseus, 2008.

Handy, W. C. *Father of the Blues: An Autobiography*. New York: Da Capo Press, 1941.

Harriss, M. Cooper. "Sightings," *Religion in* Modern Times, http://marty-center. uchicago.edu/sightings/archive_2006/0810.shtml (8/10/2006).

Harvey, Todd. "Never Quite Sung in this Fashion Before: Bob Dylan's 'Man of Constant Sorrow,'" *Oral Tradition* 22/1 (2007): 99–111.

Haynes, Todd, Dir. *I'm Not There*, 2007.

Hedin, Benjamin. *Studio A: The Bob Dylan Reader*. New York: W.W. Norton & Company, Inc., 2004.

Heine, Steven and Leighton, Taigen Dan. "Dylan and Dogen: Masters of Spirit and Words," *Kyoto Journal* 39 (1999): 4–11.

Hertzfield, Andy. "Dylan's Song Sequencing in Albums and Concerts," http://www. differnet.com/Dylan/ (3/11/1997).

Heylin, Clinton. *Bob Dylan: Behind the Shades Revisited*. New York: HarperCollins Publishers Inc., 2000.

—. *Bob Dylan: The Recording Sessions 1960–1994*. New York: First St. Martin's Griffin, 1995.

Hinchey, John. *Like a Complete Unknown: The Poetry of Bob Dylan's Songs 1961– 1969*. Ann Arbor, MI: Stealing Home Press, 2002.

Hinton, Brian. *Bob Dylan Complete Discography*. New York: Universe Publishing, 2006.

Irwin, Colin. *Legendary Sessions: Bob Dylan: Highway 61 Revisited*. New York: Billboard Books, 2008.

Johnson, Tracy. *Encounters with Bob Dylan: If You See Him, Say Hello*. Dale City, CA: Humble Press, 2000.

Jurek, Thom. "Review of *Modern Times*," *The Allmusic Blog*, http://www.allmusic. com/ cg/amg.dll?p =amg&sql=10:4ojteay84xs7~T1.

Kahn, Ashley. *Kind of Blues: The Making of the Miles Davis Masterpiece*. Cambridge, MA: Da Capo Press, 2007.

Katz, Larry. "Putting on the Brakeman: Bob Dylan's Egyptian Label Debuts with Tribute to Forgotten 'Father of Country Music'," *Boston Herald* (8/15/97).

Kazuo, Mihashi. *60 nendai no Bobu Diran*. Tokyo: Shinko Music Pub. Co., 1991.

Keohane, Ronnie. *Dylan and the Frucht: the Two Wits*. London: Ornery Pr, 2000.

Khalifa, Jean-Charles. "A Semantic and Syntactic Journey Through the Dylan Corpus," *Oral Tradition* 22/1 (2007): 162–174.

Knight, Richard. *The Blues Highway: New Orleans to Chicago, A Travel and Music Guide*. Surrey, England: Trailblazer Publications, 2003.

Landesman, Cosmo. "*I'm Not There*—The Sunday Times review," *The Sunday Times* (12/22/2007).

Landy, Elliot. *Woodstock Dream*. New York: Te Neues Publishing Company, 2000.

Lebold, Christophe. "A Face like a Mask and a Voice that Croaks: An Integrated Poetics of Bob Dylan's Voice, Personae, and Lyrics," *Oral Tradition* 22/1 (2007): 57–70.

Lee, C. P. *Like the Night: Bob Dylan and the Road to the Manchester Free Trade Hall*. London, Great Britain: Redwood Books, 1998.

Lloyd, Albertina. "Bob Dylan on screen," http://www.femalefirst.co.uk/entertainment/ Bob+Dylan-43210.html (11/03/2007).

Lott, Eric. *Love and Theft: Blackface Minstrelsy and the American Working Class*. New York: Oxford University Press, 1993.

Lutz, Tom. *Doing Nothing: A History of Loafers, Loungers, Slackers, and Bums in America*. New York: Farrar, Straus and Giroux, 2006.

Marcus, Greil. *The Old, Weird America: The World of Bob Dylan's Basement Tapes*. New York: Picador, 2001.

—. *Like a Rolling Stone: Bob Dylan at the Crossroads*. New York: PublicAffairs, 2005.

Marqusee, Mike. *Wicked Messenger: Bob Dylan and the 1960s*. New York: Seven Stories Press, 2005.

Marshall, Scott M. and Ford, Marcia. *Restless Pilgrim: The Spiritual Journey of Bob Dylan*. Lake Mary, FL: Relevant Media Group, Inc., 2002.

Mason, Catherine. "'The Low Hum in Syllables and Meter': Blues Poetics in Bob Dylan's Verbal Art," *Oral Tradition* 22/1 (2007): 197–216.

— and Richard Thomas. "Introduction [to special issue on Bob Dylan]," *Oral Tradition* 22/1 (2007): 3–13.

Mellers, Wilfrid. *A Darker Shade of Pale*. New York: Oxford University Press, 1985.

Meyer, Michel. *Rhetoric, Language, and Reason*. University Park, PA: Pennsylvania State University Press, 1994.

Muir, Andrew. *The Razor's Edge: Bob Dylan and the Never Ending Tour*. London, England: Helter Skelter, 2001.

—. *Troubadour: Early and late Songs of Bob Dylan*. Cambridgeshire, UK: Woodstock Publications, 2003.

Negus, Keith. "Living, Breathing Songs: Singing Along with Bob Dylan," *Oral Tradition* 22/1 (2007): 71–83.

Nelson, Willie and Pipkin, Turk. *The Tao of Willie: A Guide to the Happiness in Your Heart*. New York: Gotham Books, 2006.

Palmer, Robert. *Deep Blues: A Musical and Cultural History from the Mississippi Delta to Chicago's South Side to the World*. New York: Penguin, 1981.

Polizzotti, Mark. *Highway 61 Revisited*. New York: Continuum, 2006.

Ricks, Christopher. *Dylan's Visions of Sin*. London, England: Penguin, 2003.

Riley, Tim. *Hard Rain: A Dylan Commentary*. New York: Alfred A. Knopf, 1992.

Roberts, Jeremy. *Bob Dylan: Voice of a Generation*. Minneapolis, MN: Lerner Publications Company, 2005.

Rollason, Christpher. "'Solo Soy Un Guitarrista': Bob Dylan in the Spanish-Speaking World—Influences, Parallels, Reception, and Translation," *Oral Tradition* 22/1 (2007): 112–133.

Romine, Linda. *Frommer's Nashville & Memphis 7th Edition*. Hoboken, NJ: Wiley Publishing, Inc., 2006.

Romney, Jonathon. "How *I'm Not There* reveals another side of Bob Dylan," *The Independent on Sunday*, http://arts.independent.co.uk/film/features/article3276686.ece (12/30/2007).

Rosen, Jody. "Bob Dylan's Make-Out Album: The Romantic—and Spectacular—*Modern Times*," *Slate*, http://www.slate.com/id/2148563 (8/30/2006).

Rubin, Rachel. "Roundtable Discussion on Dylan's *Masked and Anonymous*," *Journal of Popular Music Studies* 16/3 (2004): 242–282.

Santelli, Robert. *The Bob Dylan Scrapbook: 1956–1966*. New York, NY: Simon & Schuster/Grey Water Park Productions, 2005.

Schieber, Curtis. "Dylan, Costello Diverge as Echoes of Anti-war Movement," *The Columbus Dispatch* (10/14/2007).

Scobie, Stephen. *And Forget My Name: A Speculative Biography of Bob Dylan*. Victoria, Canada: Ekstasis Editions Canada Ltd., 1999.

—. *Alias Bob Dylan Revisited*. Calgary Alberta, Canada: Red Deer Press, 2004.

Scorsese, Martin, Dir. *No Direction Home: Bob Dylan*, 2005.

Siegel, Robert. "Interviews: Paul McCartney," *A.V.Club*, http://www.avclub.com/content/ interview/paul_mccartney/2 (6/27/2007).

Smith, Larry David. *Writing Dylan: The Songs of a Lonesome Traveler*. New York: Praeger Publishers, 2005.

Sullivan, Jim. "Dylan Changin' with the Times," *Christian Science Monitor*, http://www.csmonitor.com/2006/0901/p11s03-almp.html (9/01/2006).

Thomas, Richard F. "The Streets of Rome: The Classical Dylan," *Oral Tradition* 22/1 (2007): 30–56.

Thompson, Toby. *Positively Main Street: Bob Dylan's Minnesota*. Minneapolis, MN: University of Minnesota Press, 2008 rpt. (1971).

Tonkinson, Carole. *Big Sky Mind: Buddhism and the Beat Generation*. New York, NY: Riverhead Books, 1995.

Toppman, Lawrence. "Everybody's 'There' Except Bob D. But the Search for the 'Real' Dylan Makes for a Fascinating Experiment in Haynes' Biopic," *Charlotte Times*, (11/23/2007).

Trager, Oliver. *Keys to the Rain: The Definitive Bob Dylan Encyclopedia*. New York: Billboard Books, 2004.

Urasawa, Naoki and Wakui, Koji. *Talkin' About Bob Dylan: Diran wo katarou*. Tokyo: Shogakukan, 2007.

Van Ronk, Dave and Wald, Elijah. *The Mayor of MacDougal Street: A Memoir*. New York: Da Capo Press, 2005.

Varesi, Anthony. *The Bob Dylan Albums*. Toronto, Canada: Guernica Editions Inc., 2002.

Various Artists. *Bob Dylan's Jukebox*. United States Dist, October 10, 2006.

Various Artists. *Classic Blues From Smithsonian Folkways*. Smithsonian Folkways, February 25, 2003.

Various Artists. *Classic Blues from Smithsonian Folkways, Vol. 2*. Smithsonian Folkways, September 23, 2003.

Vernezze, Peter and Porter, Carl J. *Bob Dylan and Philosophy*. Peru, IL: Carus Publishing Company, 2006.

Wald, Elijah. *Escaping the Delta: Robert Johnson and the Invention of the Blues*. New York: Amistad, 2004.

Wardlow, Gayle Dean. *Chasin' That Devil Music: Searching for the Blues*. San Francisco, CA: Backbeat Books, 1998.

Webb, Stephen H. *Dylan Redeemed: From Highway 61 to Saved*. New York: Continuum, 2006.

Whitehead, John W. "No Shelter from the Storm: Bob Dylan's Apocalypse," *The Rutherford Institute*, http://www.rutherford.org/articles_db/commentary. asp?record_id=535 (5/27/08).

Williams, Paul. *Bob Dylan: Performing Artist: The Early Years, 1960–1973*. New York: Omnibus Press, 2004.

—. *Bob Dylan: Performing Artist 1974–1986: The Middle Years*. New York: Omnibus Press, 2004.

—. *Bob Dylan: Performing Artist: Mind Out of Time 1986 and Beyond*. New York: Omnibus Press, 2004.

Williamson, Nigel. *The Rough Guide to Bob Dylan*. London: Rough Guides, 2006.

—. *The Rough Guide to The Blues*. London: Rough Guides, 2007.

Zuckerman, Matthew. "If There's An Original Thought Out there, I Could Use It Right Now: The Folk Roots of Bob Dylan," *Dylan Influences*, www. expectingrain.com/ kok/div/influences.html (3/21/08).

Zwigoff, Terry. R. *Crumb's Heroes of Blues, Jazz and Country*. New York: Harry N. Abrams, Inc., 2006.

WORKS ON ZEN AND COMPARATIVE THOUGHT

Abe, Masao. *A Study of Dogen: His Philosophy and Religion*. Albany, NY: State University of New York Press, 1994.

Aitken, Robert, trans. *The Gateless Barrier: The Wu-Men Kuan (Mumonkan)*. New York: North Point, 1991.

Ando Yoshinori. *Chusei Zenshu bunseki no kenkyu*. Tokyo: Kokusho inkokai, 2000.

Barthes, Roland. *Empire of Signs*. New York: Hill and Wang, 1982.

Bodiford, William M. *Soto Zen in Medieval Japan*. Honolulu, HI: University of Hawaii Press, 1993.

Cage, John. *Silence: Lectures and Writings*. Middletown, CT: Wesleyan University Press, 1961.

Carroll, Lewis. *Alice's Adventures in Wonderland and Through the Looking-Glass*, ed. Hugh Haughton. New York: Penguin, 1998.

Carse, James P. *Finite and Infinite Games: A Vision of Life as Play and Possibility*. New York: Ballantine, 1986.

Ching-te ch'uan-teng lu (Jap. *Keitoku dentoroku*), 1004, Taisho, vol. 50.

Clarke, J. J. *The Tao of the West: Western Transformations of Taoist Thought*. London: Routledge, 2000.

Cleary, Thomas, trans. *Book of Serenity: One Hundred Zen Dialogues*. Hudson, NY: Lindisfarne, 1990.

—. *No Barrier: Unlocking the Zen Koan*. New York: Bantam, 1993.

Denkoroku, 13th c., Taisho, vol. 82.

Dougill, John. *Kyoto: A Cultural History*. New York: Oxford Press, 2006.

Droit, Roger-Pol. *The Cult of Nothingness: The Philosophers and the Buddha*. Chapel Hill, NC: University of North Carolina Press, 2003.

Eihei koroku, 1236–53, in *Dogen zenji zenshu* [hereafter DZZ], vols. 3–4.

Eliot, T. S. *The Waste Land and Other Poems*. New York: Barnes & Noble Classics, 2005.

Faure, Bernard. *The Rhetoric of Immediacy*. Princeton, NJ: Princeton University Press, 1991.

—. *Double Exposure: Cutting Across Buddhist and Western Discourses*. Stanford, CA: Stanford University Press, 2003.

Goto, Seiko. *The Japanese Garden: Gateway to the Human Spirit*. New York: Peter Lang, 2003.

Heine, Steven. *Opening a Mountain: Koans of the Zen Masters*. New York: Oxford University Press, 2002.

—. *The Zen Poetry of Dogen: Verses from the Mountain of Eternal Peace.* Mt. Tremper, NY: Dharma Communications, 2005.

—. *White Collar Zen: Using Zen Principles to Overcome Obstacles and Achieve Your Career Goals.* New York: Oxford University Press, 2005.

—. *Zen Skin, Zen Marrow: Will the Real Zen Buddhism Please Stand Up?* New York: Oxford University Press, 2007.

Herrigel, Eugen. *The Method of Zen.* New York: Random House, 1974.

—. *Zen in the Art of Archery.* New York: Vintage Books, 1971.

Hori, Victor Sogen. *Zen Sand: The Book of Capping Phrases for Koan Practice.* Honolulu, HI: University of Hawaii Press, 2003.

Hsu tsang ching (Jap. *Zoku zokyo*), 150 vols. Taipei: Shin Wen Feng, n.d..

Ishikawa Rikizan. "Transmission of *Kirigami* (Secret Initiation Documents): A Soto Practice in Medieval Japan," in Steven Heine and Dale S. Wright, eds, *The Koan: Texts and Contexts in Zen Buddhism.* New York: Oxford University Press, 2000, pp. 233–243.

Ives, Christopher. *Zen Awakening and Society.* Honolulu, HI: University of Hawaii Press, 1991.

James, Simon P. *Zen Buddhism and Environmental Ethics.* Hampshire, England: Ashgate, 2004.

Kana Shobogenzo, 1231–53, in DZZ, vols. 1–2.

Kawamura Kodo et al. ed. *Dogen zenji zenshu* [DZZ] 7 vols. Tokyo: Shunjusha, 1988–1993.

Kenzeiki, 13th c., ed. Kawamura Kodo. *Shohon taiko Eihei kaisan Dogen zenji gyojo-Kenzeiki.* Tokyo: Tanshūkan, 1975.

Kim, Hee-Jin. "The Reason of Words and Letters: Dogen and *Koan* Language," in William R. LaFleur, ed., *Dogen Studies.* Honolulu, HI: University of Hawaii Press, 1985, pp. 54–82.

Leighton, Taigen Dan, and Shohaku Okumura, trans. *Dogen's Extended Record: A Translation of the Eihei Koroku.* Boston, MA: Wisdom, 2004.

Lin-chi lu (Jap. *Rinzai roku*), 12th c., ed. Taisho, vol. 47.

Mana Shobogenzo, 1235, in DZZ, vol. 5.

McPhail, Mark Lawrence. *Zen in the Art of Rhetoric: An Inquiry into Coherence.* Albany, NY: State University of New York Press, 1996.

Mishima Yukio. *Temple of the Golden Pavilion.* New York: Perigee, 1959.

Mitchell, Donald, ed. *Masao Abe: A Zen Life of Dialogue.* New York: Tuttle, 1998.

—. "Remembering Masao Abe," delivered at American Academy of Religion Conference, San Diego, CA: November 2006.

Nishimura Eshin, ed. *Mumonkan.* Tokyo: Iwanami bunko, 1994.

Pai-chang yu-lu (Jap. *Hyakujo goroku*), 12th c., HTC, vol. 119.

Pi-yen lu (Jap. *Hekiganroku*), 1163, Taisho, vol. 48.

Shobogenzo zuimonki, 1236–1238, in DZZ, vol. 6.

Taisho shinshu daizokyo, 85 vols. (Tokyo: Taisho Issaikyo Kankokai, 1924–1932).

Ts'ung-jung lu (Jap. *Shoyoroku*), 1224, Taisho, vol. 48.

Tung-shan lu (Jap. *Tozan roku*), 13th c., Taisho, vol. 48.

Wumenguan (Jap. *Mumonkan*), 1228, Taisho, vol. 48.

Yun-men yu-lu (Jap. *Unmon goroku*), 12th c., Taisho, vol. 47.

Glossary of Asian Mystical Terms

Datsuraku — Casting off the trials and tribulations that plague body and mind in Zen

Dharma — Buddhist truth

Dukkha — Buddhist notion of suffering

"Gateless Gate" (*mumonkan*) — The paradoxical gateway to nirvana in Zen Buddhism

Honkadori — The notion of allusive variation in Japanese poetry

I-Ching – Ancient Chinese text concerning the flux of existence

Jakugo — The capping phrase that comments ironically from the standpoint of a particular thinker's spiritual perspective on a Zen saying

"Just sitting" — Zen Buddhist form of meditation

Kannon — Buddhist goddess (Guanyin in Chinese/Avalokitesvara in Sanskrit)

Karma — The inevitable effects of moral causality (i.e., good begets good, evil begets evil)

Katto — Disentangling tangled vines in Zen writings

Koans — A pedagogical puzzle or riddle that triggers the insight and illumination of a Satori in Zen

Mono no aware — Sadness at the passing of things (relationships and circumstances) in Japanese poetry

Mu — Zen notion of ultimate reality as the realization of nothingness

Muen — Literally means "unaffiliated or disconnected," and refers to an outcast in Japanese society

Muenbotoke — Unattached Buddha, or one who rises above the petty concerns of the masses

"Nine-turn bridge" — An East Asian-style bridge with multiple twists and turns

Nishida Kitaro – A 20th century Japanese Zen Buddhist philosopher

Other Power — Path of devotion based on faith in the saving powers of the Buddha or other divine force(s)

Sakyamuni Buddha – The founder of Buddhism in ancient India

Satori — The experience of a sudden, eureka-like moment of awakening; a Zen epiphany

Self Power — A dedicated commitment to self-discipline or self-reliance as the key to realization in Zen

Sunyata — Buddhist notion of emptiness (or nothingness)

Ugetsu monogatari – *Tales of Rain and Moonlight*, a Japanese folklore collection

Yin/Yang — State of flux in Chinese thought where pro and con factors complement rather than conflict with one another

Index

BLUES

AAB structure, *see* Twelve-bar rhythm
American folk music 41
Beat Blues 22, 59–65
    see also Delta Blues
    and Greenwich Village 45, 51, 60, 163
Blues ballads/lyrics 34, 52, 64, 202
bluesmen 41, 42, 46, 48, 51, 53–4, 56, 59, 112, 168
"call and response" technique 47
Clarksdale (Mississippi, epicenter of Delta
    Blues) xv, 48–9
Chicago (among St. Louis, Kansas City,
    Detroit) 46, 50, 56
Cross Road (intersection of highways 49
    and 61 near Clarksdale) xv, 48–9, 117
"cutting heads" (Blues competition) 57
Delta Blues (Mississippi Delta/Classic Country/
    Deep) xv, 9, 17, 45–51, 58, 60, 175,
    202–5, 209–10, 239n.7, 240n.16,
    247n.24, 248n.33
folk revival period (1960s) 45, 51
Grand Ole Opry (country music style) 145, 163
"Hellhound Blues" 42, 101, 130, 168
Highway 61 ("Blues Highway"/New Orleans to
    Duluth) xv, 49–51, 60, 63, 65
"Holy Blues" ("Preachin' the Blues") 42, 99
Jefferson, Blind Lemon 41–2
Johnson, Lonnie 196, 205
Johnson, Robert 46–48, 51, 56, 59, 64, 170
minstrel (minstrel tradition/minstrelsy) 29, 47,
    142
    and blackface 29, 47, 53, 160
    and whiteface 29, 160–1
Mississippi Delta 117
    and Mississippi River flood (1927) 48, 212
Parchman Farm (Mississippi State
    Penitentiary) 48
Patton, Charley 34, 42, 47, 48, 51–3, 193,
    247n.24, 248n.31

Rainey, Ma 72
Southern crosses the "Yellow Dog" 49, 72, 74
twelve-bar rhythm (African polyrhythmic
    ritualism) 46, 53, 57, 64, 156, 201–2, 206
Williams, Big Joe 238–9n.14, 240n.14

DYLAN, BOB

Life of
    Americana (Dylan in context of) 44–5, 139,
    150, 207
    Baez, Joan 20, 137, 161
    Miller, Charley 116, 245–6n.15
    Dinkytown (near University of
    Minneapolis) 60–1
    Duluth (Dylan's hometown) 50–1, 60, 127
    divorce 10, 103, 151, 154, 168
        see also Sara
    motorcycle accident 80, 93–4, 103, 134, 138,
    150
    Hibbing, Minnesota (Hibbing High
    School) vii-viii, 79, 115–16, 245n.12,
    246n.15
    Judaism (Jewish upbringing) 9, 35, 39, 97,
    115–16, 165, 248n.27
    "Judas" (Dylan as) 27, 137–8
    Live Aid and Farm Aid concerts 195, 237n.19,
    251n.7
    March on Washington 145, 246n.16
    Never-Ending Tour 20, 31, 93
    Newport Folk Festival 27, 75, 79, 145, 146,
    244n.7
    Rolfzen, B. J. 75, 116, 245–6n.15
    Rolling Thunder Revue 10, 28–9, 63, 93, 136,
    152, 250n.14
    Sara (Dylan's first wife) 3–4, 10, 137, 145, 151,
    168
    Woodstock 145

ZEN AND EAST ASIAN CULTURE